**PRAISE FOR *A MORE PROSPEROUS PLANET, THE NEW FORMULA FOR A PROSPEROUS GLOBAL ECONOMY***

"Felipe Tudela provides a novel explanation and a new meaning to the age old problem of why some nations are wealthier than others. His book is clear, concise, and goes to the root of the problem, showing that the wealth of countries depends on the world view of their leaders and populations alike. Every person interested in world economics will benefit from owning this book." -Javier Pérez de Cuéllar, Former United Nations Secretary General

"Felipe Tudela's book explains, in a new and powerful way, the core of the wealth creation process. A must read!" -Hernando de Soto, author of *The Other Path: The Economic Answer to Terrorism* and *The Mystery of Capital: Why Capitalism Triumphs in the West and Fails Everywhere Else*

"In A More Prosperous Planet, Felipe Tudela presents us with a creative way of thinking about our global economy and its key issues." -Eduardo Aninat, Former Finance Minister of Chile, former Chairman of the Board of Governors of the IMF and World Bank, former Deputy Managing Director of the International Monetary Fund (IMF); author of the novel *Economia de Desamparados*

"Felipe Tudela provides a highly compelling, readable account of the sources of prosperity. He provides an excellent integration of the importance of cultural dynamism with that of a legal framework supportive of free enterprise. Finally, his provocative and entirely appropriate arguments on behalf of inequality through the process of creative dynamism adds spice and verve to the book. Billions of people could have better lives if Tudela's principles were implemented." -Michael Strong, co-founder of Conscious Capitalism, lead author of *Be the Solution: How Entrepreneurs and Conscious Capitalists Can Solve All the World's Problems*

"Felipe Tudela masterfully explains how wealth is created, and what are the essential elements leading to prosperity. A More Prosperous Planet is an essential book that every politician and every businessman should read as soon as possible. It is an instant classic." -Guy Milliere, Distinguished Senior Fellow at the Gatestone Institute, New York

" I'm sure this book will become a classic. It's the good news the world desperately needs right now." -Kevin N

## Also by Felipe Tudela

*Trading Triads, Unlocking the Secret of Market Structure and Trading in Any Market*, John Wiley & Sons, Ltd., 2010

*The Secret Code of Japanese Candlesticks*, John Wiley & Sons, Ltd., 2010

"La Quatrième Révolution Monétaire" article, *Revue des Deux Mondes*, Juin 2000

# A MORE PROSPEROUS PLANET

The New Formula for a Prosperous Global Economy

FELIPE TUDELA

ISBN-13: 978-0692804452
ISBN-10: 0692804455

Kindle Ebook published in 2015 by Avantangle
Paperback published in 2017 by Avantangle
www.avantangle.com

*Dedication*

To my parents and grandparents

# Contents

# Acknowledgements

I want to thank all the people who in the last two decades provided the support and intellectual stimulus that enabled me to create and develop my Prosperous Economy Formula™ as well as the many ideas contained in this book.

A special thanks to Bernard Cherlonneix, Philippe de Rougemont, and Céline Berthet from the Bank of France, as well as to Philippe Nataf and to Guy Millière, whose conversations at our lunch time breaks, while we lectured for the Bank of France, or enjoying a cup of coffee in a Parisian café, stimulated my thoughts and helped me sharpen my ideas. Thanks also to John Laughland, Henri Lepage and the late Martin Pot, friends whose thoughts on economics, monetary policy and politics were enlightening.

A big thanks to my friends Nathalie de Baudry-Dasson, former editorial director of *La Revue des Deux Mondes* who pushed me to write "La Quatrième Révolution Monétaire," the article that was the trigger for this book, and Philomème d'Arenberg who introduced me to Nathalie.

Thanks also to my friend Michel de Poncins, whose book *Tous Capitalistes*, and the conversations we had at his Paris home gave me first-hand insights on the high-level bureaucrats and what their actions meant for the French economy.

I also want to thank the late Sorbonne professor Francois Bourricaud, with whom I used to have coffee on Thursdays at the Angelina tea room, in Paris, and who had deep insights on what being a world citizen meant, and about how entrepreneurs were victimized and constantly swindled by politicians.

Thanks to Ramon Prat who authorized me to use the photo in page 24 from his book *Desert America*, (Actar, 2006). His photo was finally not used but the idea behind it was reshaped into the satellite photo used for this book.

A very special thanks to Mike Reid, who gave attentive and focused care to the edit, and whose suggestions helped improve this book in many ways.

Also, a big thanks to Angie, Dion, Greg, Kevin, Lidia, Mich, Rufus, Singh, Karu, and all the people at AvantAngle, without whom there would be no book today.

Most of all, I want to thank Annie, my wife, whose love, help, and support have made this book possible.

Lastly, I thank all of my other friends and students whose names do not appear here, but who helped me along the way.

# Introduction

The purpose of this book is to explain in a new way why some countries are wealthy while others are not.[1]

What I intend to show is that three elements are needed for a country to become wealthy and developed. To the extent that any of those elements is missing, a country's development and wealth is hindered.

These three elements are (1) the gap between wealth levels; (2) a critical mass of creative, scientifically minded people whose conditions enable them to foster a wealthy and prosperous society; and (3) freedom from government regulations. These three elements combine to create the formula for wealth development.

To reach this conclusion, I will begin by explaining the conditions—economic, historical, and technological—that have enabled those three elements to develop and to lead to prosperity. And I will explain how, in order for prosperity to be achieved, the dynamic mind-set of *wealth creation* had to displace the older, static mind-set of *permanently limited wealth.*

---

[1] I use the term "country," and not "nation," for the reason that I think modern nations have already outlived, or almost outlived, their reasons to exist. Modern nations, as well as governments, are bound to disappear. See chapter 10 for more on this surprising conclusion.

Once the foundations of the dynamic mind-set are explained, I will develop in depth each of the three elements of our formula—the gap between poor and rich, the critical mass of creative people, and the environment free from regulations. Then I will try to give a picture of how our world is changing, what the key agents of change are, and how governments are soon going to be superseded.

Finally, I will explain the role of the individual within those changes. The individual is the main actor and agent in the emerging new world order we are witnessing. Therefore, I end by discussing the individual choices and actions each person can take to survive and to achieve wealth and freedom for himself and for society.

But just as there is a formula for wealth, so there is a formula for poverty. So far, the laws of economics have been applied in many countries in ways that create failure, poverty, and corruption.

This is partly because it is easier to apply the formula for poverty than the formula for wealth. Destroying wealth is faster and easier than building it. Imagine having the patience to watch a tree grow from seed to maturity. On the other hand, no patience is needed to watch a tree being cut down. You need only a few minutes.

The idea that such a formula existed came from my research, my writing, and my lectures for financial institutions, coupled with my market and business activity in first- and third-world countries. Writing this book enabled me to develop the formula into its present form.

Our goal, as we have said already, is to supply a formula for the generation of wealth for countries, a sort of algorithm that can replace the recipe for misery that most countries continue to follow.

A fundamental idea in this book is that the gap between the rich and the poor must be enlarged rather than reduced. No, what I have said is not a typo. I mean it.

We constantly hear politicians and economists telling us that the gap between poor people and rich people should be reduced and that wealth is not trickling down to the less privileged sectors of society. When they say this, they are not only obstructing the path to prosperity; they are providing an economic recipe that is sure to guide their countries into poverty and misery.

To this myth that the wealth gap ought to be reduced, we can add other faulty beliefs. For instance, we can add the belief that capital should not be permitted to move around the world, but should remain in those countries where it was initially created or invested.

Another problem is the myth of democracy. All third-world politicians and economists swear by "democracy," although it is only an empty word to them. It means nothing to them, except following the herd in order to be politically correct. The truth is that those pseudodemocrats are the ones who are responsible for the misery of their countries' inhabitants. If they properly understood democracy and its role as a power-shifting mechanism within a republic, their countries would be rich and prosperous, instead of what they are—failed worlds.

We will see how all of the preceding derives directly from the laws of economics, just as a watercourse follows gravity.

However, we will go beyond a consideration of free economics. All economic principles are based on the belief that free will is the ultimate foundation of economic behavior. This book endeavors to show how economic freedom, as the foundation of economic thought, has consequences beyond those that are usually recognized.

The concept of freedom applies not only to economics but to all reality. Economic freedom works because it is an image of a higher freedom. Reality is always bound to win. In this book, I will try to explain why.

The explanation will result in a formula, or algorithm, that every country must follow in order to be wealthy.

Learning about the formula will transform your understanding of reality as it did mine. I promise that after you read the chapters that follow, whatever your economic or political thinking is now, you will never see things in the same way again. Your outlook will be changed forever. To discover why this is so, let's continue reading.

# Chapter 1

# The Hidden Origin of the Modern World

*With Gutenberg Europe enters the technological phase of progress, when change itself becomes the archetypal norm of social life.*

— Marshall McLuhan, The Gutenberg Galaxy, 1962

Why are there rich countries and poor countries? What is the secret behind countries' prosperity and poverty? Let us look for an answer from a new angle.

## THE INFORMATION REVOLUTION

The revolution that gave birth to the modern world came about because of an individual, Johannes Gensfleisch Gutenberg. He was born in Germany in the city of Mainz around the year 1400. After completing his university studies, he became a jeweler. However, he was exiled from Mainz because his family had taken part in a rebellion against excessive taxes.

Gutenberg set up his jeweler's business in Strasbourg, and there—inspired by a press used to make wine—he invented the printing press with mobile type. This invention allowed him to produce books very quickly and inexpensively compared to the old method of copying by hand.

He built his own publishing business based on this technology, and in 1442 he printed the Bible at a low price and with high quality. Although he died in 1468, his new technology was so successful that by 1500, practically all of Europe had adopted it.

Gutenberg's invention had many consequences: the mass distribution of knowledge that previously had been reserved for an elite group; the birth of modern, large-scale, public education; and horrific wars of religion.

But the printing press was responsible for much more than that. It also caused the destruction and disappearance of monarchies and the old world order. Indeed, the printing press is the reason that we have modern democracy and an industrial society today. If we were to remove the printing press from the fifteenth century, our entire modern world would disappear as if by a simple wave of a magic wand.

However, this technology began as just a dream, an idea in the mind of Johannes Gutenberg. In that sense, he was the greatest revolutionary of all time.

## *Revolutions and technological breakthroughs*

True revolutions happen because of technological breakthroughs. They are not the result of the theories of philosophers or politicians. These theories come later, when reality has changed and society must adapt to the new conditions.

The power of the technological ideas that underlie social change is akin to the power of the laws of nature that underlie geological or climatic events. For example, a natural catastrophe, such as the approach of a glacial period, is caused by a principle of climate or geology that is inherent in nature itself.

Another example may help to illustrate this. All things on the earth are bound to it by gravity. If we drop a ball, the ball falls. This happens because of a principle of nature, a law.

These laws are also why you can make a plane soar, or a rocket fly to the moon. The inner laws of nature enable you to do it. They also enable nature itself to work out its own answers.

Reality always wins. In a natural catastrophe, driven by the laws of nature, each species must adapt or die. Something similar happens in human societies when a technological change occurs. The change can have unpredictable consequences for the future of mankind, but man's societies must adapt to it.

Here is an example. In the transition from the Paleolithic Age to the Neolithic Age around 12,000 years ago,[2] a scientific and technological revolution led to harnessing and modifying the genetics of food. We humans went from being hunters and gatherers to being farmers—planters and cultivators.

The first genetically modified plants in history were born. Although probably less healthy for us than the wild foods that they replaced, these new plants made it possible to feed many more people.

With agriculture, men did not need to travel great distances to hunt. Agriculture, with domesticated plants and animals, brought a transformation of the social order from nomadic to sedentary. Men could remain in one place and work the land—and thus become the workforces of kings and emperors. Thus, cities were born.

Cities were a result of the domestication of crops. You could say that cities and empires are nothing but the dreams of a domesticated vegetable world. If you could suppress agriculture, you would also

---

[2] The transition from the Paleolithic Age (which began about 2.5 million years ago) to the Neolithic Age (which began about 12,000 years ago) meant a huge scientific and technical revolution. Plants were domesticated, giving rise to agriculture and the first genetically modified crops. (The wild varieties of plants differ from their domesticated counterparts. For example, wild rice is not agricultural rice.)

erase cities, kingdoms, and empires. It would not be easy to feed an entire city by means of nomadic hunting or by collecting nuts and berries.

Empires were not born because of the ideas of some early philosopher, nor because of the victories of some tribal chief who had conquered many other peoples. Conquests and empires came instead as a consequence of sedentary life—and sedentary life is a consequence of the invention of agriculture.

The key idea here is that a single technological invention can have such an impact that it can change history and the destiny of mankind. In fact, the advent of the printing press and the Gutenberg revolution did those very things.

## *The printing press as the first information mass-production machine*

If there ever was an apocalypse, it was the one caused by the printing press. Stars fell from the heavens, and the demons of the world were released. Chaos blanketed the earth while, at the same time, the light of a new world was emerging.

We live in a world that would have been unfathomable to those who lived before the printing press. Even today, few people realize the depth of the Gutenberg revolution and the transformations that it brought about. We are the postapocalyptic children of Gutenberg.

His invention made possible the massive dissemination of information. For the first time in history, information achieved a critical mass and turned on itself in a sequence of interactions, hastening the increase of knowledge. Many thinkers discovered new ways in which to transform society and nature without realizing that behind them, as the active cause, was the power of a new machine, the printing press.

## *The printing press made the impossible possible*

Before the printing press, calligraphy and the arts were the tools used to convey written or visual images. Books had to be copied by hand. The process was slow. For instance, copying the bible by hand could take up to 6 years.

Monasteries had rooms called scriptoria with many scribes working at once (together, they could reduce somewhat the total time needed to copy the Bible). A scribe taking dictation could use up to 80 quills per day.

All this made books difficult to obtain. They were expensive luxury items, and the monks who copied them were highly paid. The Sorbonne, in Paris, held only 1,722 volumes in 1388.[3] Only a small elite could read and write.

A library was a privilege that only a very fortunate few could afford. The same could be said of writing and reading. A book was a high-tech object, one so expensive that only large institutions or wealthy people could afford one. Thus the technology of information resided in only a few hands, and as a result most knowledge was available to only a few people. It could not have been different.

Then, suddenly, as if in a dream, this new device enabled rapid information exchange, with low production costs for each book. Without any warning at all, the era of high-speed, low-priced information exchange had arrived.

By 1452 two hundred copies of the two-volume Gutenberg Bible had been printed. It sold for 30 florins per copy.[4]

Over time, information became cheaper and cheaper. Books, reports, and printed data of all kinds became readily available. As a result,

---

[3] Annette Lamb, "Early Libraries: 1300s CE," History of Libraries, 2013, Eduscapes, IUPUI Online Courses, http://eduscapes.com/history/early/1300.htm.

[4] "Gutenberg Bible," *Wikipedia*, last accessed 29 November 2014, http://en.wikipedia.org/wiki/Gutenberg_Bible.

science and technology exploded. And in so doing, they swept away the old world.

## *Freedom and the technological loop*

We must draw attention here to the role of the mind. The printing press was merely a mechanical device that enabled minds to gather together and expand knowledge more rapidly than ever before.

This brings us to a key factor—freedom.

Without the freedom to think and the freedom to exchange, assemble, and circulate, the interactions that enabled such a rapid accumulation of knowledge could not have occurred.

From this freedom, a technological loop was born, in which a mechanical device made possible mental synergy on a scale never seen before. In turn, this mental synergy reinforced freedom and began to destroy all obstacles in its path.

## *The greatest revolution in history*

The first and greatest changes wrought by the Gutenberg press were in the mind itself. There was nothing in the past to compare with the new collaborative power of human minds. The mode of learning in all areas, from religion and metaphysics to natural science, changed. In addition, all practical applications of knowledge began to change.

Society modified its beliefs. Religion, government, and finance took on new meanings. Education expanded on a new scale, technology evolved into new patterns, and science explored new fields.

Johannes Gutenberg was a technological genius, a sort of new messiah for a new world. His role in history is more important than that of many emperors, kings, or politicians.

History is mostly propaganda, even if historians are not always aware of this. This propaganda is a veil that makes it difficult for us to see the real agents of change. When you visit the history section of a bookstore, you will notice that most history books are about persons who were in government or government institutions—mostly political or military figures. History today is biased toward politics. There is another kind of history that is largely missing. The history of inventors, scientists, and entrepreneurs is more important than the history of politicians.

When the average man thinks of "history," he thinks of Wellington or Napoleon or Kennedy, rather than Newton or Galileo or Gutenberg. The teaching of history would make more sense if, by history, we primarily meant the stories of men of thought and enterprise, instead of men of government, political power, and war. It is the thinkers and entrepreneurs who create the most profound changes in society.

The bias toward political events in the usual outlook of history is probably the reason Gutenberg is not widely valued as the transformer of society and the creator extraordinaire of a new world.

To rectify this bias, let's review some consequences of the Gutenberg revolution. We will begin with religion.

## *Religious wars: Gutenberg and the upheaval of Christianity*

The new printing technology made possible the mass production of the Holy Bible and, as a result, its mass distribution.

This development involved one of the main principles of economics: that a supply can create its own demand. There was no demand for the steam engine and railway train. However, when these machines arrived, they solved a large-scale transportation problem.

Similarly, until the Wright brothers flew their airplane at Kitty Hawk there was no demand for such a machine. But once the airplane had been invented (by the Wrights and others), it became a great success, later making possible even intercontinental travel by air.

The same thing happened with the Bible and other books. Once the printing press had made them available, that is, once the printing press *supplied* them to the public, the books became great successes, and everyone wanted his or her share of them. Furthermore, this technological feat and the new good that it supplied affected religion and society.

## *The printing press blew away the religious monopoly*

The Bible became the first bestseller in history, and today it continues on the list of bestselling books. Everyone has an opportunity to read what previously was restricted.

Before Gutenberg, only the priests and a fortunate intellectual class had access to the Bible. To suddenly have access to the most important book of his world, thanks to a new technology, must have been an unforgettable experience for a layman.

Now, all of the new readers of the Holy Bible not only enjoyed the scriptures, but also began to think in different ways about what they were reading. As a result of this reading by many new readers, many opinions were bound to emerge. Where you have free minds, you have many opinions. Similar, but differing, interpretations of the Bible naturally arose.

The Catholic Church's interpretation had hitherto been accepted as the only correct way of reading and interpreting the Bible. This interpretation was based on tradition.

The Bible was, and still is, interpreted by the Catholic Church in accordance with the doctrine of all previous popes and councils, and the thoughts of such church fathers as Saint Augustine of Hippo and Clement of Alexandria.[5] The church fathers were followed by the church theologians, such as Saint Thomas Aquinas or Duns Scotus.[6] In

---

[5] Saint Augustine (Aurelius Augustinus Hipponensis, 354–430) was Bishop of Hippo (which is now Annaba, Algeria). He was the author of more than 100 surviving works, including *Confessions* and *The City of God*. He is one of the Church Fathers.

[6] Saint Thomas Aquinas (1225–1274), who was known as Doctor Angelicus, is considered to have been the most important of the 33 doctors of the Catholic Church. He is mainly known for his *Summa Theologica* and his *Summa Contra Gentiles*.

this way, the Catholic Church developed a doctrine based on the distilled and continually perfected thinking of its most brilliant minds.

This vast intellectual heritage convinced the Catholic Church that it was the possessor of the true faith and the only valid interpretation of the sacred book, the Holy Bible. It was logical and natural that any opinion, that contradicted the doctrine of the Church should be considered heretical. The Catholic Church could not fathom the possibility of someone differing in his interpretation.

Then, suddenly, it happened. The printing press arrived.

## *The printing press gave away the secret book, the Bible*

The Bible was now exposed. Anyone could read it—and, what was even more dangerous—anyone could interpret it. This danger was probably not even anticipated in the early days of the printing press, because it takes some time for a society to feel the impact of a new technology. The consequences of people being able to read and interpret the Bible for themselves were not at first visible.

But the Church soon sensed the risk that its very foundations might crumble, and it fought to prevent itself from being overtaken by the many differing interpretations that arose. However, these differing interpretations, and new Christian denominations based on them, did grow and thrive. And from early on, the leaders in the new interpretations of the Bible, for their part, saw the Catholic Church as an enemy that they had to fight.

Everything was set for the European wars of religion. In the past, the Church had fought heretical minority groups, such as the Cathars, and it had always prevailed.[7]

---

Duns Scotus (1265–1308), called Doctor Subtilis, believed that universals were real as opposed to nominal (i.e., they were not just names without an underlying reality).

[7] The Cathars were a Gnostic and dualistic sect, a Catholic heresy that appeared in the Languedoc region of France in the twelfth century.

However, this new sequence of wars became a fire that would envelop all of Europe in flames. It was a religious and political catastrophe of unprecedented dimensions.

The wars of religion arose from the Protestant Reformation. The first war was the German Peasants' War (1524–1525), supported by the Protestant clergy in German-speaking Central Europe, in which a hundred thousand peasants and farmers were slaughtered. The religiously motivated conflicts that followed included the battle of Kappel in Switzerland (1524–1525); the Schmalkaldic war (1546–1547) between Charles V and the Lutheran Schmalkaldic league in the Holy Roman Empire; the Eighty Years War (1568–1648) in the Low Countries; the French Wars of Religion (1562–1598); the Thirty Years War (1618–1648) in the Holy Roman Empire, Habsburg Austria, Bohemia, and France; and the Wars of the Three Kingdoms (1639–1651) in England, Scotland, and Ireland.

Among these, the French Wars and the Thirty Years War, a battle between European Catholic and Protestant states, were the most devastating, taking a toll of around three million casualties each.

The new world was emerging, even though its foundation, the printing press, was invisible to the public. What people saw, instead, were books and authors.

They took for granted the new technology that made the books possible. It seems as though every true revolution is invisible at first.

## *The printing press made everyone think*

When a large number of persons begin to read and think on the same topics simultaneously for the first time, new and exciting things happen.

In post-Gutenberg Europe, a pool of new knowledge began to accumulate and to be publicized in books. At the same time, books by ancient authors began to be printed and distributed, popularizing older thoughts alongside the new.

Reading propelled thinking to new heights. The distribution of the Holy Bible allowed people to think independently about its contents. Tens of thousands of ordinary people were now reflecting on what they read, exchanging opinions, and debating them among themselves. Thus, thinking in society increased in quantity, quality, and speed.

Reason was soon to be heralded, because a machine that stimulated reason had arrived, and all were benefiting from it. The advent of an age of reason, the age of great thinkers like Desiderius Erasmus and, later, René Descartes, was the age of a new machine.[8]

The world became a world of writers and readers. Higher minds came together by means of a unique object, the book. The book became the emblem of reason and intelligence. Authors became the leaders of a new world. Readers shared in their aura of intelligence and culture. A new civilization of the book was emerging.

Supply creates demand. This is nowhere more evident than in book publishing. An author writes a book about a new subject, a subject that no one ever thought of before it was born in the mind of the author. When, it is published it becomes a success, although there was previously no demand for such a book.

---

[8] Erasmus (1466–1536), whose full name was Desiderius Erasmus Roterodamus, was born in Rotterdam. He was a Dutch Catholic priest, philosopher and theologian who was called "the crowning glory of the Christian humanists." He was an advocate of free will against the doctrine of predestination upheld by some Protestant Reformers. He considered the reading of the Bible to be essential.
René Descartes (1596–1650) was a French philosopher who wrote the *Discourse on the Method*. In it he tried to formulate a method to enable research to isolate true principles that no one could doubt and from which all truth could be derived. He postulated this as the principle "I think, therefore I am."
Aside from the validity or invalidity of his findings, Descartes is important for having been the first to write a work about method itself. The book's title gives the key to his thinking, which provides a blueprint or method for scientific research.

Original thought and new ideas in fiction and nonfiction create a market, as long as what is offered can arouse the interest of a large number of readers. Books are the boundless reservoir of the new.

The novelty of thought in all fields created a new world where the rate of progress quickened exponentially. In turn, this progress accelerated history itself.

In books, a central reference point for knowledge in all fields had appeared. Human intelligence could thus relate to itself differently. A new kind of community of thinkers was formed that had no precedent.

Archimedes, Heraclitus, Plato, or Aristotle in the ancient world or Saint Albertus Magnus, Scotus Eriugena, or Robert Grosseteste in the Middle Ages never had even a hint of this new age. The old intelligence was not severely limited in depth or scope. A single thinker like Plato or Aristotle could achieve a great deal. However, the material that could be handled and the number of exchanges possible among minds and among different fields were necessarily limited. The old intelligence was a mind of the minority, because those who could read and write were few.

The large-scale diffusion of information enabled minds to communicate more efficiently in all fields: both philosophy and religion, both physics and metaphysics.

In addition, the world of European thought had expanded and now included distant continents and their minds. New religions and philosophies arrived. The West was not alone.

In the seventeenth century, the Jesuit missionaries in China discovered the *I Ching* and used it to underscore the affinities between the Bible and the Chinese classics with the goal of winning converts. The Jesuit Joachim Bouvet (1656–1730) tutored the Kangxi emperor. It is thanks to Bouvet that the *I Ching* caught the attention of Leibniz (1656–1716) and other European philosophers. Leibniz and Bouvet believed the *I Ching* could help to create a universal scientific and mathematical language that would transform the act of thinking into a binary calculation.

Meanwhile, the French Orientalist Abraham Hyacinthe Anquetil-Duperron (1731–1805) discovered the Zoroastrian religion. In 1772 he translated the *Zend Avesta* into French.

The British Orientalist Charles Wilkins (1749–1836) was the first to translate the Baghavad Gita, which he published in 1785.[9]

Through the linguistic and religious achievements of men like these, Eastern religions and Eastern culture were able to penetrate and mingle with Western thought. This stimulated debates that led to many new ideas.

Thus, the era of philosophical invention was born. It would also be an era of technological invention.

## THE EDUCATIONAL AND TECHNOLOGICAL REVOLUTION

The printing press made possible a massive diffusion of technical and scientific knowledge. The reinterpretation and criticism of old ideas that had occurred in the religious field also arose in the scientific and technical fields.

As a consequence, a new kind of science came into existence. The world saw the emergence of a new philosophy, a new mathematics, a new physics, a new astronomy, a new chemistry, and a new medicine.

### *Gutenberg, the grandfather of a million inventions*

Our science today is the immediate consequence of the printing-press revolution. Without the printing press there would have been no Louis Pasteur or Marie Curie, no Nikola Tesla or Albert Einstein or Alan Turing—nor their discoveries. Therefore, we must see Gutenberg as the grandfather of Pasteur's vaccine for rabies, Curie's research in radioactivity, Tesla's fantastic invention of the alternating-current

[9] Guido Abbattista, "European Encounters in the Age of Expansion," European History Online, Jan. 24, 2011, http://ieg-ego.eu/en/threads/backgrounds/european-encounters/.

generator (on which all our present electrical power systems are based), Einstein's theory of relativity and Turing's pioneering work in computer science.

Without Gutenberg, we would not have the printing press; and without the printing press, none of these achievements would have been possible. By its massive dissemination of information, the printing press allowed scientists and inventors to exchange ideas and pass on their discoveries much more rapidly than ever before.

Thus, the printing press increased significantly the probability that *someone* would discover *something*. This probabilistic function of the printing press was important. It is highly significant whether the same information is used by only a few thousands of people or by millions of people. Sheer numbers do matter.

The key to this transformation was the possibility of having free minds sharing and studying information. The important word here is *free*. The printing press could only work its miracle where people had the freedom to own, to think, and to exchange.

Free minds combined with the printing press to cause an educational revolution.

## *The educational revolution of the individual*

Public and private schools became possible in numbers that had never even been considered previously. You see, you need to produce hundreds, if not thousands, of copies of the same books to enable a large number of students to read the same material.

However, education in its new form was fundamentally a consequence of the individual freedom to learn. The great minds often educated themselves. That is, free learning was an individual phenomenon, rather than a collective one. It was not mass education. It was the opposite.

At the same time, a part of that education consisted of the intellectual elite exchanging thoughts freely among themselves.[10] A large scientific community was born because of the freedom to learn by oneself.

The mass distribution of relevant information developed large-scale individualism: many people felt that they had a right to learn what they wanted, when they wanted, and in the way that they found most useful.

Thus, the printing press marked the beginning of the era of large-scale education.

The era of the individual had arrived. Its arrival was accompanied by the beginning of a sort of war, a conflict that is neither military nor religious nor scientific. It is a war of another kind.

The war that we speak of is the war of the individual against his (and her) enemies of all kinds. The war began with this era of the individual and will exist as long as there are free individuals and forces that oppose them.

The era of the individual is the achievement of the Gutenberg revolution. The enemies of the revolution take many shapes and faces, including that of the Gestapo officer, the Communist commissar, the Cuban dictator, the abusive bureaucrat, and many others. As times have changed, the same kinds of totalitarian, anti-individualist, and antifreedom persons or institutions have assumed different forms in different countries, but in essence they remain the same.

What these enemies did not realize in the past and do not realize now is that their conflict is a result of the same machine that has doomed them. The printing press provided the deathblow against collectivism of all kinds.

It was not the only blow, although it was decisive in its action. Other blows were to come, reinforcing the power of the individual and exalting his freedom of spirit. We will come back to these in part 3 of this book.

---

[10] We have many examples of correspondence between scientific minds. Edison kept extensive files of correspondence.

The printing press educated the minds of free men. Gutenberg came as a messiah, heralding freedom for all. He did this not by a famous speech or a military victory, but by the consequences of his invention. He gave us the generosity of a new machine.

Technology made us free.

## *The link between education and technology*

Technology was not a result of education. Instead, education was a result of technology. Without the right tools, education is impossible. (Here we refer to large-scale education.)

The printing machine made large-scale education possible. Teachers did not. Schools did not. In short, the new technological marvel enabled education. This was impossible to achieve by political will.

Philosophers thought that mass education was their achievement. The goddess of reason had revealed to them the benefits of education. But philosophers—and the politicians who attempted to put the philosophers' ideas into practice—did nothing about it by themselves.

Widespread education resulted from the simple fact that the printing press existed. Education on a large scale was inevitable. All that thinkers and politicians did was to rationalize, ex post facto, something that was already there, and try to control and manipulate it.

When books became available, the most brilliant minds used them, not because of schools, but simply because books were available. These individuals could obtain food for their minds at a reasonable price in a selection and quantity that had never been possible before. They used books to learn what other minds were thinking, to consider it, and to exchange ideas. They invented and created.

Educational revolutions are primarily the results of new technologies. The first educational revolution was the change from oral transmission to the written word. The next was the advent of the printing press.

Today, the computer and the microchip have made the Web possible. A new revolution is again changing the world and changing education. Once more, a new technology is at work behind the scenes.

When politicians and educators begin to formulate policies to address the need for education, the policies are already obsolete. Real education for real people comes about in a different way. When a new technology enables education, the pupil goes ahead and seeks a teacher. No one watches TV unless he wants to watch TV. Anyone who wants a TV goes out and buys one. It is the same with books or printed information or websites. New technology opens a window of opportunity for many people.

Education exists because when it was offered, people wanted it—they expressed a demand for it. The new technology, the printing press, produced the printed material that people wanted. When the product was supplied, it created a demand. And this product changed the world.

## *The deep link of technology to itself: the accelerating loop*

Technological progress and its acceleration were possible because of a machine that enabled the distribution and exchange of technological ideas. This distribution and exchange enabled an enormous variety of new technologies to be created and perfected.

Technology began to build on itself in unforeseen ways. Just a few centuries after Gutenberg, technologies arrived that defied imagination, such as the train, the car, the airplane, electricity, and the computer.

These are the products of a self-sustaining growth process. Each technology fascinated and captured the imagination of men and women, who then envisioned further possibilities. One technology created another, and so on.

An era of endless invention and creation of new machines, new technologies, and new methods was born. Technology evolved progressively from simple mechanisms to electrical mechanisms, and from electricity to electronics.

Furthermore, a new concept of reality and of wealth was developing progressively as new discoveries and inventions made man conscious of the powers of his own mind and the power of the laws of nature, which until then had not been fully freed.

## THE BIRTH OF A NEW WORLD: A DYNAMIC VISION OF WEALTH

The scientific community had expanded vastly, and these new creators began to consider new ways to transform nature in order to master space and time.

To achieve their goals, scientists needed material support. Thus, the financier and the entrepreneur entered the picture.

### *The link between technology and social order*

Science, finance, and business enterprise went together in this new civilization made possible by the printing press. The links among these three forces were necessary for our new world to arrive. The scientists created the new ideas, the financiers provided the required investment money, and the entrepreneurs (in the early days, these were usually industrialists) turned those ideas into reality.

The pecuniary fortunes of the financiers and industrialists were the monetary expressions of the value of the new technological achievements. Thus, there was an interaction between the expansion of practical knowledge and the emergence of new financial and industrial empires.

A power of a new kind was born. Invention, finance, and industry created new pools of wealth that were more powerful than medieval kingdoms had ever been. Wealth expanded and benefited more people than ever before.

The result was a world of industry, finance, and learning. Its three modern heroes were the entrepreneur, the financier, and the scientist-inventor.

The financier and the entrepreneur became the powerful figures of this new world. The old monarchs and aristocrats had to yield their privileged places to these new powers. The old social, political, and economic order could not continue. It had lost the foundations of its power and its reason to exist.[11]

## *The dynamic and static concepts of wealth*

The cause behind this loss of the old order was a radical and invisible change in the concept of wealth. The older *static* concept was replaced by a new *dynamic* concept. This change explains why our new world of entrepreneurs and financiers replaced the old world of the monarchs.

In a static concept of wealth, wealth is thought of as being limited in quantity and nonrenewable. Wealth is finite and bounded.

In contrast, in the dynamic concept, wealth is conceived of as limitless and renewable. It knows no boundaries in itself. As the Gutenberg revolution took hold, this new concept became the foundation of the new technological civilization.

The reason for the predominance of the static concept of wealth in the Middle Ages is that it was an image of property in land. Land, in itself, is limited and bounded. When wealth is conceived as an image of land, wealth too must be finite and bounded.

---

[11] The French Revolution is an example. It occurred because of the bankruptcy of the monarchy and the unjust tax levies and exactions that it imposed on landowners, industrialists, and merchants. Industries were farmed out as official monopolies. The French revolution at first dismantled the previous regulations, enabling free enterprise and making possible the formation of hundreds of banks of issue.

We can call the static concept of wealth an "earthly" concept, in the sense that it uses as its model land and its boundaries.[12]

## *Monarchy, the power structure of an "earthly" vision*

In the Middle Ages, people who had land held it for generations. To own land, you usually had to inherit it or obtain it by war.

Land is not elastic. It cannot grow or change. This finite supply explains why there were many wars of conquest. Wars enabled aggressors to conquer new territories when they could not purchase them or acquire them by other means. War, in short, can provide a means of expansion and acquisition when things, such as land, are strictly limited in supply. (Wars were also sometimes a legitimate way to defend property against invasion.) Thus, a static and "earthly" concept of limited wealth is conducive to war and violence.

The feudal lords, or in other words the landowners, were the powers of this world.

Because physical territory—land—meant power, those who had more and better land were more powerful than those who did not. So landowners in premodern times had to be organized and arranged in a hierarchy according to their relative power.

The lords' titles (e.g., duke, count) differed according to their relative land power. At the top of the pyramid was usually a king. His kingdom encompassed the holdings of numerous lesser landowners.

All of this power and wealth was based on land as the foundation. In this way, we can see that monarchy is a land-based power structure that is founded on a static, "earthly" concept of wealth.

---

[12] The Physiocrats, a group of eighteenth-century French economists, believed that land is the source of all wealth. Jacques Turgot and François Quesnay were their chief representatives. They had a typical mind-set of static wealth. We must say in favor of the Physiocrats that they foresaw the need for free markets and the free circulation of capital. Turgot had brilliant insights, such as the noncommensurability of value, meaning that the economic value of different eras could not be compared, owing to changes in circumstances.

The static concept, a remnant of the old landowning system of power and wealth, still makes many people think that wealth is bounded, limited, and nonrenewable. However, this model is no longer valid.

The new, more valid concept of dynamic wealth does not debase or belittle the monarchies of old. The monarchies and their aristocratic structure probably were the best system to rule a world efficiently when wealth was seen as static and bounded. Because monarchies were an adequate system for a landowning structure of power and wealth, they formed the worldwide power system and lasted for thousands of years.

Nevertheless, monarchy and its power base had to die.

## *Dynamic, "heavenly" wealth*

In contrast to this "earthly" concept of wealth, we have the dynamic concept of wealth.

In the static, "earthly" concept, wealth is never created but merely possessed. In the dynamic concept, wealth must first be created to be possessed; possession comes from an act of creation that has the unbounded, free human mind as its source.

In this way of thinking, wealth is unbounded and unlimited, because its foundation is not bounded material property, but unlimited creative intelligence.

If land was the image of the limited and static concept of wealth, the heavens are an appropriate representation of the dynamic concept of wealth and its products. The earth is the symbol of hard, quantifiable matter. The sky has always been a symbol of the higher and unlimited powers of the mind.

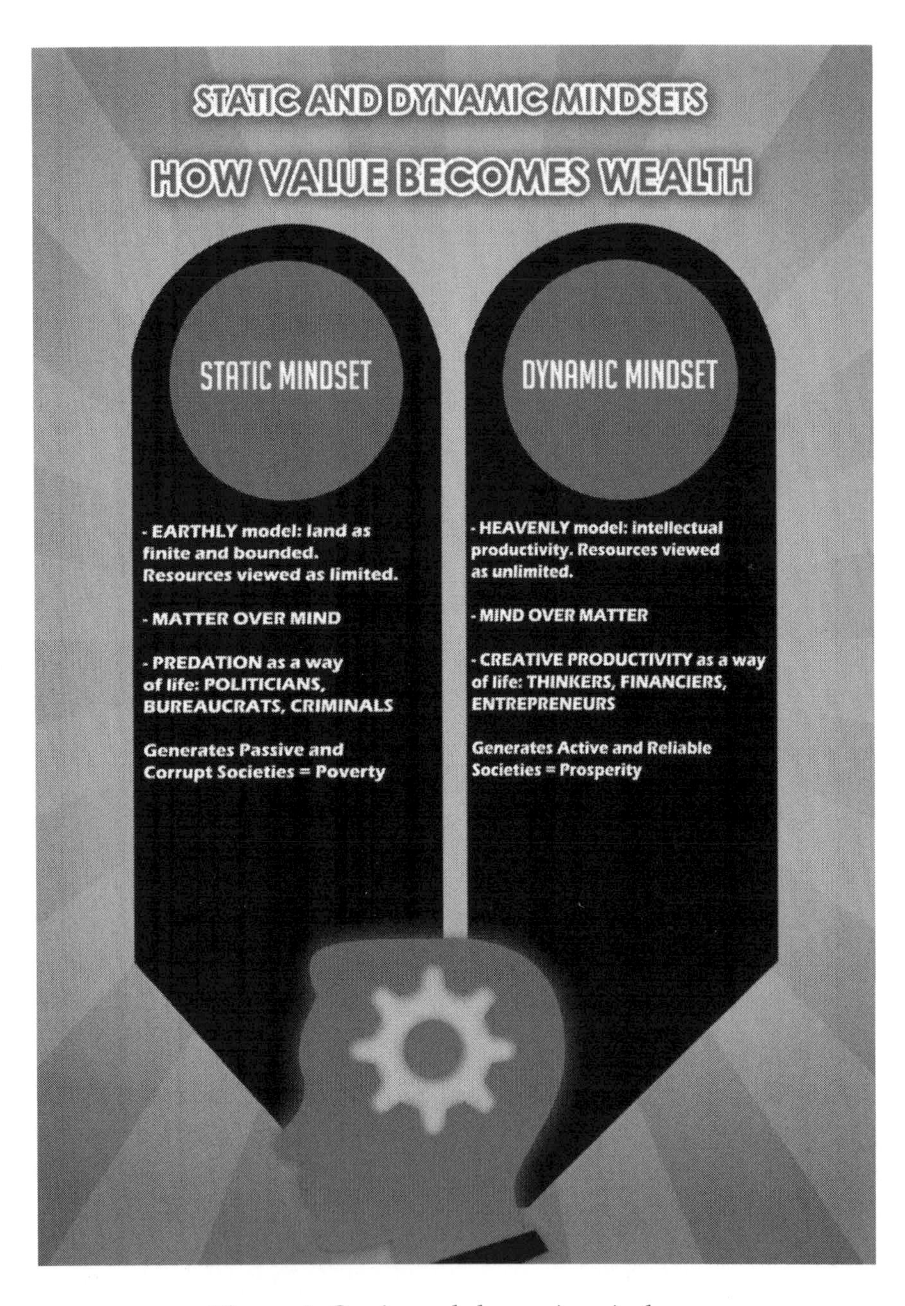


Figure 1. Static and dynamic mindsets

### *The birth of the dynamics of wealth*

The change from a static to a dynamic concept of wealth meant a heavenly ascension in which the human mind and its products became more and more free of material bondage.

The new world order was based on creators of wealth. Inventions and discoveries, rather than land, became the main sources of abundance and prosperity.

There thus arose a meritocracy in which power was no longer based on land and its limits.

The change of paradigm from wealth as static to wealth as dynamic occurred because a new kind of knowledge machine, the printing press, made it possible to exploit the unlimited resources of creativity and invention.

Gutenberg's invention made learning, researching, discovering, and inventing easier. New machines were invented, new scientific principles were discovered, and new information was obtained about nature, the cosmos, and the human race and its geography.

Never before had humanity been on a path that was conducive to unlimited, renewable wealth. A new technology was silently instating a new world order. The printing press had made possible the large-scale creation of wealth through the growth and exchange of knowledge.

The understanding of prosperity shifted toward the new, dynamic, creative concept. The static vision of wealth—and the feudal society built on it—had to go.

The revolutions and the violence that, in some places, accompanied this transformation were superficial phenomena of no consequence. Similarly, all the philosophers and politicians who believed that their arguments for or against monarchy were winning or losing the struggle were mistaken.

Monarchy collapsed, not because of violent revolutions or new political ideologies, but because new, underlying powers were advancing, even without anyone's being aware of them. The rulers of the land were not capable of ruling a technological and financial world.

It was this change that disposed of the old form of government and replaced it with a new one. The new world structures asked for it. Most politicians were not even aware of the shift of society from a static to a dynamic world view.[13]

## *The new world order of ideas*

The source of the new, dynamic wealth was intangible, encapsulated only in intellectual property. Thus intellectual-property rights became relevant. Patents, copyrights, brands, and professional secrets became property.

The material side is secondary in importance. The new machines had their origins in ideas, and the ideas were the source of their value.

Inventors and authors began to make fortunes with their intellectual property. In this way, property and wealth changed hands from owners of land to owners of intellectual property.

The new wealthy individuals were those who benefited from the businesses that were created from intellectual property. The new wealthy countries were those that managed to accumulate the most intellectual property. New empires were built upon this new kind of property.

Even today, however, most people don't consider ideas to be real. Although they see new machines around them, they don't realize that the value of those machines is not in the material objects themselves, but in the ideas behind them.

---

[13] Note that it was possible, although uncommon, for a republic to appear and thrive before the Gutenberg revolution. What matters for creating a republican form of government is the mental attitude that focuses on freedom. Therefore, it is possible to sustain either a republic or a monarchy in a pretechnological society, although it is very difficult to sustain a monarchy in a technological society. See chapter 3 for more on republicanism and democracy.

When we purchase a book, its value comes not from the ink and paper on which it has been printed. Its value and the price that we pay at the bookshop is what we pay for the ideas that the book contains. We cannot reduce a book to simply ink and paper.[14]

The same is true of any machine. Take a car, for example. Its price is not the price of the materials that are used in its construction. What we are paying for when we buy a car is the inventors' idea that has given a form and function to the materials.

Raw materials are not the primary contributors to the worth of a book or a machine. The raw materials have to be organized according to the mind so as to behave in the way that gives the product its function. Price is mind.

When we buy something, we buy ideas, not things.

The persons who have a dynamic perspective on wealth are the wealth creators of our planet. It is thanks to them that the world's population can satisfy its needs and wants.

---

[14] Here we use the term *value* to mean the intrinsic utility of something aside from its material support. Value is mind-bestowed.
Economic value refers to price. For example, a book has an intrinsic value because of the use we can give to its content. A single idea contained in a book could be easily worth millions of dollars to someone even if the price he paid for the book was ten dollars. The price, therefore, is not the real value. The price only expresses the sum of services needed to make the book available to us.
The real value of the book as such is free of charge. We are not paying for the book, but for the services needed to get it into in our hands. Its price is the price that we paid to have people give us the book. The same is true of everything.
Oil, for example, is free. The intrinsic value of oil for us, unlike its price, is nil. We are not paying for the oil itself and the use that we can make of it, but for the chain of services that made oil available to us.
Another example is gold. The price of gold is higher than that of other metals because it is scarcer and no one will make it available for the same price as something easier to obtain. The person who sells gold charges the buyer for the extra trouble of having to obtain it when, for the same amount of time invested, he could have sold us something that is easier to deliver.

The static concept of wealth also has supporters and representatives. Alas, they still form a majority of the human population. But fortunately, their influence has not been sufficient to destroy the new world of technology and invention.

People who support a static concept of wealth are found today mainly in third-world countries. Their belief that wealth is static and "earthly" is the reason that these countries experience poverty and misery. It is in fact their distinctive characteristic. Let us now consider their plight.

# Chapter 2

# The Shadows of Modernity

*It takes effort to destroy a country like Argentina—a country which should have succeeded effortlessly. Serious effort—idiocy at this level is not an accident. It has to be coordinated.*

— Mike Konrad, "How to Destroy a Rich Country," American Thinker, September 20, 2013

The static, "earthly" concept of wealth is prevalent in third-world countries, although it also exists in first-world countries as well. Neither the majority of the populations of these third-world countries nor their ruling political classes understand the nature of the origin of wealth—its dynamic dimension of creativity.

This lack of understanding is found all along the political spectrum, from elected officials to ordinary people.

## THE THIRD WORLD: A STATIC VISION OF WEALTH

Many if not most of the people in third-world countries believe that rich countries exploit and abuse them by acts of legerdemain and are solely responsible for the poverty of their nations. Rich countries, they believe, are to be blamed for the evils of all the other countries of the world.

For those who possess this mentality, it is always the "others," the rich countries, who are responsible for the poor countries' misery and who have a moral obligation to rescue them from the evils that they have brought about. This is an argument that is heard frequently at all levels of society in these third-world countries.

The attitude at the root of this static perspective of value, which places the blame on others, is one of servility and hate. (These are two sides of the same coin.) Servility and hate are found especially in the ruling sectors of third-world society. By denying their responsibility for the poverty and misery in their countries, a segment of the population and the ruling elite of third-world countries are indefinitely postponing the creation of their own future wealth.

It is enough to hear ten seconds of Fidel Castro or Hugo Chávez to understand this. The guilty party is always the "other" party. "Imperialism" is to blame. Such an attitude creates and reinforces a mentality of poverty and misery.

People like Castro or Chavez, or their disciples, provide us with an effective formula to attain poverty and misery in the least possible time. They believe that there is a static, limited amount of wealth in the world, and that if they do not have as much as they want, it is because the rich have stolen it from them.

Poverty and misery are the necessary consequences of perceiving wealth to be static and then acting on this belief. The static mind-set is the invisible attractor that joins all the actions of people who hold such a belief. Their behavior does all that is possible to destroy the prosperity mentality and supply a home for its counterpart.

Such is the power of a single belief. It can structure life positively or negatively. A single belief about the core of social or economic reality can polarize an entire society around it. Such a belief will emerge in that society in several forms and become the center that organizes other beliefs. In the end, all the expressions of this society will bear its mark.

The belief that wealth is static will polarize all of social life toward its own perspective.

The belief in the static nature of wealth is found not only among politicians, but also among most third-world businessmen. For most third-world entrepreneurs, wealth is static. Only a minority of them holds a different viewpoint.

A large segment of third-world countries' businessmen are the best allies of Marxists, socialists, and all those who hold, as a core tenet, the belief that wealth should be distributed according to the needs of each.

For such people, wealth must be acquired by distribution, by an act of social "justice"—rather than through the inherent dynamism of value creation. When wealth is seen as static in nature, it must be taken by force from someone else—it cannot be newly produced. These people have a predatory view, which is that you can and should take wealth away from anyone who has it. Lying and dishonesty accompany this mentality, and words then become meaningless.

This predatory attitude is why some countries' businessmen approve of every kind of government regulation that will favor them. A classic example is the support of tariffs to prevent free international competition. Preventing competition then becomes more important as a goal than creating wealth itself.

## *The premodern businessman*

Furthermore, the third-world entrepreneur usually has a pretechnological vision of the world (as does the third-world politician). Such an entrepreneur will tell himself and others, "I am modern. The machines in my factory are the latest generation of machines and use the newest technology available today."

He will immediately add, "The products of my factory are as good as, if not better than, those that you can find in America or Europe." Our businessman wholeheartedly believes this, and so does his entourage.

However, this businessman is the victim of a delusion. This delusion has its origin in his static concept of wealth, which prevents him from understanding what "modernity" or being "modern" means.

The businessman to whom we are referring can be described as premodern, even if his factory produces the latest generation of high-tech products. He is with all those other people, still the majority in the world, who do not understand modernity.

And this, even though they live in the midst of modernity and its benefits! Let us find out why.

## *Invention, value, wealth, and capital*

The inventions themselves that changed the world are secondary to the spirit that enabled those changes to happen—the spirit of invention itself. Inventing is the foundation of our new world.

We may *use* as many inventions as we like, but without an inventive spirit, we will lack the key that enabled an entirely new world to develop.

The inventor holds the keys to our world's present and future. He has in his hands the ultimate source of power and wealth in our world. This source of power can be likened to an ever-flowing fountain of invention and creation that creates new value and wealth.

Here it is important to explain the difference between wealth and value, and how they relate to invention and entrepreneurship. *Value* is an incorporeal reality: the potential usefulness of a thing or an idea. A wrench, for instance, is potentially useful for turning nuts on a bolt. As soon as you invent a wrench, it has value—potential usefulness—even if nuts and bolts have not yet been invented.

When the usefulness of a thing or an idea is finally found, put into practice, and rewarded, this reward is wealth. For instance, if you invent a wrench and offer it to me in your store, I may be willing to pay you $20 for it. In that sense, the value of the wrench has turned into $20 of wealth.

In other words, value becomes wealth when a product's usefulness is discovered, and the product is offered, and accepted.

However the conversion of inventive and creative value into wealth is not always immediate. A mathematical discovery, such as Galois theory, can wait years before finding an application whose offer and society's acceptance of it becomes wealth.[15] (Originally developed by the mathematician Évariste Galois, who died in 1832, today Galois theory enables us to prove the impossibility of exact algorithms for problems that concern various models of computation.)

The same is true of many technological inventions that occur before their time has come. They must wait for the appropriate circumstances—often other inventions—that will let them express their full value and transform them into wealth.

However, a scientific discovery or an invention, even if it is not converted to immediate wealth, can be a step in helping to make new, valuable discoveries or inventions, some of which will be converted to wealth.

Furthermore, financial wealth can be used as capital. Capital is wealth that assists in creating new value. For instance, capital can provide the resources scientists and inventors need to do their research.

Therefore, wealth is achieved through value creation by invention, and then this wealth can be used as capital to contribute to the creation of more value.

This cycle of value, wealth, and capital is what third-world countries lack. Even worse is that they do not realize that they are lacking it.

---

[15] Evariste Galois (1811–1832) was a French mathematician. He developed a theory of the solvability by radicals of polynomial equations. He died at the age of twenty. His "Galois connections" in computing sciences, for which abstraction is needed to simplify problems to make them computable, help define such abstractions.

Figure 2. The border between a third-world and first-world country

## *Third-world countries live in the shadows*

Those who are not at the inventive centers of science and technology are blind to the origins and causes of wealth. Their world view and concept of value are still static. Therefore, they must suffer the consequences of their lack of vision.

Third-world countries think of themselves as modern countries. In fact, they are not modern, because they have invented nothing of importance. They only use the inventions of other countries.

Their inhabitants, ruling classes included, live in the shadows of modernity. These shadows are the technological products: for example, an airplane, a television, a computer, a microwave, sophisticated machinery, chemicals, or medical equipment. Most people confuse these shadows with the reality behind them.

Living in a city where there are modern buildings, where the inhabitants buy the latest cars and technological goods, and where there are even factories manufacturing such goods, furthers the illusion of being modern. You see, it is possible to benefit from modernity without being modern. Third-world countries, at their best, use the technology and science that has been discovered and developed in first-world countries. The key difference here is between actual invention, or discovery, and the mere use of knowledge invented by others. To be modern means to invent technology and new goods—not merely to reproduce them.

Here, then, is our first fundamental equation: Modernity = Invention.

Third-world countries' factories do not invent or create technology. They reproduce or build what was invented or discovered elsewhere. Discovery or invention never occurs in a third-world country.

For example, the inventions of IBM or HP are created only in first-world countries. If companies in third-world countries could begin to invent, they would help to turn their homelands into first-world countries. Indeed, when a country invents a significant technology, such as the airplane or the microchip, it belongs to the first world by this act alone.

Think of this: Not one third-world country has invented anything of significance for our world. No fundamental invention or discovery has come from them; not from Bolivia or Rwanda or Iraq. Here, we are thinking of such important discoveries or inventions as electricity, the airplane, the double helix, or the microchip.

Of course, a third-world country can have minor discoveries that are extensions of a major invention (though even this rarely happens). The ball point pen was invented in Argentina, but not the telephone or nuclear fusion.

If a person who was born in the third world discovers something important, its discovery and development normally takes place in a first-world country and not in a third-world country. Third-world countries are not at the source of modernity, but at its periphery.

We do not fly in airplanes or use telephones or computers that were invented in third-world countries. Not a single fundamental invention has come from countries such as Bolivia , Rwanda, or Yemen.

We must emphasize this point. When we understand that the technologies that we presently use were not invented in third-world countries, we will see these countries in a different light. We can understand their lack of modernity.

Because they limit themselves to using or reproducing modern technologies, third-world countries are still more backward in the twenty-first century than England was in the seventeenth century.[16]

Such countries lack the source of wealth creation that defines our modern world. Although secondary wealth and value are created in those countries, they depend ultimately on tools that those countries have not created, invented, or discovered. For example, many countries export textiles. They can create textile designs and export the finished materials, but they cannot invent machines like those used to produce textiles.

They depend on centers of invention whose spirit they do not understand. This requires an explanation.

## *The third-world state of mind*

The reason that third-world countries have no inventions or discoveries that matter in science and technology can be found in their collectivist state of mind.

Although those countries have printing presses and computers, and they do disseminate knowledge, these technologies have not stimulated

---

[16] The Industrial Revolution began in England in the eighteenth century and then spread to the rest of Europe.
In Textiles, Richard Arkwright invented the "water frame" used to spin cotton. Samuel Crompton invented the Spinning Mule, patented in 1769, which gave rise to a multitude of cotton mills. Steam power was developed with the James Watt steam engine that was patented in 1775. These are some key innovations of the period.
Today, in our twenty-first century, no third-world country has had an innovation comparable for our times with those that took place in England. Third-world countries are from this point of view more backwards than eighteenth-century England.

in them an inventive mind-set in the fields of science and technology. It seems that the tools of discovery and invention cannot find fertile ground in these countries.

Above all, the first reason for not inventing is having a static concept of wealth and value, instead of a dynamic concept . Note that this concept is not necessarily held consciously.

In a world that has a dynamic concept of value, the emphasis is on the mind and its potential. This is the opposite of what happens in a world that holds a static concept of value. In such a world, the emphasis is on matter—on producing or having or distributing things—and not on inventing them. Static-minded people see inventing as secondary to possessing and distributing.

With this mentality, there is always a dependence on someone else. Entrepreneurs must sell or produce things that someone else has invented. They must mine natural resources using a science and a technology that people in their country did not discover or invent.

## *Every first-world country has its inner third world*

In third-world countries, persons who have a static, "earthly" mind-set outnumber the others and give such countries their defining spirit. This is why the main force of gravitation tends toward the static mind-set and its actions.

However, it is also true that there is a set of people in first-world countries who have "earthly," static mind-sets. To these people, it seems that wealth is permanently limited, and so it must be protected and distributed by government regulations.

The attitude of these people is an aggressive one that embodies the predatory spirit. Most bureaucrats, many businessmen, and most ordinary employees have such an earthly, static mind-set.

These people, although they have good intentions, lack an awareness of their own way of thinking. Their main characteristic is a belief that limiting the free market by a set of regulations will solve any economic problem.

History shows that this has not been the case. Regulation has solved nothing (see chapter 7).

For now, it is enough to say that regulations have been the outcome of a static, "earthly" mind-set. This mind-set has been behind many financial crises that could have been avoided or diminished by leaving free-market forces alone.

The concept of leaving the free market to its own initiative arises from a dynamic, nonpredatory attitude. It results from a belief in the dynamism of free minds in the free market.

In first-world countries, the dynamic mind-set outweighs the static one. It is the prevalence of this dynamic concept of wealth that has made first-world countries what they are.

If the static, "earthly" concept had prevailed, these countries would also belong to the third world.

## *The third world as a state of mind*

In this sense, the third world is a mental attitude rather than an external reality. Third-world countries, or at least their cities, share a familiar landscape—a common look or atmosphere. Whether it is La Paz in Bolivia or Kigali in Rwanda, they look the same. The capitals of these countries may have some nice neighborhoods, but as soon as you go beyond them, a shabby urban landscape prevails.

On a trip to Athens, I looked out from the window of my hotel and saw the rooftops of the city, decrepit and covered in waste. They looked exactly the same as the rooftops in Lima. Even Al Gore has noticed this phenomenon in Cairo, where, he says, "It is not uncommon to see garbage taken to the roofs of the ramshackle homes to decompose in the sun."[17]

---

[17] Al Gore, *Earth in the Balance*, (New York: Rodale Books, 2006) p. 155.

All these third-world cities are similar in their lack of harmony, their unfinished buildings, badly kept roads, and general shabbiness. However, the defining element is the mind-set that prevails.

Poverty and misery cannot exist where there is a dynamic concept of value and wealth, whatever the limitations may be. In contrast, when the static mind-set prevails, physical and mental surroundings are perceived to be limitations that can be overcome only with external help. Man is seen as a helpless victim of someone else or something else.

The static-value-minded individual only follows those who offer to help him. If he is not helped, he grumbles and complains. This professional complaining always begins with politicians and bureaucrats.

This political and bureaucratic complaining extends to government-dependent businessmen and the rest of the population. An attitude of helplessness develops, with blame always directed at other people. This mentality permits the individual to avoid responsibility.

When this attitude is combined with the static, "earthly" concept of value, the poverty machine is set at maximum speed.

With his complaining, the political predator in disguise becomes fully operational and successful. His goal is not to create new value and wealth, but to seize someone else's property. He believes that if he does not pursue this strategy he will obtain nothing.

When the complainers are successful, they obtain what they do not deserve and, in so doing, harm themselves and their countries—as well as the army of those who agree with their complaints.

The result is a misallocation of resources. However, a misallocation of physical resources is the lesser of the two evils in this situation. The greater evil is the misallocation of mental resources, and the reinforcement of the static-value mind-set and the habit of denying all responsibility.

In short, these complaining politicians, bureaucrats, and businessmen are the main destructive forces today, and they are responsible for misery and poverty around the world.

Gutenberg and his revolution are foreign to them. They still live in, and believe in, the poverty mind-set. Their belief translates into actions that transform whatever they touch into deprivation and suffering.

In contrast, when the concept of dynamic value and wealth is ingrained in the population's mentality, poverty and misery never last long, but are only accidental and temporary. In the end, the dynamic mind-set always results in prosperity.

The dynamic attitude sees every desert as something that can be transformed into a garden paradise, and each region of difficult land or topography as something that can be converted into a commercial empire. Poverty and the misery of physical surroundings exist only in the eyes of the beholder.

There is only one true solution to the problem of poverty in the world, and that is for people to acquire a dynamic vision of value and wealth. There is no other road to prosperity.

## INVENTION AND MODERNITY

As mentioned previously, a modern country is not defined as one that offers its inhabitants all the facilities of modern life and has a high-technology industry. Instead, a modern country is one that creates its science and technology and lives off its creations as its source of national income. A modern country creates incorporeal value—new ideas. All the industries of developed countries are born from a discovery, idea, or invention. An inventor is always behind the value creation that changes into wealth.

## *Creativity released*

From such value creation, organizations that are today's household names, such as General Electric, Coca Cola, and 3M were born. These corporations were each created to enact a profitable idea.

As indicated previously, when we purchase something, we do not purchase the physical article but its idea instead. In the end, we are purchasers of ideas. The matter in which ideas are embodied is secondary. It is the idea that gives the value.

The mass of plastic, metal, or silicon in a computer is, for all practical purposes, worthless. The value of a computer is in the "form" into which matter has been molded and which then becomes the material expression of its idea.

The same is true in the arts. The marble of a sculpture is not what gives it value. The Pietà of Michelangelo is not valuable because of the material it was fashioned from. The value is in the artist's idea that was conveyed in the sculpted form.

The same can be said of the canvas and oils of a painting masterpiece, such as those by Rembrandt or Picasso. Canvas and oil are not what give value to the work of art. The value lies in the artist's idea and his expression of it.

The same principle can be applied to a work of literature. If paper and ink were the only criteria for valuing such a work, writing would be valueless. The value comes from the ideas conveyed by the vehicle of paper and ink. An idea is what gives value to a book.

This principle can be extended to labor. It is not the work of the laborers that provides the value of something, but the idea behind that work. The idea will give the thing its usefulness and thus its value.

When a worker uses a machine, he can be thought of as using "leverage," in the sense that by using the machine he is doing work that he is unable to do by himself. The machine's "leverage" is the idea behind it. Such a worker acquires his worth because of the machine. Without the machine, he would produce far less, his income would be lower, and his employer's profits would be lower. Without the machine, the worker might not have a job.

A computer, for example, enables us to do things that we could never imagine doing so efficiently without it. Writing with the aid of word-processing software, or doing complex calculations using spreadsheets, gives us tremendous "leverage." We are indebted to machines for much of what we do.

### *Wealth is in the mind*

True value is never defined by the amount of work, but by the quality of the work. It is the idea and its usefulness that are the true measures of value.

The entrepreneur is the vehicle that enables ideas to assume material form and to serve society. His function is to create products or services around ideas, thereby making them useful.

We should distinguish between entrepreneurs and businessmen. The businessman is not always an entrepreneur. Many businessmen base their wealth on government monopoly and regulations. They could not operate in a free market. For instance, some insurance businesses and some industries exist only because of regulations.

I prefer to reserve the use of the word "entrepreneur" for its original meaning, which is attributed to Jean-Baptiste Say, the French economist (1767–1832). The entrepreneur is the main character in Say's economic model. Say was the first economist to consider the entrepreneur as an active force.

According to Say, the entrepreneur is the person who creates new possibilities of value and wealth. He is the antithesis of the government official. He enables new value to be distributed to all corners of the earth.

Think, for example, of the commercial electric light bulb, which we owe to Thomas Edison. He was not only an inventor but an entrepreneur. He created, among other businesses, the Edison Electric

Light Company, which later became General Electric. GE is the oldest company in the Dow Jones Industrial Index, and it still creates new products in its R&D laboratories.

The entrepreneur who invests and who pays salaries is taking a risk for the sake of an idea. Each additional salary that he pays is an additional unit of risk for him. The entrepreneur's generosity makes him the backbone of society. Entrepreneurs accomplish the dreams of mankind and give them reality in often-unexpected ways.

Entrepreneurs come in many guises. An inventor is an entrepreneur; so are a writer and an industrialist. An artist is an entrepreneur just as much as is a merchant. The entrepreneur is the one who directs the passage of an idea from the stage of its initial conception all the way to its enactment.

The entrepreneur sacrifices his time and effort and, above all, his comfort and security. He does this without knowing in advance the outcome of his actions: He could succeed or he could lose it all. He gives up a part of his life for a reward that he may not ever receive. As careful as he is in estimating and controlling his risk, which all entrepreneurs who deserve the name attempt to do, he cannot guarantee his success.

According to Say, the entrepreneur is the agent who enables knowledge to be applied to create a useful product. To achieve this, the entrepreneur pulls together all the people and things necessary for the task.[18]

Thomas Edison's achievements were made possible, not only by his own genius, but also by the team he assembled to work with him. There were around forty or fifty men, most of them specializing in different branches of science and engineering. Edison built a lab for his team in Menlo Park, New Jersey. The main lab was a two-story

---

[18] Jean-Baptiste Say, *Traité d'Economie Politique* (Paris: Guillaumin, 1876) book II, pp. 393, 396. For Say, the goal of the entrepreneur is "to apply existing knowledge to the creation of a product we can use."

wooden building. Two or three of the houses near the laboratory housed the staff and their families.

Among his key coworkers we can mention Charles Batchelor, an Englishman who came to the United States to work with Edison as his principal assistant in laboratory experiments; Francis R. Upton, employed as mathematician; John Kruesi, a Swiss trained in mechanics, who was able to understand and execute accurately Edison's ideas and sketches.

Edison and his team were able to achieve so much because they lived in a milieu that did not put obstacles on entrepreneurs and inventors. They were a community of like-minded men living in a country where a critical mass of achievers in science and business gathered together from all around the world, because they found the conditions favorable to the development of their minds and talents.

Menlo Park became the birthplace of the incandescent lamp, the phonograph, the dynamo, the electric railway, the carbon transmitter that became the heart of modern telephones, the first storage battery, the dictaphone, and multiple other inventions.

Edison had 1,093 separate patents in his name. No one else comes even close. Edison achieved all this because he invented a *method of invention*, gathering like-minded individuals to work together in the first modern research facility.

The creative seed of ideas and invention is at the base of all progress and development of countries. This seed enables countries to create dynamic and infinitely renewable wealth. We find in it the keys to economic and political power.

## *Never impose limits on reality*

Material goods embody the seed of creativity. However, these goods owe their value, not to matter, but to a creative mind that discovers an idea that can become corporeal and thus overcome the old limitations of reality.

Reality, then, always surprises us. When someone says that something cannot be done, sooner or later an inventor comes along who does it and, in so doing, erases that boundary or a frontier.

One example was the case of the Wright brothers. At the turn of the century, a member of the London Royal Academy, Lord Kelvin, argued that an airplane carrying men could never usefully fly, saying, "I have not the smallest molecule of faith in aerial navigation other than ballooning." But in the end, reality disproved this brilliant man's contention through the achievements of two humble bicycle makers, Orville and Wilbur Wright, at Kitty Hawk.

When almost nobody else thought that an airplane could be a viable means of human transport, the Wright brothers did. They created value from nothing—out of thin air. Their source of wealth was not land or war, but mind, creativity, and invention.[19]

Again, we have a lesson to learn. The lesson is to never put limits on our concept of reality. We must always leave a door open to the opportunities or possibilities that reality can offer us. The base of all value and wealth is, finally, reality itself, whose possibilities are unlimited.

This unlimited concept of reality provides the basis for our dynamic concept of wealth—the concept that has enabled wealth to be created on a scale never seen before.

The unlimited concept of reality is the ultimate foundation upon which the creative seed has grown. And the creative seed of invention and discovery is the basis of all progress and development of societies. This seed enables the production of dynamic and inexhaustible value and wealth. It encompasses the keys to all power in politics and economics. However, it requires a condition that enables it to blossom to its fullest.

---

[19] The Wright brothers' key invention was the three-axis method for controlling a plane's flight, which made airplane flight safe enough to be used.

This condition is none other than freedom. Only in free countries with free people can creativity develop its maximum possibilities.

The wealthiest countries are those that have the greatest freedom. The poorest countries are those that have little or no freedom. There is a simple reason for this: Where freedom exists, the restrictions on reality are less, enabling us to develop more of its infinite possibilities. And these possibilities provide the opportunities to create value and wealth.

## *Science and the Gutenberg revolution*

Remember that technology and industry have a long past. They did not appear because of the printing press. Science and technology have existed since the beginnings of humanity.

The difference is that mankind did not have a vehicle for large-scale dissemination of knowledge until the printing press entered the picture.

One unequivocal measure of the wealth of countries is what we could call it the "reading index of wealth." In general, the wealthiest countries are not only those with great freedom, but also those where people read the most.

According to the OECD's PISA 2000 Report,[20] third-world countries have lower levels of reading skills than the developed world.

For one study on reading habits in third world universities, Michael Smithies from the Nanyang Technological Institute of Singapore chose a "fairly typical third world institution, the Papua New Guinea University of Technology." The study showed that most students read nothing outside their course readings. Thirty-three percent of the students read nothing other than their textbooks. Most of the others

[20] Ray Adams and Margaret Wu, eds., *PISA 2000 Technical Report* (Paris: OECD [Organisation for Economic Co-ordination and Development] 2002), http://www.oecd.org/edu/school/programmeforinternationalstudentassessmentpisa/pisa2000technicalreport-publications2000.htm.

read one book in two or more months. And 27 percent had never used the reference section of their university library.[21]

Reading is the Gutenberg act par excellence. It is where the distribution and exchange of knowledge occurs. So the "reading index" can show us the state of the Gutenberg revolution daily.

The Gutenberg revolution is as real today as it was in the days when Gutenberg invented the printing press, if not more real. In addition, the consequences for mankind not only continue, but are increasing exponentially.

## THE NEW WORLD ORDER AND THE NEW KINGS

A new world of creativity, invention, and industry needs a political order that provides the freedom necessary for this development to take place—a development based on a dynamic concept of value.

Once a large number of people accept such a dynamic concept of value and wealth, reality opens its treasures to humanity as never before. The old, accepted limitations of matter cease to constrain us.

### *From the alchemist to the scientist and the inventor*

Imagine the medieval alchemist. He attempts to convert lead into gold. To him, all matter will be valuable once he learns the secret of its transformation.

Alchemy is more real today than ever before. Scientists and inventors embody all the powers of the alchemists of old. Alchemists were supposed to change base metals into precious metals. The scientists and inventors of today can change almost anything into something valuable. With the unlimited concept of reality, the material world becomes plastic, full of possibilities, with no ultimate boundaries.

---

[21] Michael Smithies, "Reading Habits at a Third World Technological University," *Reading in a Foreign Language* 1, no. 2 (Oct 1983), http://nflrc.hawaii.edu/rfl/PastIssues/rfl12smithies.pdf.

Creative minds can reorganize this raw material almost as alchemists once believed they could.

Matter is accomplishing its plastic potential to its fullest. The limits of what is thought to be possible recede every day, and new frontiers are being discovered. Just think of analysis of the genetic code and the possibility of interplanetary flight. As each limit is vanquished, it generates new possibilities for prosperity.

With this expansion of knowledge, all sciences and technologies also expand. They combine in new ways.

Each invention and discovery opens up more potential avenues of invention and discovery. This reciprocal action compounds. Just as an exponent increases the power of a simple number, each new invention or discovery has its exponential growth and takes us beyond the previous inventions or discoveries.

This growth happens in two stages. The first is a stage where new technologies appear and accelerated growth begins. For example, from the fundamental technology of electricity and generators came new electrical machines, ranging from the radio to the telephone and the washing machine.

The second stage is a plateau. Science reaches an apparent limit, and the new technologies remain at the same level. Each new discovery uses the same ideas, but in a different way. For example, the refrigerator and the doorbell both use mechanisms that operate on electricity.

Then, suddenly, a new technology causes a new leap forward in all other technologies. The new technology not only changes the way in which our technology used to work, but changes our way of thinking and behaving.

Here is an example. In the premechanical age, transportation involved walking or riding a horse or perhaps a horse-drawn carriage. Medicinal plants were collected and used for their healing powers. Defense used human power to operate arrows, spears, and swords.

Then technology became mechanical. Mechanical devices and machines, such as clocks, windmills, watermills, or steam locomotives, harnessed natural forces. The next step involved using electricity to power all these inventions.

Electronics followed, and, after it, computing power.

A bicycle, a steam locomotive, and a steam ship are examples of mechanical transport. The first is fueled by human power, the second and third are fueled by a combustible agent that produces heat.

The next step involves electricity, as in a motorcycle, a car, or a diesel-motor-propelled ship. Each requires electricity to ignite an explosive gas that activates the motor. In the electric car or train, electricity itself becomes the motive force. A further step refines electricity into electronics, transforming force into information that controls systems.

A medical ventilator is a machine to move breathable air into the lungs. The first and simplest ones were hand-operated machines. Ventilators later became powered by electricity and electronics—their motion and later much of their controls not depending on direct human effort.

Laparoscopic surgery uses electricity and electronics in a machine called a laparoscope, which enables the surgery to be conducted through a small incision. This allows surgeons to avoid making a large cut in order to perform a procedure such as an appendectomy. The laparoscope uses a tiny fiber-optic line to illuminate the operative field inside the patient, and transfers images through a video camera to the surgeons.

Guns and cannons are mechanical defense devices. Each one triggers an explosion that launches a projectile. The company BAE Systems has developed for the US Navy a rail gun, a weapon that uses electricity instead of traditional explosives to shoot high-speed projectiles.[22] A Taser is another example of an electrical weapon. It is used in personal

---

[22] Sharon Weinberger, "The Navy's Electric Cannon Fires Its First Shots," *Popular Mechanics*, Feb. 28, 2012, http://www.popularmechanics.com/technology/military/weapons/the-navys-electric-cannon-fires-its-first-shots-6969929.

defense to give an electroshock. Nowadays, missiles are guided by radio and radar, in what can be called the electronic era of weapons.

The examples above show how mechanisms that are initially human powered refine themselves and become enhanced first by fuels ignited by mechanical force, then by fuels ignited by electricity. Later, electricity itself becomes the motive force, and finally electronics makes those mechanisms "intelligent" in the sense that they not only manipulate raw force but manage information to regulate their own operations.

Thus, every technology is elevated to a higher degree: mechanics is enhanced by fuels, the fuel mechanisms become electric, then electricity replaces the fuels, and ultimately electronics takes over the mechanisms as their guidance and control systems.

## *The inventive society*

As a result of the Gutenberg revolution, and of the refinement of the scientific procedures of thought, what was once spontaneous discovery or invention was eventually refined into a science of method. Ways to collect, consider, refine, and test information began to be developed. Rigorous procedures of thought and verification were established.

An inventive society was born. It was the society of entrepreneurs—of dreamers who each dared to imagine something new and transform it into reality. Many enterprises flourished, and our world is the result.

Think of it: at the end of your day at the office, you turn the lights off, you take the elevator, and you get into your car. Then you can go to the airport and board a plane that will take you anywhere in the world, while you work on a spreadsheet on your laptop computer.

All of these technologies had to be invented and produced and sold by someone. The number of inventions that you depend on in your daily life is staggering. But someone came up with each of them.

These inventors are the people on whom our daily world rests. In turn, they and their achievements depended on the freedom to communicate, create, and exchange.

Many of those people built up enterprises, such as ITT, Coca-Cola, General Electric, Dow Jones and Co., Hewlett-Packard, and 3M. Behind all of those companies were inventor-entrepreneurs who dared to think in new ways.

They were not isolated individuals. They could do what they did because they teamed up with others to achieve their goals. Often the team consisted of three people—the inventor "entrepreneur," the manager and accountant, and the salesman.

One example of a three-person team is Dow Jones and Co., which Charles Dow and Edward D. Jones created together with Charles M. Bergstresser in 1882. Dow was the thinker, who invented new ways of analyzing and understanding markets. Jones was the salesman, accountant, and manager. Charles M. Bergstresser managed the business and provided start-up capital as a silent partner.

In other cases, the inventors were forced by circumstances to do what they did. In 1902 five men, Henry S. Bryan, Hermon W. Cable, John Dwan, William A. McGonagle, and Dr. J. Danley Budd, all of them shrewd businessmen, set out to work a mine in the Lake Superior town of Two Harbors, in Minnesota.

Their goal was to mine the mineral deposits for grinding-wheel abrasives. For this, they created the Minnesota Mining and Manufacturing Company (3M. But as soon as they tried to work the mine, they encountered a seemingly insurmountable obstacle: the mineral deposits had no value for their intended purpose.

The businessmen were not deterred by this failure. On the contrary, they struggled and persevered until they transformed failure into success.

They reoriented their company's resources (over the course of the next decade) in order to make a sandpaper called "Wet or Dry," the first waterproof sandpaper. From then on, 3M went from success to success, growing continuously even to today.

Among their achievements we can count Scotch Tape in 1925, the Thermo Fax copying system, the dry silver microfilm in 1960, and Post-it Notes in 1980. Besides that, they created products for defense in World War II, and for pharmaceuticals, radiology, and energy control.

In 2008 they developed an ultracompact LED projector that could be integrated into personal electronic devices. In 2009 they introduced the 3M Littmann Electronic Stethoscope Model 3200, with Bluetooth technology.

The outstanding inventive record of 3M is due to their corporate culture. They invented a corporation whose job was to stimulate invention in all its employees. The success of 3M is due in part to the fact that anybody in the company can submit an idea. Mind power has been and is the most important capital behind 3M. Its success is living proof that a mind-set of dynamic value and wealth has no limits, because that mind-set is anchored in the infinite and boundless essence of reality.

That's what these five unique businessmen understood when they confronted that initial failure in 1902 and converted it into success, abolishing the limits that matter seemed to impose on them.

Their long-lasting success was not the result of any particular invention. Instead, their legacy of success came from the creation of an entrepreneurial culture that democratized creativity, stimulating it at all levels and helping it achieve its potential.

This is an example of a company that not only turned a setback into an opportunity, but also developed it into a procedure, an inventing methodology that became the backbone of their business.

3M holds the secret of how the prosperous countries of the first world came into being. Value-creating entrepreneurs, thinking with a dynamic concept of value and wealth, built them.

### *Creators need their own social order*

The new power centers that emerged from this way of thinking and creating required a new kind of social order to support them. This new system was representative democracy. Land-based monarchy gave way to open-ended, mind-based leadership, and the new king of this new world was the entrepreneur.

The entrepreneur, whether his role is that of writer, artist, scientist, industrialist, financier, or merchant, is the ruler of the new society. The Edisons, the Bells, the Teslas, the J.P. Morgans, the Carnegies, and the Picassos have become the new masters of the planet.

Above all, these new kings needed freedom. The freedom to create and to express oneself embodies their ideas. Achieving freedom was not always easy.

For many of these entrepreneurs, the old world of land-based monarchies and static wealth had become an obstacle. A new world was then born, and America came to have a special place in it as the land of freedom, opportunity, and the future.

But a question remains unanswered. How have the developed countries managed to create a world that is the image of their ideas and projections? Why have these countries become what they are today? And why haven't the majority of countries been able to follow those developed countries in this unique adventure of the human spirit?

We will now examine the difference between the successful countries and the others.

The answer lies in capitalism.

## CAPITALISM: ITS TRUE NATURE AND ITS SECRET MEANING

Our point of departure is that the countries that we call third-world countries have not understood the nature of capitalism or modernity. Further, they have not understood the link between the two. Capitalism is a natural, nonartificial system of private ownership of the means of production, ideally in a completely free market.

We constantly hear leaders of third-world countries proudly mentioning their natural resources as the main source of all wealth. "Our country has everything, gold, silver, copper, agriculture," we hear them saying.

For them, wealth means the material possessions of the land. They do not understand the difference between their third-world countries and first-world countries, except that they are poor and the others are not.

This kind of reasoning goes so far that a few third-world economists believe that the exportation of industrial products from developed countries is merely a stratagem to overprice raw materials. In other words, when Germany sells a harvesting machine to Bolivia, some third-world economists see that machine simply as a way to sell overpriced iron or copper. They cannot see that the value does not come from the copper used, but from intellectual property, the value of the idea behind the harvesting machine.

An example of this way of thinking is provided by Argentinean economist, Raúl Prebisch, an advocate of import substitution, the replacement of imports by domestic production, in third-world countries (to avoid being cheated in this manner by first-world countries). For the countries that adopted the Prebisch plan—Argentina, Bolivia, Brazil, Chile, Ecuador, Mexico, Peru, Uruguay, and Venezuela—the results of his beliefs were catastrophic.

These countries ended up paying more for their imports than before. Instead of importing the finished article, for example a car, they imported the parts with which to assemble it in their country. In the end, the cost of importing the parts was higher than that of importing the finished article.

At the same time they banished imports of raw materials; resulting in inefficiency, low quality, and higher costs of production. Protectionism and import substitution made those countries poorer than ever.

This protectionist attitude is born from a defensive reflex that seems fully justified—if we are unaware that value and wealth are dynamic. If wealth and value were static and not dynamic, those economists would be correct in their reasoning. If this were the case, value would lie almost exclusively in land or land-like property of some kind, or perhaps in the number of hours worked. Only raw possession and brute working force would account for value.

In this view, no account would be taken of the intellectual quality of the final product—the value of the idea behind the good. In such a case, it would be normal to resist having to pay for the idea, instead of paying only for the raw matter.

If ideas are of no significance, there is little reason to pay for them. It would be logical to refuse to pay for any kind of added value. This lack of perception may seem so obvious that we may think that no one would fall for it.

Unfortunately, this is not the case. Even a mind like that of the famous British economist David Ricardo (1772–1823) fell into this limited kind of thinking. To Ricardo, the only measure of value was the number of hours worked. He could not conceive of any other way of defining value beyond pure raw quantity of input.[23]

---

[23] Ricardo tells us that "the quantity of labor employed on commodities determines the rate at which they will exchange for each other," this being for him the "rule for measuring relative value." However, a month before his death, he wrote, "I cannot get over the difficulty of the wine which is kept in a cellar for three or four years, or that of the oak tree, which perhaps had not 2 [shillings]. expended on it in the way of labour, and yet comes to be worth £100." Quoted in Mark Skousen, *The Making of Modern Economics*, (Armonk, NY: M.E. Sharpe, 2001), pp. 107, 108.

He believed this so strongly that his greatest puzzle was why antique furniture could be worth more than the material it was made from plus the hours spent by the worker to finish the product. Ricardo could never solve the problem. Because of his limited idea of value, Ricardo unwittingly became the father of Marxism,, which considers time worked as the only measure of value.

For a Marxist, one Einstein hour is worth the same as one plumber's hour. No difference. No added value—or, more accurately—no value at all.

In the static view, value is conceived merely as a quantity of raw materials and labor time. This comes from an inability to perceive the true source of value, and it leads to a defensive attitude. This belief is common among third-world country leaders and their populations.

In short, creation has no meaning for them—nor does real value. Only raw materials and raw work time matter.

All of this originates in the atavism of "earthly" ideas, where wealth is still considered to be static and where mafias reign. These mafias exist because the chief wealth-acquisition methods, when creation is not possible, are depredation and corruption.

We never hear about "invention" in those countries, because it is a meaningless word for them. The corrupt customs officer does not envision or care about invention as a source of wealth.

## *Creators of value in the third world*

The entrepreneur, in the meaning that Jean-Baptiste Say gave to this word, is the creator of value. It is this sort of person that enables a country to become rich. Becoming rich implies having a dynamic, alchemist's mentality in which wealth and value come from an act of creation.

In third-world countries, this kind of mentality is absent, except in isolated individuals. These isolated persons must do everything by themselves, because there is not even an echo of collective support for a creative or inventive act.

Such a lack of collective support probably explains why creators in third-world countries must take refuge in the arts, as writers, painters, or musicians. People in those fields do not require complex social support to succeed. When there is no collective support, technological creation cannot take place. This is why third-world countries have first-rate sculptors and poets, but lack scientists who make discoveries of significance or inventors who create important new technologies.

Despite these artistic creators, there is practically no wealth being created from a dynamic source in the third world. All wealth in those countries comes from nondynamic sources, static sources. With a static mentality, resources, which are ostensibly limited, are defended at the expense of creating new wealth. By concentrating only on possessions, the people forsake the creation of new wealth.

The people do not invent or conduct sufficient research to have significant results. Habits that are conducive to thinking, knowing, inventing, and discovering, such as reading books, are not common. It is not often that you see people in third-world countries reading in cafés, parks, or buses as you do in rich countries.

In short, the main results of the printing press, discovery, and invention, are absent. Modernity still has not arrived.

## *The social order must adapt to the creation of value*

We see in third-world countries that churches, associations and other kind of organizations adopt the defense of the "less favored." This action of defending the "less favored" is misleading and produces results that are the exact opposite of those that are expected or sought.

The one who adopts the defense of the weak is a victim of the same illusion that makes third-world countries what they are, poor countries. The reason is that the defenders have a static concept of wealth and value, which they want to impose on everyone else.

For them, poverty has exclusively one source—"social injustice"—whatever that means. As wealth and value are available only in limited quantities (from their static viewpoint), the acquisition of wealth can only be an act of aggression and force, stealing what belongs to others.

When there is one pie for all, justice can only mean cutting it into pieces of equal size. So all differences of wealth must be the results of injustice, aggression, or abuse.

This is why, in the mentality of many third-world people, there is a deeply rooted belief that all wealth comes from a primal crime. They lack the insight to perceive that dynamic value is the origin of all wealth. As long as they lack this insight, neither they nor their countries will ever shake off poverty.

# Chapter 3

# Democracy and Its Misrepresentations

*All the great governments of the world—those now existing, as well as those that have passed away—have been of this character. They have been mere bands of robbers, who have associated for purposes of plunder, conquest, and the enslavement of their fellow men.*

— Lysander Spooner, Natural Law, 1882

~

*"Liberalism, recognizing that the attainment of the economic aims of man presupposes peace, and seeking therefore to eliminate all causes of strife at home or in foreign politics, desires democracy....*
*Democracy without Liberalism is a hollow form."*

— Ludwig von Mises, Socialism: An Economic and Sociological Analysis, 1951

Democracies do not work in third-world countries. The governments look like democracies, but they are not.

We have seen that monarchy as a form of government is linked to, and goes along with, a static and "earthly" concept of value. Monarchy and its static concept of value are not compatible with an industrial, techno-scientific society, except as a decorative remnant of the past.

## THIRD-WORLD COUNTRIES ARE CONCEALED DICTATORSHIPS

As to third-world countries, their continuing static concept of value is the main reason why democracy is not, and cannot be, their natural system of government. Third-world countries can only be dictatorships, despite whatever appearances they may give.

Democracy in those countries is a political artifice that a clique uses for its own benefit at the expense of the people. Because the citizens live within the rules of a formal democracy, they believe that they are democrats. But the country lacks all of the elements that are necessary for a democracy to function.

For those third-world populations and their leaders, democracy comes from the outside. It has been imposed upon them by a few rich countries. They know this but will never publicly admit it.

They will never admit that their democracy is a parody for the simple reason that they have constructed their jobs, their lives, and their survival around this political travesty.

If democracy in third world countries is a parody and a travesty of real democracy, the opposite is true in rich countries. Democracy for the latter is not only a legitimate form of government that works relatively well, but much more.

For rich countries, democracy is the historical, legitimate, and natural form of government that flows from their social and economic structures. Democracy is their natural form of efficient government.

This takes us to the source of all differences between poor, third-world countries and rich, first-world countries.

On one side we have a kleptocracy, an association of delinquents that is natural to third-world countries. Kleptocracy derives from a static vision of wealth and value in which, because wealth is static, it is only natural to take it from others by force. The people of third-world countries still hold the old-fashioned view that wealth and value are composed of material possessions, landownership, natural-resource exploitation, or traditional industry.

On the other side, we have the defenders of a dynamic concept of value and wealth, who seek, as their natural way of government, a democracy within a framework of law and freedom. Rich countries, for which wealth is dynamic and springs from inventions that create value, hold this view.

The supporters of a dynamic concept of value believe that, because you create wealth, you do not have to steal it from anyone. You do not need to become a predator and victimize the legitimate creators of value.

## *Politics, privileges, and pretechnological businesses*

The leadership of third-world countries consists mainly of a few families whose members are landowners, politicians, or businessmen in traditional industries.

Also, those families and people all know one another. They form a small group. We could say, instead, that they resemble an enlarged family that may be linked through friendship, marriage, or business alliance.

This small group of people will try to establish a democracy in order to rule the rest of the population. In doing this, they think of themselves as modern and avant-garde. They think that they are at the edge of the spirit of their times.

In this belief, they delude themselves. Nothing could be further from democracy and modernity than the kind of rule that they have created.

What they have done in good faith and ignorance is to superimpose an incompatible system onto their countries. They have superimposed the external form of democracy onto a society that has an "earthly," static, and feudal concept of value and wealth.

This is why third-world countries' democrats are in fact absolutists. Their democracies do not work and will never work.

Their government regulations are intended for the benefit of politicians and their business associates. A system of predators is in place, attacking and harassing the creators of wealth. Thus, business is based on privileges that depend on proximity to the holders of political power.

Furthermore, as explained before, the kind of business done in these countries is the kind that existed before the technological era. Mining, real estate, landownership, and textiles have existed since the beginning of civilization.

Of course, these pretechnological businesses now have high-tech machines and tools and management systems. But what they do is not modern at all.

In a third-world country, not only is business pretechnological, but politics exists to prevent any competition or new market share that would put the friends of the government out of business.

Thus, politicians are gang leaders whose primary concern is the conservation of their privileges and the enhancement of their power. To these people, political principles are tools to be fashioned as needed to satisfy the credulity of voters.

This is true for politicians across the entire spectrum. Ideas do not matter. Principles do not matter. These politicians excel in the art of cheating and dissembling. Public image is all that matters to them.

## *Third-world politicians are mafiosos*

Politicians are enslaved to public image because deep in their hearts they have no belief in themselves or their countries. The politicians realize that they are not needed and must create false visions and play on the people's fear and greed to maintain their influence over the population.

These are the mafiosos who create the dangers that cause you to ask them for protection. All third-world problems are created by governments themselves, which must make radical changes to justify their existence.

For example, many third-world governments have created hyperinflation, which they have had to combat, or terrorism, which they have had to suppress violently. Of course, they *had* to address these problems, but this is not the point. The point is that they created the problems in the first place.

Not only were the politicians responsible for such evils, but many politicians or government officials actually benefited from them. In free, unregulated countries, these things rarely happen.

The reason that they happen in third-world countries is that the countries suffer from a political regime that is not suited to them. The regime is not suited to them because the wealth of these countries does not come from research, scientific discoveries, or technological inventions.

These countries do not have enough scientists, researchers, or inventors to create original value that transforms itself into wealth. There is no alliance or partnership between businessmen and inventors in these countries.

The research in these countries is marginal and not integrated with the economy or society. Consequently, their democracies can be only external—third-world democracy is a simple formality that enables politicians to better depredate their victims.

In a third-world country, democracy is purely artificial. It serves as the chief alibi for mafioso-politicians. It is an easy-to-believe facade that conceals their true intentions.

## *Why politicians are predators*

The goal of the third-world politician is to accumulate power at any cost. To achieve this, he must get rid of all competition.

His is a game of "whoever gets caught lying first, loses." Regardless of what a politician says, you should never believe him. He has his own agenda and will say whatever is needed to gain your support. He can never be trusted to keep his word.

The politician knows that he lies. More than that, he has turned lying into a fine art and a sophisticated game. The rules of the game are simple. He must outguess his opponents and render their lies public, while avoiding exposure of his own lies.

For every one of his opponent's lies that he discovers (or can claim to have discovered), the politician wins a point. For every one of his own lies that he manages to conceal, he avoids losing a point. In the end, the winner is the one who manages to conceal his own lies and corruption while exposing and making public those of his opposition.

In the Philippines (often considered the most corrupt country in Asia), the *Economist* reported in 2014 that two opposition senators were jailed and "accused of stealing public funds." And "the opposition says the round-up is simply a political vendetta, and that in a genuine campaign members of the ruling coalition could be jailed, too."[24]

Meanwhile, the British Arabic news site *al-Araby* reports that "Corruption in Iraq is the norm, so much that politicians regularly

[24] *Economist*, June 28, 2014.

accuse each other of corruption, to deflect accusations against themselves."[25]

The politician does all this shamelessly. That is what the business of being a politician is all about. The happiest moment for the politician is when he has managed to make his public believe that he is honest. He has won the politician's game. Wealth and fame will be his.

Every politician in the world knows that he cannot create anything. His wealth comes from preying on other people's businesses in ways that make people think that what he has done was in their interest.

To understand a politician's mind, imagine that Al Capone has managed to win the presidential election. Now ask yourself, What would Al Capone do if he had political power over the entire country?

Not much imagination is needed to solve this riddle. Well, the politician is already where Al Capone might have wished to be in his most secret dreams. Full power to ransack and plunder is the politician's privilege.

Finding new ways to tax and extract money from the unwilling and unsuspecting public that voted for him is every politician's job. He must use his creativity to find new methods of doing this while making everyone believe that it is for the common good.

This predatory role of the politician is compounded in third-world countries, because there is no new wealth from creative sources in those countries. When there is little wealth and it is in only a few hands, depredation becomes the number-one economic activity. The small number of entrepreneurs will become the victims of politicians, bureaucrats, and lawyers.

The magic of political depredation is complete when those same entrepreneurs become willing victims and feel guilty for the wealth

---

[25] Mundher al-Adhami, *al-Araby*, April 24, 2015, http://www.alaraby.co.uk/english/comment/2015/4/24/iraq-is-suffocating-under-an-oil-slick-of-corruption.

which they have created and without which their poor countries would not even survive.

Not only have the politicians and bureaucrats stolen the entrepreneurs' wealth, they have also fully turned their minds. This alienation of minds is far worse than the alienation of their material wealth, for recovering money is easier than recovering one's mind.

### *Why Marxists are royalists*

Marxists, of course, have a static concept of wealth and value. We must point out that Marxism has many names. However, "socialism," "collectivism," and various systems of "social justice" are all the same. They are just some of the many clothes that predators and their friends use to disguise themselves.

In their static world view, Marxists believe that quantitative work is the only measure of value. Any profit in excess of quantitative work is, to them, stolen wealth that must be distributed equally. To achieve this, the wealth must be taken by force.

That is the simple truth about the "class struggle" promoted by Marxists. The Marxists' goal is a revolution in which proletarians will fight capitalists to take their wealth, which they consider to be the fruits of exploitation. Their intention is to have a society in which all property is owned collectively. The proletarians must take by force the wealth that is not yet under their control. So Marxists attempt to create the conditions for a revolution. They seek to increase the differences among classes—to accentuate to the maximum what they call the contradictions in society, until the proletarians finally wake up and revolt.

For Marxists, ideas and principles do not matter. These things form a mere superstructure above reality that is without real existence. They are mere "ideology." For Marxists, this is nothing more than a word game in which you say whatever is convenient in order to ransack and plunder the wealthy.

In the end, Marxism is a pretext to steal, defraud, blackmail, and prey on the population. This predation arises from the belief that wealth is static and limited. When someone else has wealth, you must take it from him by any means possible.

In this, Marxists share the world view of the monarchies of old. The old regimes were based on a hierarchy of landowners in a static, nondynamic concept of wealth. The hierarchy was absolute. Each member enjoyed special privileges according to his level in the pyramid.

The same happens with Marxist governments, as seen in Cuba and the former Soviet Union. A privileged class, the nomenklatura and the commissars, hold all power in the name of the people.

There was a joke in communist Romania. They used to say that all Romanians, thanks to communism, were able to eat caviar—through their authorized representatives.

Marxism in government is a static pyramid of privileges. In this, it resembles the pyramids of the absolute monarchies just before they fell, when they had become bureaucracies of predators.

Remember that monarchy was the best system to rule a country of landowners in a world where wealth and value were primarily static. The technology to make possible a world in which wealth is conceived dynamically did not exist at that time. So the rulers did the best that they could.

Marxist rulers and their followers hold a static concept of value in a world that has a dynamic concept of value. This explains why they must fail in the end.

They belong to a static past that is at odds with modernity.

## *The creation of value is always shifting*

In a modern society, one that perceives wealth and value to be dynamic, things are constantly changing. To begin with, science and technology change, and as they change they modify the human landscape.

New technologies arise and bring change with them. Automobiles need roads and highways to be built. Airplanes need airports. So cities progressively change their appearance.

Every home has an electric lamp, then a radio, then a telephone, later a television, and then a laptop.

Inventors, inventions, and technologies build up, one upon the other. Furthermore, the new technologies displace the old technologies, fulfilling their functions more and more perfectly.

For example, the function of transportation began with walking and progressed from there to riding on horseback, driving in a car, and flying in an airplane. In all cases, a new technology enhanced the old function.

Similarly, the telegraph was displaced by the telephone and the radio, and now the Internet has entered the picture to foster a planetary leap forward in communications.

Behind these new technologies that enrich our lives, there are people. These people invented, then built, and finally distributed what had begun as an idea. As new technologies develop and replace old ones, new businesses replace old businesses. New entrepreneurs take the places of the former power figures, so the leadership of business is constantly shifting and moving.

The old moguls must surrender their place to rising entrepreneurs who bring new and unexpected sources of value into existence. And each of these new moguls will be replaced in turn.

This mobility of technological and financial power is the natural result of the dynamic concept of value, which allows us to constantly create new and unexpected value and wealth.

As new power centers evolve, they displace the old ones. In the Gutenberg revolution, the old power was that of monarchies, and the new power that emerged was that of industrialists and financiers, who are the spokesmen for the new science and technology. As they became more powerful than kings, these industrialists and financiers became unwilling to accept the rule of a monarch for very long, simply because monarchy is not the right system for a technological and industrial power if it is to evolve and thrive.

Entrepreneurs and financiers need an appropriate power structure for themselves and their dynamic society. This power structure must satisfy a few interrelated conditions: it must allow for a free market, it must allow for mobility of power, and it must contain a higher law to defend freedom.

## *Dynamic wealth needs a free market*

A free market enables the entrepreneurs, discoverers, and inventors to finance themselves efficiently. Every new idea needs backers who will provide the capital to put that idea into practice. So the free market is as essential as the freedom to learn, to conduct research, and to create without restriction.

Freedom cannot be found everywhere. In the Soviet Union, you were not even allowed to think as you wanted. When your mathematical ideas were not properly aligned with Marxism, you were sent to Siberia to rethink your positions. Cuban films today must conform to the party line. This should make us consider what the privilege of freedom really means. It means the life we live.

If entrepreneurs, inventors, and scientists are to gain financial support, achieve technological results, and offer those results to society, they must have a free market.

If they are successful, financial wealth will come to them from the accumulation of thousands of people's decisions to accept a new technology or product. We call this the demand for that product.

There is a considerable element of the unexpected in the wealth that new discoveries and inventions bestow on their creators, because supply creates demand. There was originally no demand for airplanes, trains, cars, cell phones, computers, the Internet, or spaceships.

Someone had to invent them first and offer them to society. What is taken for granted today did not even exist in people's minds in the past.

The underlying principle here is that value must first be created and then offered if people are to accept the new product and reward it with wealth. Supply creates demand. Thus, value must be created before wealth can exist. But the fact that value exists is no guarantee that wealth will come too.

Value becomes wealth only when the offer is accepted. Vincent van Gogh died poor because the value of what he offered was not accepted during his lifetime. For him, value and wealth did not coincide in time. This gap in time also made future art dealers rich with the poor man's value.

When an entrepreneur does gain wealth, it means that people are saying, "We like your idea. We want it. Please give it to us." The conversion of value to wealth means that the new idea has been socially and practically accepted and that people want it. In that sense, wealth gained in the free market is the greatest acknowledgement of success that value can receive.

In the end, the outward manifestation of the success of a new technology will be wealth. In this context, political power must be the power of the wealthy, because their wealth represents the power of an offer, technological or scientific, that has been accepted.

## *Dynamic wealth needs mobility of power*

The second condition that the creators of wealth require in the political system is mobility of power.

As new technologies are offered, those that are successful and accepted create new wealth. Thus, these successful technologies give rise to new fortunes and new moguls.

In a world where feudal lords no longer exist, the new rulers are the people who control the leading enterprises. A John Pierpont Morgan or an Andrew Carnegie needs to be able to influence political power. The way for them to achieve this is by having a candidate to endorse and attempting to have that candidate freely elected.

These moguls must be able to influence power according to their needs, without obstructing or restricting the people's freedoms in any way. Democracy within the framework of republicanism is all about allowing creators to influence politics from behind the scenes.

Now, even though one of the proper goals of government is the creation of the framework for a free market, in practice democracy enables different groups to exercise their influence for their own goals, whether or not their goals favor a free market.

For example, one proper exercise of power through democracy would be the abolition or reduction of taxes or tariffs or quotas, such as those in agriculture. However, in a perverted way, tariffs and controls seeking to obliterate competition or to give someone a government-based monopoly could also arise in a democracy. This is because some businesses live by restricting free markets, and they use democracy to advance their positions.

When a group has the power to regulate, it will use that power for its own benefit. Regulations are the favorite tools of mafias and dictators to enhance and strengthen their powers and to advance their interests in general. When they have attained power, they will protect it by regulations.

The only way to stop regulators from abusing people is to have a system that will reduce to a minimum the struggle for power through regulation. To do this, the system must first enable mobility of power, in order to avoid having a single ruling group that always advances its own interests.

Democracy is only a tool. Its purpose is to prevent a single group from remaining in power continuously, and to give an opportunity to other groups, permitting an interplay of forces.[26] Democracy enables mobility of power, and this mobility enables power to better mirror the reality of value, wealth, and innovation.

But even in a democracy, the group in power—politicians, bureaucrats, and cliques of businessmen—will attempt to regulate for their own sakes.

Politicians are only servants of the economic interests that pay them (by helping them with their projects, giving money to their political parties, etc.). In turn, these economic interests represent value converted to wealth. These interests that the government serves thus do not stay the same; they are mobile because they change with technological advances. But of course the interests that wield political power at a particular moment will attempt to perpetuate their power and eliminate competition. To ensure competition, we must ensure freedom in the interplay of forces under the rule of law.

Here, we are at the intersection between the real and the ideal. The struggle of forces looking out for their own interests is legitimate, as long as they do not infringe upon the freedom of others. However, behind any regulation, there is always aggression against freedom.

## *Dynamic wealth needs a higher law*

This is why democracy is dangerous all by itself, without the framework of a constitution that defines government's nature and

---

[26] Karl Popper wrote,

> We may distinguish two main types of government. The first type consists of governments of which we can get rid without bloodshed—for example, by way of general elections; that is to say, the social institutions provide means by which the rulers may be dismissed by the ruled, and the social traditions ensure that these institutions will not easily be destroyed by those who are in power. The second type consists of governments which the ruled cannot get rid of except by way of a successful revolution—that is to say, in most cases, not at all. I suggest the term "democracy" as a short-hand label for a government of the first type, and the term "tyranny" or "dictatorship" for the second.
>
> *The Open Society and Its Enemies* (London: Routledge 2002) p. 136.

limits its actions. Such a constitutional higher law is the third condition that dynamic wealth requires of the government.

Democracy in itself is nothing but a blind mechanism. Democracy is neither the best system nor the worst—nor even a "lesser evil." Democracy is simply a mechanism whose direction must come from something else. Because it has no higher law of its own, democracy has the potential to become dictatorship.

This is why we must make the distinction between a democracy and a *republic*. Any government limited by a higher law upholding individual freedom and limited government, whether or not that government is a democracy, is a republic. The entire content of the republican ideal can be expressed in one word—freedom. The United States Constitution and Bill of Rights are one example of such a higher law.

A republic is defined by its higher law, in other words its constitutional key idea. The form of government suited to a modern, technological society with a dynamic concept of wealth is a democracy that is also a republic, that is, a democracy with a higher law that preserves freedom.

Democracy is only a tool. Today, it is the republican higher law of individual freedom and limited government that gives content to democracy. Thomas Jefferson expressed this doctrine.[27]

---

[27] For Thomas Jefferson, America was to be the "Empire of Liberty," whose goal was to promote republicanism. He drafted the Declaration of Independence of the United States, which takes freedom as its foundation in the sentence "We hold these truths to be self-evident, that all men are created equal, that they are endowed by their Creator with certain unalienable Rights, that among these are Life, Liberty and the pursuit of Happiness."
Thomas Jefferson was an inventor and polymath who made contributions to architecture, linguistics, anthropology, horticulture, archaeology, paleontology, music, and political philosophy.
He invented the automatic door and the swivel chair, and improved the polygraph (a machine with two pens, one of which creates a simultaneous copy of whatever is written with the other). He suggested that the origins of American Indians could be traced through their languages, of which he proposed a compilation. He was the founder of the University of Virginia and designed its campus plan.

Democracy should obey republican law and not vice versa. The rule of republican higher law over democracy will ensure that a government rules for all people within a dynamic concept of value and wealth.

This *should* guarantee the existence of a free market, but the fact is that different groups have different goals. Thus democracy, as such, can do nothing more than give the creators of value a tool to try to preserve the conditions of a free market. This is possible when democracy operates within the limits of a constitution that has freedom as its foundation.

Within a free republic and its free market a permanent state of war exists between those who seek to pervert freedom and those who want to preserve it. Like a pendulum, freely elected governments will have an oscillatory behavior, going in the direction either of freedom or its denial.

When a democracy cannot preserve the freedom of the republican ideal, it becomes a dictatorship and the worst of tyrannies. This is why dictators and bureaucrats love democracy—but only as an empty word that they can manipulate at will.

## *Rule by politicians*

Democracy is a tool whose primary function is not to elect a government or to express the people's will. Instead, as explained above, its function is to provide a check on power in order to prevent the restriction of the very freedom that was required to create it.

---

Jefferson's life and work embodies a dynamic concept of value and wealth where the mind is the first agent in the development of a happy life.
The distinction between republic and democracy were essential ideas of Benjamin Franklin and of James Madison, father of the Constitution. Section 4 of the Constitution emphasizes republican government as the cornerstone: "The United States shall guarantee to every State in this Union a Republican form of Government."
It is evident, therefore, that the form of government is not democracy. Democracy is subordinated to republicanism.

Democracy is not rule by the people. It is rule by the groups or persons who manage to be elected. The function of the people's vote is to enable power rotation and change, not to decide the laws.

This may seem to be a paradox until you realize that your choice of laws when voting is limited to whichever choices the political salesmen stock in their ideological stores. Here, offer always comes first. You can only choose from among the things they offer you. People do not rule in a democracy, political salesmen do. Ask a politician.

Where there is creativity, innovation, and invention, the entrepreneurial groups of creators manage to have some of their ideas inserted into the political choices available. That enables them to have a role in the exercise of power.

Through democracy, they can defend themselves and their freedom from abuses and depredation. Where there is no freedom, and therefore no proper democracy, what will prevail is depredation, under dictatorship posing as democracy.

Such false democracy is what third-world countries have. Their static framework impedes the emergence of new powers that come from the creation of inventive sources of wealth.

Remember that democracy is just a tool for freedom. We must use it well.

## GOVERNMENT AND FREEDOM

Above all, remember that freedom belongs to an individual and not to a society. Only individual consciousness can be free to choose. A society, as such, is not free. Only the individuals who compose it are free.

Furthermore, only the individual is responsible for his or her freedom. To believe that society will make us free is the first step toward delegating our freedom to someone else and becoming that person's slave. This someone may be a politician, a bureaucrat, or whoever else wants to prey on us.

## *Only individuals can be free*

Even in a democracy, freedom is individual and never collective. When we vote, our vote does not decide the result of the election. Nobody knows in advance who the winner will be. The result is purely mechanical and blind.

When we vote, our freedom ends with each of us making our choice. The results are in the hands of raw numbers. Rule by numbers, a blind and purely mechanical procedure, is not free by any means. Thus, society cannot be free. You and I can be free.

Democracy itself works only because of our freedom as individuals. Society is composed of free individuals who set its course, which is a nonfree vector. This is good. However, this takes us to our main concern.

This main concern is how to preserve and enhance our freedom as individuals. Liberating our consciousness and opening its range of possibilities creates value and generates prosperity.

Now let us determine how we can be free.

## *How to maximize your freedom*

Freedom originates in the consciousness. It does not originate in collectivity or in governments. At the most, government and society can prevent freedom from being limited. They can defend the right of everyone to freedom, but they cannot create freedom. Freedom is, in the last instance, our responsibility as individuals and conscious beings.

So it is up to us to take every precaution and every means in our power to ensure and maximize our freedom. No government and no circumstance can limit our will to be free. External conditions may limit our freedom, but it is ultimately our determination to be free that really matters.

The determination to be free is the source of every outer condition designed to guarantee our freedom. Without this determination, freedom cannot be preserved.

A determination to be free means that first, and above all, we must do everything in our power to be free. When a country gives us conditions that are favorable to exercising our freedom, that is good. However, when the country doesn't, it is up to us to ensure our freedom by any means available.

## *Freedom is the ultimate law*

When government seeks to abridge your freedom, you must, when necessary, disobey the government to safeguard your freedom. No collectivity or institution has any right to restrict your freedom, whatever politicians and bureaucrats may say.

To sacrifice yourself to the collective good is your decision and no one else's. Only you, as an individual with free will, can decide to sacrifice your life for someone else.

However, only extreme circumstances require this. Most sacrifices of lives are actually for the sake of politicians and bureaucrats. They want you to forsake your freedom for their personal agendas, disguised as the public or common good.

When your freedom is at stake, you are not obliged to obey anyone or anything, whether God or the Devil.

Anyway, if anything is worth sacrificing your life for, it is the defense and preservation of your individual freedom. Without freedom, you cease to exist as a human being who can exercise free will. So the utmost good is freedom, and you should do everything in your power to preserve it and to develop it.

To do this, you must oppose and circumvent any measure taken by others to limit your freedom. By safeguarding your freedom, you achieve something fundamental for yourself, your family, and society.

Safeguarding of your freedom, whoever you may be, means safeguarding your mind against depredation. It means ensuring that your mind has the optimal conditions to build value and, in so doing, generate prosperity.

## THE HEART OF THE PROBLEM

The best illustration of freedom at work is the creative use of capital, which leads to innovations. This is a key difference between third-world countries and developed countries.

### *Prosperity and the creative use of capital*

Capital as a source of innovation and new value creation has such strength that it can often enable economic growth in the midst of regulations and government meddling. However, when regulations intrude too much—and that is what happens in third-world countries—neither the tools nor the equipment are available for potential entrepreneurs. Further, they cannot find the financial backing they need, which a free market could provide.

Freedom enables invention. However, something in addition to freedom is needed. This something else is a mind that possesses the necessary motivation and desire, and an ability to create and invent. Freedom allows such minds to gather and create.

Systems that restrict freedom restrict the ability of minds to discover new value.

### *The origin of social prosperity*

Rich countries are able to find prosperity in scientific research, invention, and creative enterprises because of their dynamic vision of value and wealth. Third-world countries cannot do this because they are currently blind to this dimension of reality.

Poor countries seek value and wealth where they will never find it. Prosperity, these poor countries wrongly believe, is found in "sharing" and fighting for the rights of the "less favored." Such beliefs lead to poverty. These countries will forever continue to chase rainbows unless they change their views.

True wealth is not "shared," nor won by fighting, but created. The key resources are creative minds. A country's capital is its creative individuals..

Simply thinking about forcing others to "share their wealth" distracts the mind and diverts its energy from the actual creation of value.

The answer to the poverty of third-world countries is a change of perspective. How can they change from an "earthly," static concept of value and wealth to a dynamic one?

To achieve this shift in their perception, poor countries must turn their eyes to the development of scientific and technical creativity and invention.

When this shift of perspective occurs, the entrepreneurs of poor countries will become the vehicles for discoveries and inventions created in their countries. At that point, those countries will cease to be third-world countries, and will join the first world.

Now we must study the conditions that make possible a society where inventors and creators develop new things, and where entrepreneurs make discoveries and inventions that enhance the quality of life of their fellow citizens.

## *Regulations kill the mind*

In poor countries, creative minds face insurmountable obstacles to their efforts to obtain the tools of their trades.

Hordes of petty bureaucrats and politicians are there to hamper the free circulation of goods that would enable free creative minds to work. At every opportunity they plunder or degrade whatever they can.

There are restrictions on the free circulation of books, and the list goes on and on, from scientific tools to machines, software, chemicals, and all kinds of products that are needed to develop what the mind conceives.

The effect of each regulation is worse than that of the preceding one. Regulations keep creative minds away from these poor countries, because creative minds cannot work comfortably in such environments. A residual kind of person remains there—the relatively incompetent person.

Regulations are tangible obstacles to freedom. They leave you without tools for your craft. Bureaucrats and politicians pocket their "take" and prevent the free circulation of goods.

The loss in time, energy, and money required to circumvent or comply with regulations is enough to stifle the creative drive.

All that third-world countries need to do to become wealthy is to eliminate all regulations. Everything would work at its highest potential. The foundations would be laid for anyone to obtain whatever he needs.

The poor countries believe that they are better and "stricter" than the "stupid" first-world countries. What they don't realize is how ridiculous their own attitudes and minds are. They are so strict that nothing works in their countries. Of course, their "strictness" includes predation.

The sin here is a sin against life. These are countries where respect for other people's lives is virtually nonexistent. The inhumanity of the authorities and bureaucrats is appalling. But this lack of humanity is part of the typical and necessary predatory attitude.

Regulations stifle minds and, by doing so, kill the creative and inventive drive of the population. They stifle not only minds but also lives.

This is why poor countries are poor. When you stifle the mind, you stifle everything.

### *The only natural resource is our minds*

Above all, matter is what our minds make of it. Mind is the resource that is always available and never diminishes. In fact, it is the opposite of nonrenewable; the more you use it, the more you have of it. The more that the mind creates, the more it *will* create.

The foundation of dynamic wealth is the constant growth of the mind. All value comes from the mind, and, as a consequence, so does all wealth.

The difference between mind and matter, which at first seems insurmountable, becomes dimmer as we approach it in our mind's eye. What seems to be only matter is never devoid of form.

Matter is always something that we can identify. It can be a stone, a flower, a tiger, or a barrel of oil. The underlying energy that becomes all of these things is only seen with our mind. No one has ever seen "matter" directly.

All that we see has form, and the form is provided by our mind. We see reality in a way that fulfills our needs. Ants and tigers do not see things as we do. They see the world in ways that fit their own needs.

What has this to do with value and wealth? I am merely saying that it is our mind that gives value and form to the things around us. Consider oil, for example.

Strictly speaking, oil has no value in itself.

If oil had no use, human minds would only have seen in it a material form—like a specimen in a mineralogical display case. Oil owes its value to the function humans use it for—to the service it provides for us. That function is given to it by the minds that invented the technologies that use oil.

The inventors' minds are what gave oil value.

Other examples are iron and copper, which obtain their value and use from the technologies that use them. Automobiles, boats, and motors give utility—that is, value—to the minerals and metals from which their components are built.

Minerals and metals are valuable because they are used to build things that originated in an inventor's mind. The values of these material resources are not fixed. The mind is the magic wand that gives them value, and the mind can also make their value disappear.

Take the case of coal. For many years it was, thanks to the mind, the energy source for steamboats, locomotives, and other machines. Today, it is one of the materials used to produce electricity, although oil, water, and nuclear energy are also used for this purpose.

Every energy source can be replaced—except for the mind itself.

The forms into which we put matter are not fixed, but plastic. Value is not static, but dynamic. Wealth is not limited, but virtually unbounded.

### *True government enables the mind*

The function of government is to guarantee the condition that will enable the mind to free itself from all conceivable obstacles. When this has been achieved, a society achieves prosperity.

The prosperity achieved in this way is not only material but also spiritual. Reality in its highest degree offers nearly unlimited possibilities to achieve value and wealth. Knowledge of nature and man opens itself to society. Then progress is achieved.

Government must seek to eliminate obstacles to the mind, so that we can achieve further prosperity and progress. This means eliminating all regulations that slow invention, discovery, and creativity in every field. This also implies leaving the minds of all individuals to their own free way of invention. The Wright brothers invented a workable, controlled-flight airplane, although they did not belong to a governmental or academic center of research. They were normal people like you and me.

Many unknown individuals have a potential for invention that is unfathomable. All that one must do is let those people emerge by themselves.

Now, they do need certain environmental conditions. The right ecology is one of the mind. This is the ecology that all governments usually despise, because their bureaucrats and politicians can receive no profit or power from it. The first and only measure that any government must adopt to create the environmental conditions for freedom is to abolish all regulations and leave government in its minimal expression.

This would make government the center of a wheel that is rotating at high speed—a wheel of creativity, entrepreneurship, and prosperity. However, governments are reluctant to do this, because it would jeopardize the power and profits of the armies of politicians and their associated bureaucrats.

The proper function of government is to liberate the mind, which is our unique source of value and wealth. No country can have lasting wealth of any other kind. It only has the minds of its citizens.

Wealth does not come from oil, natural gas, gold, copper, or mineral resources of any kind. Ultimately, wealth does not come from biotechnology or computers or big business or high-end research either. Those are not sources of value and wealth; they are merely products of the true source.

The true source of value and wealth is the mind, and nothing else.

## *True social order optimizes asset allocation*

With true social order, the mind can function unhampered. From this follows not only prosperity but also social equilibrium and harmony. When minds are free, men are happy.

Happiness is the ultimate source of wealth and value. The word "happiness" is just a way of saying that an equilibrated and harmonious mind exists, a mind that works for the benefit of itself and all who surround it.

This kind of mind is a generous mind—one that generates value and wealth. Everyone benefits from it. It gives itself away in its actions, its creations, its inventions, and its discoveries.

The opposite of a generous, inventive mind is an ungenerous, predatory mind. This mind, which should be called an antimind, is closed in on itself and seeks to plunder or diminish the wealth that others have created.

The antimind is the mind of politicians and their hordes of bureaucrats and mass-media slaves. They accomplish wealth destruction and plunder by putting obstacles in the paths of creation and freedom of the mind. In short, they are seekers and creators of regulations.

To these people, regulations are like the fisherman's net or the hunter's gun. The regulations are designed to capture the innocent prey who will become their victims. The mass media are the drum beaters who surround the prey so that it will not escape capture.

Regulations break the natural flow of interactions among members of human society so that the mind is blocked. Rupturing the flow of social interactions creates a misallocation of resources.

Creation and invention and every kind of action become artificially restricted. Yes, I do mean "every kind of action." By restricting one unit of action, regulation blocks and slows all others.

For example, when computer imports are regulated, not only computer users will be affected, but also all people whose businesses or lives depend in some degree on computer users. No regulation operates in a vacuum.

The more regulated a society is, the less prosperous it will become. All poor countries are overregulated.

To solve this problem of regulation, it is necessary to go to its root, the human mind. We must ask why those politicians and bureaucrats are antimind. Why does freedom of the mind mean nothing to them?

The answer lies in their static concept of value and wealth. It is necessary to change their thinking so that they will understand that all people require an environment favorable to technical and scientific creativity, discovery, and invention.

This necessary shift in their thinking can only come from education—but not education "politician style."

# Chapter 4

# Education and Its Impersonators

*To achieve the greatest fulfillment, we must passionately learn, challenge and experiment to create value as we apply sound theory and practice in every aspect of our lives.*

— Charles G. Koch, The Science of Success, 2007

The people most in need of an education are the politicians and bureaucrats. Our actions reflect our education. When a person's actions are ineffective, the failure of his education is the cause. Politicians and bureaucrats are living testimony of a failed educational system.

Their concept of education is not education. They are the people least qualified to speak about such a sensitive and important subject. So where should we look for an answer to the problem of education, if not into the sterile minds of politicians and bureaucrats?

Subsidized education by governments and international institutions through their foreign-aid programs does not work.

Third-world politicos fill their mouths with the word "education"[28] as if it were the panacea for poverty. However, several studies show a lack

[28] William Easterly, who was an adviser for the World Bank, says that foreign aid from international organizations, such as the World Bank or the IMF, "appears to be determined by the strategic interests of donors, not by policy choices of the recipients." *The Elusive Quest for Growth: Economists' Adventures and Misadventures in the Tropics* (Cambridge, MA: MIT Press, 2002), p. 110. Easterly also tells us that one of the motives of international organizations in donating money to third world countries is not generosity but because "Most donor institutions are set up with a separate country department" and, "the budget of this department is determined by the amount of resources it disburses to its recipients." He then goes on to tell us that the department that does not spend its allocated budget "will likely receive a smaller budget the following year." Finally, he confesses that "larger budgets are associated with more prestige and more career advancement." He concludes by telling us that those international organizations end up by disbursing "even when loan conditions are not met" (p. 117).
He adds in Chapter 7 that the methodology of lending used by the World Bank, the IMF, and "other bilateral donors" results in lending to "irresponsible governments" (p. 133).
The perversion of international organizations is thus revealed. They are tools of predation that contribute to a misallocation of resources, while they advance the careers and fill the pockets of "donors" and politicians alike.
David Osterfeld, in his book *Prosperity versus Planning: How Government Stifles Economic Growth* (Oxford: Oxford University Press, 1992) tells us that foreign aid has been followed by a "parasitic government bureaucracy whose very existence undercuts the recipients' ability for sustained economic growth" (p. 142). He gives many examples of the disasters that follow foreign aid.
For instance, in Tanzania, the economy collapsed while bureaucracy increased by 14 percent as a result of foreign aid. In many countries, such as Micronesia, India, Egypt, Haiti, Peru, or Guatemala, such aid has had the result of "driving local producers, especially farmers, out of business" (p. 142).
Osterfeld mentions that former U.S Assistant secretary of Agriculture George Dunlop said that the dumping of U.S. wheat in India in the 1950's and 1960s may have caused the "starvation of millions of Indians." In the Ethiopian famine of 1983–1984, millions of dollars in loans provided by the World Bank for famine relief were used by the government to buy trucks instead of food (pp. 142, 143).
Osterfeld also tackles the problem of corruption. He tells us that the use of government as "a vehicle for plunder, is quite common, especially in the Third World." He concludes that the corruption of the public sector in such countries

of correlation between education and economic growth. This has been the case in much of Africa.

William Easterly, an ex-adviser for the World Bank, explains this in his book *The Elusive Quest for Growth: Economists' Adventures and Misadventures in the Tropics.* He argues that corruption, low salaries for teachers, and lack of adequate teaching materials destroy the possibility of quality education. He mentions that in Pakistan, for example, teachers are without scruples, and they routinely intimidate their students. Teaching jobs are given as patronage and the teachers are unable to pass the exams they administer to their students. In another example, he explains that in Vila Junqueiro, Brazil, not only do schools lack hygiene and safety, but the teachers do not show up for weeks at a time.[29]

Such situations occur in all third-world countries. The World Bank and other donors have wasted huge amounts of taxpayers' money in useless educational programs whose only beneficiaries are the bureaucrats from those international organizations.

The educational concoctions of bureaucrats have not worked. Further, they have been a source of social disruption. By biasing a society's outlook, they plant the seeds of violence and hate.

In many third-world countries, these educational projects advance the static vision of value and wealth. They convince the students that government is the answer to everything.

What such an education tells these people is that they should favor an ordered world where each person has his or her place and a livelihood assured at birth. The bureaucrat and politician become the paradigms of social success, wealth, and power. In short, a collectivist mind-set rules these schools.

The result is frustration. Life soon shows these people that government is not the answer to their problems. The same thing happens to the politician himself. He knows that the educational

stifles wealth production by placing obstacles that enable government bureaucrats to plunder (pp. 210, 211).

[29] Easterly, *Elusive Quest for Growth,* pp. 73–83.

problem is unsolvable. He is as frustrated as the uneducated or poorly educated population. But the more frustrated the politician becomes, the more he will insist in his speeches that education is the answer.

Indeed, true education *is* the answer. But it is not to be found within the government's educational system.

## *Education by government is only a ruse with which to assign blame*

The politician knows better than anyone else that all of his efforts to educate will fail. However, his predation will succeed in making money and obtaining votes for him and his associates.

The politician knows that the frustration of the uneducated population will increase, but he is powerless to do anything effective to provide real education. However, his static and "earthly" concept of value comes to his rescue. The politician will explain to his people and to the international bureaucrats that if his country cannot be educated, it is the fault of selfish entrepreneurs who do not distribute their wealth to everyone else.

The population will endorse the point of view of the politicians and bureaucrats. The seeds of hate and social unrest then become deeply rooted. The population will hate corporations and big business for their selfishness, accusing them of all evils. The businessman will even learn to hate himself.

The only person who will not be accused is the politician, who is the perpetrator of the whole scheme. He assumes the role of just another victim of the selfishness of big business. He wants to educate the entire country, but he cannot. It is not his fault.

Once the stage has been set to blame someone else, there will be consequences. A message of hate, envy, and guilt can only produce more hate, envy, and guilt. Thus we have a spiral of violence and poverty. Terrorism, guerilla warfare, violence in the streets, hunger, and abuse of all kinds occur wherever someone else can be blamed.

The media echo the message of hatred, resentment, and envy on a grand scale, mesmerizing entire populations.

## EDUCATION BY FORCE: THE WRONG ANSWER

Forced education—that is, misallocated education, education without any purpose beyond getting votes—destroys the free, creative mind, whose natural impulse is to learn. Forced education does not come from a real need, but from political fiat.

When education is the result of a real need, and the means for obtaining it are not restricted, nothing can prevent it from taking place.

Yet the taxpayers' money is used in inefficient educational programs that were born in the minds of bureaucrats whose only goal is to enhance their own power. Money that would have gone where the market directed it is instead forced to go to education.

The result is a purposeless education that is wasted on the minds of its recipients.

Thus, in third-world countries, schools and universities are often created for the sole purpose of creating propaganda by including them in statistical annuals. Such propaganda helps politicians to obtain power through votes—as well as financing from international organizations, thereby increasing the bureaucrats' salaries and "pocket money."[30]

Useless educational projects cost the taxpayers money and educate no one. All they do is reduce what is available for legitimate educational purposes.

---

[30] Peter D. Schiff, in his book *Crash Proof 2.0: How to Profit from the Economic Collapse* (Hoboken, NJ: John Wiley & Sons, 2009), p. 215, remarks that the rise in tuitions is a consequence of "borrowing under government programs to finance education," the reason being that subsidies make things more expensive. Even though Schiff's remark is about the United States, it applies worldwide.

Misallocated funds, taken away from the market and controlled by bureaucrats, have a rebounding, negative effect on education. For example, the misallocated funds mean that someone's salary will not be paid, reducing the possibility that the children of one or more households will receive a true education.

Such conscious misallocation is criminal. It is responsible for a loss of time, energy, and revenue.

## *Why bureaucrats hate free education*

The misallocation of educational resources by government shows that there should be a separation between education and the state, just as there is between religion and the state. Somewhere in the depths of their unconscious minds, where a remnant of a link to reality still remains, bureaucrats know this to be true. The weakness of their link to education creates a state of fear in them. Their worst fear is that someone might tell the truth, namely, that government is not needed to deliver education. The fact is, government is an obstacle to any efficient system of delivering education.

To hide the fact that they are an obstacle to the delivery of education, politicians and bureaucrats will do anything in their power to persuade the population that government is needed to provide an education. They argue that the private sector will not take charge of the education of the needy, and therefore the government must take those people who cannot afford to pay tuition in its hands and provide for them. The politician will add that government does not have any profit motive in educating the people.

Let us decide whether these assertions are true. Let us verify that politicians and bureaucrats have no profit motive of any kind when they so outrageously defend the need for government to take over something as important as education.

And let us try to explain why they fear so much the possibility of a separation between education and the state.

# EDUCATION IS TOO IMPORTANT TO BE LEFT IN THE HANDS OF GOVERNMENT

The first reason for politicians to keep an iron hand on education is that control of education helps them get the votes they need.

## *When education means votes*

Education is one of the best sources of votes. It is the easiest way to show concern for society without achieving anything. The more backward the country and the poorer its population, the more the politician fills his mouth with the "need for education."

In this process, the politician will always take care to blame someone else for the failure of education (reflected in the fact that masses of citizens are persistently poor and uneducated). Blaming someone else is essential to retaining his power and influence.

Also, the politician needs uneducated people in order to always have an educational market of votes ready for him. He knows this. He knows that discontent of any kind is the fuel that will enable him to overcome his competitors.

## *When education means empty statistics*

A second, related reason for the politician and his bureaucrat fellows to keep the education business to themselves is to gain prestige by using education statistics as an ideological tool.

This prestige—achieved with only a little ink and paper—will be the source of more votes and more educational projects financed by international institutions. Politicians' and bureaucrats' prestige will ensure that there is lots of pocket money along the way.

In third-world countries, many "paper universities" have been created by the fiat of politicians and bureaucrats. These institutions deliver degrees to people who don't deserve them and who, as a consequence, cannot find jobs that correspond to the diplomas that they receive.

In 2007, UNESCO published the book *Corrupt Schools, Corrupt Universities: What Can Be Done?*, by Jacques Hallak and Muriel Poisson.[31] The authors mention "paper mills and diploma mills." Some countries do not accept professionals who come from certain universities because they do not have acceptable qualifications, they have worthless diplomas. The authors fail to mention the corruption implied in the creation of universities for only political reasons that underlies many "paper" universities. I may add that the teachers of many third-world country universities do not have the level of knowledge of many high school students from first-rate, first-world schools.

Two examples of diploma mills are the Enugu State University of Technology in Nigeria and the Universidad Nacional San Cristóbal de Huamanga in Peru. The aforesaid Peruvian university seeded the Shining Path guerillas that murdered thousands of defenseless children and women.

Whether or not the university provides any genuine education is irrelevant to the politician, who at the end of his term can show statistics that "prove" a "large national advance in education." Meanwhile, these "paper degree" professionals end up driving taxis or working in other menial jobs due to their lack of ability in what they were "trained to do."

The politician's interest is in the statistics that show a significant increase in the number of diplomas delivered during his term. That's all that matters to him.

## *When education means self-promotion*

Here is another motive for politicians and bureaucrats. Their "concern" for education is an ideal platform from which to secure foreign aid and project financing from international organizations.

Every year, a new plan for building schools and buying teaching materials is designed by international organizations, whose bureaucrats

---

[31] (Paris: UNESCO International Institute for Educational Planning, 2007) http://unesdoc.unesco.org/images/0015/001502/150259e.pdf.

are eager for projects to include in their résumés to advance their own careers. Bureaucrats endorse projects for which there is no need. This is like selling sand in the middle of the desert. Thus, a school will be built without taking into account the need for qualified teachers and students.

The only result is an increase in government expense that will burden the taxpayers and slow the economy.

Meanwhile, politicians, bureaucrats, and their allied businessmen become rich by leading a naïve population to believe that they are selflessly seeking to foster education.

The waste of resources sometimes will be hidden by the relative success of one of the schools or a few meaningless samples of students who succeed.

Statistics in this regard can easily be manipulated by lowering the standards for success.

All told, the politician's main reason for showing concern for education is to build a strong propaganda platform. There is nothing better than publicizing his actions as being for selfless, nonprofit motives.

No one can raise his voice against the politician without being considered a soulless, egotistical, capitalistic, monster. The politician finds his alibi in "education." He can prey upon the taxpayer with impunity. He has created the perfect propaganda machine. This machinery, while also bringing in some bucks, will be the most powerful vote-generating instrument, thus ensuring the success of the politician and his bureaucrat followers.

So, as we can see, profit is the only motive for the politician's or bureaucrat's concern for education. Nothing else matters. If it did, education would not be left in the hands of government.

Whatever the government does can be done by individuals in the private sector. All of the problems in government undertakings could be solved simply by forbidding government from taking them on.

Whatever argument government may give to justify its existence, the fact remains that it is a mafia that has only the benefit of its leaders and associates as its goal. There is no area of government (except maybe justice and security) that an in-depth analysis would not show to be ultimately useless.

## *Freedom is the true spirit of education*

In order to achieve full education, we must *free* education from restrictions. When all materials needed to teach and to learn are available, and when bureaucratic regulations and restrictions that make it difficult to learn have been lifted, education takes place.

In short, freedom is the spirit behind true education.

Freedom is the fuel of education. The freer a country is, the more educated is its population. The inverse is also true. The less freedom there is, the less educated is the population. The link between freedom and education is powerful. But which comes first, freedom or education?

Freedom can be achieved only where there is a particular level of consciousness and intelligence. Uneducated populations do not understand the need for freedom or the benefits of it. Consciousness breeds freedom.

Consciousness of the need for freedom begins with the ruling class. When it is absent at this level, government overregulates.

Without freedom, education cannot develop in any fashion. The results of schooling will be very short-sighted and will generate no prosperity. An example is the Soviet Union, which was able to send rockets into space, thanks to an educated minority of scientists, while an uneducated and fearful population was starving to death, despite propaganda to the contrary.

True education can only develop in a climate of freedom and prosperity. Given those conditions, education takes place by itself. No additional action is needed, besides suppressing the government obstacles that may hinder the natural tendency of education to expand.

People need and want to be educated, and they will do anything in their power and go to any length to acquire the best education available. But first the proper conditions for education must be restored.

## THE SECRET KEY TO EDUCATION IS THE ENTREPRENEUR

The natural link between the creation of enterprises and the need for qualified people to run them and work in them is the motivating force behind true education. When we release this force from obstacles, education will occur by itself.

### *Entrepreneurs need education*

Entrepreneurs need teams at every level of their activity. At each level, the best-qualified people are the best because of the education that they received, and they have jobs because their skills are needed.

Imagine an oil company that has no geologists. Imagine an aeronautical company without any aeronautical engineers. Imagine a construction company that has no architects or engineers or qualified laborers. Imagine a software company that has no programmers.

Indeed, there would be no entrepreneurs if they did not receive the education that they need for their work.

Entrepreneurs crave being educated and having educated people around them.

What do you think entrepreneurs would do if public schools did not exist? They would finance their own schools. And they would do it in the best way to satisfy their needs for knowledgeable employees.

How likely is it that a company would hire someone who doesn't know how to read, write, or do elementary arithmetic? Would you hire someone who has no education? Would you outsource a job to someone who does not read or write or know arithmetic? You probably would ask for much more than these basic skills before hiring anyone.

Entrepreneurs need educated people around them. Education is their source of human capital. So in a free society, entrepreneurs will provide all the education necessary for the society's survival. The real hindrance to education is government, which makes us believe that we need it to educate us.

## *Entrepreneurs can create education*

Where entrepreneurs are free and market freedom rules, the need for education and the means to satisfy that need will grow constantly and naturally. Growth in education will be accompanied by an equivalent growth in prosperity for the entire society.

When private investors contribute money to education, they do so to ensure successful education as a return on their money. They direct their funds for education according to the needs of the market. If, for example, there is a shortage of computer scientists, the educational market will react to this, and funds will flow to fill this need.

Indeed, this is already happening in some of the poorest places in the world. In James Tooley's book, *The Beautiful Tree*, he shows that entrepreneurially minded teachers have established private schools for poor children in places like Hyderabad, India, and Kibera, Kenya. By focusing on serving the real needs of those children rather than on fulfilling government mandates, these schools have achieved better educational outcomes with much lower budgets than the "free" public schools.

Far from receiving any assistance from the government, many of these schools must operate in careful obscurity to avoid attracting the attention of predatory bureaucrats. The regulators might simply extort bribes, but might equally well shut down a successful private school in order to prevent any embarrassment to the inept government-school administrators.[32]

When entrepreneurs create education in this way, they will increase society's educational resources. These resources will also be free of regulatory constraints and thus will not be misallocated. The entrepreneurs will allocate the optimal quantity of resources at the optimal time for education.

In contrast, politicians provide public education not because of a market need but because of their own opinions and their own egotistical agenda. The resulting misallocation of resources results in using money for education in ways that are inefficient and even useless. For example, many governments create new universities for political reasons. These universities lack teachers and resources. The money would be better spent by endowing existing universities with the resources needed to be successful.

Imagine if our society's educational level were a hundred times what it is today. Such a level can be attained if education is left to private enterprise, instead of the state. There would be no misallocation of resources. Everyone who had received an education would have a job and an income.

The key to education is the entrepreneur.

## *Education, value creation, and capitalism*

What made modern education possible was the Gutenberg revolution. Through mass distribution of printed information it made our techno-scientific society possible. This techno-scientific society can only exist if there are qualified people to build it and contribute to it.

Our techno-scientific civilization therefore rests on education as its foundation.

---

[32] James Tooley, *The Beautiful Tree: A Personal Journey into How the World's Poorest People Are Educating Themselves* (New Delhi: Penguin, 2009).

We should add that this techno-scientific civilization is, above all, a capitalistic civilization. We should perhaps use "techno-scientific-capitalistic" to tell the whole story.

Furthermore, capitalism and education converge. We have here a formula: Capitalism = Education

Here is why.

Capitalism rests on the principle of capital acquisition and capital saving. Capital acquisition originates in the creation of value. In turn, value is transformed into wealth. In this transformation, we obtain new capital.

Capital, and wealth in general, are the visible signs of an invisible reality, the creation or discovery of value. Value is the invisible potential, and wealth is its visible actualization.

To create value, which is the primal source of capital, one needs knowledge, and so education is essential. In other words, education is the basis on which capital creation rests. And entrepreneurs can turn the newly created capital into more education.

In contrast, in collectivist schemes the mafia that rules the collective body steals the capital that value creation produces. Regulations and the fear of punishment further hinder value creation. And as for the little value is still produced, its conversion to wealth and thus to capital, and its free flow to create more value through education, is slowed. The final result is ignorance as well as poverty and misery. We have witnessed this in all communist countries.

A techno-scientific-capitalistic society, on the other hand, will seek education to achieve its goals of value creation and capital conversion. No effort will be spared to do this in the least possible time and with the greatest possible efficiency.

We do not need government to educate, because education is the foundation of all human capital, enabling value to be converted into wealth.

By creating wealth, education comes into existence by itself. Education and prosperity are the two faces of one and the same reality. We can express this in another way. We can regard it as a chain of equivalent terms:

**Wealth = Value = Education = Human Capital = Enterprise**

In summary, as indicated previously, Capitalism = Education.

The agent of education is the entrepreneur. In other words, the motivation for education is the profit motive. This is the motivation to create value and convert it to wealth, which will make possible a better life.

## *Education teaches happiness*

So in the end, education is the way to happiness. Education enables you to transform yourself and your environment; in both cases, the goal is a good life.

Education is the first step in making the most of yourself and the reality that surrounds you. It is the instrument that enables you to find or create value and to transform yourself or the world.

By doing so, you transform value into wealth, and you become wealthy. Value and wealth contribute to greater wealth and value through constant synergy, in an indefinite and accelerating progression. Then the accumulation of knowledge and learning becomes enormous and in fact has no limits. Consequently, some people will become richer in knowledge, becoming beacons of science and wisdom in their world.

The knowledge society is not egalitarian. Even assuming that everyone has the same opportunities, not everyone will achieve as much as others. Some people will be much richer than others in wisdom, knowledge, and ideas.

The idea-rich people, when left unrestricted in their acquisition of knowledge, benefit all others who do not have the same level of intelligence. Someone like Srinivasa Ramanujan, a great Indian mathematician, benefited the world with his unique knowledge and ability.

If his ability had been hindered, mathematics and science would have suffered. Because Ramanujan was free to explore and develop his mathematical abilities to the utmost, he became what he was—one of the greatest twentieth-century mathematicians.

The fact is that there is a gap between the average man and the scientists, inventors, and discoverers like Ramanujan, who are behind the inner workings of our techno-scientific civilization. Not everyone could have discovered relativity or invented the computer or painted like Picasso.

So it is a fact that our world is ruled by the king-thinkers of our age. These are the men who can not only conceive, but also build and maintain, the technological marvels that are part of our daily lives today. It is thanks to this minority of thinkers and developers of technology that our world endures.

It is good that there is a gap between the average and the higher levels of mind and knowledge. The greater we allow the gap to become, the better our world will be. Furthermore, the general average will also rise with time.

Imagine a world where the freedom to become idea-rich is forbidden. Imagine a world where everyone is restrained from excelling in science or other fields. There would be no freedom in that kind of world, nor anything else of value.

# Chapter 5

# Let Us Widen the Gap between the Rich and the Poor

## THE GAP AND THE TWO ROADS OF ECONOMIC DESTINY

We often hear in the media that efforts should be made to reduce the gap between the rich and the poor. The media and politicians are constantly telling us that the rich are becoming richer while the poor are becoming poorer.

In addition, the same people do their best to impress on us that the cause of all social evil is the widening of this gap, with the rich, of course, being the ones who are responsible for it. Politicians or newsmen are, as usual, free of all guilt and responsibility. Their role is rather that of saviors who, identifying the ultimate root of all evil, rend their garments in a display of despair and suffering. Thus, it is now widely accepted that the gap between the rich and the poor should be reduced. The politicians' message of guilt has become the politically correct attitude in this matter.

## *The road to poverty*

However, the truth is the opposite. All of this wailing by the media and the politicians to lessen the gap between the rich and the poor is a road, not to increasing the wealth of countries, but to further poverty and misery.

The more that the gap is reduced, the poorer the poor countries will become. In this process of impoverishment, not only will the poor become poorer, but also the rich will become less rich until they also attain poverty.

The attempt to reduce the gap between the rich and the poor will ultimately lead to the failure of government and the collapse of the state.

## *The prosperity gap*

What should be done instead of trying to diminish the gap between rich and poor? Exactly the opposite. The road to prosperity consists of *increasing the gap* instead of reducing it.

We should:

1. Let the rich become richer.
2. Let the poor become less poor (which follows from the first point).
3. Enable the gap between rich and poor to become permanent.

Let us examine the reasons for this.

The gap between the richest and the poorest segments of the population is greater in rich countries than in poor countries. The poorer a country is, the smaller is the gap. Conversely, the richer a country is, the greater is the gap.

The gap between the richest inhabitant of the USA and its poorest inhabitant is greater than that between the richest inhabitant of Rwanda and its poorest. The same applies to a comparison of any rich country and any poor country.

According to CelebrityNetWorth.com, Aliko Dangote, a Nigerian and the richest man in Africa, has a net worth of roughly $25 Billion. Tribert Rujugiro Ayabatwa, the richest man in Rwanda (and the richest tobacco industrialist in Africa), has an estimated fortune of $200 million.

In Rwanda, the average assets per person are $583. In Nigeria the average assets per person are $1400. And in the USA the average assets per person are $184,000.

The *arithmetical gap*, the difference between the richest individual's and the average person's assets, is greater in the rich countries than in the poor countries. The difference in the USA between Warren Buffet's assets of $58 billion and the average person's assets of $184,000 is $57.9 billion.

The difference in Nigeria between Aliko Dangote's $25 billion and the average citizen's assets of $1,400 is $24.9 Billion. And the difference in Rwanda between Tribert Rujugiro Ayabatwa's $200 million and the average citizen's assets of $583 is $199.9 million.

Additionally when we compare the average assets between them, the countries with the bigger arithmetical gaps have the higher average assets. So we get here a proportionality that is instructive.

US average assets per person are 131 times the Nigerian assets per person, and the Nigerian average assets per person are 2.4 times the Rwandan average assets per person. US citizen Warren Buffet's fortune is at least 2.3 times greater than Nigeria's Aliko Dangote's fortune and Dangote's in turn is 125 times greater than the fortune of Rwanda's Tribert Rujugiro Ayabatwa.

In sum, the greater the arithmetical gap between the richest individual's assets and the average assets per person, the richer the country, and the higher the average assets per person. So, great gaps in wealth favor the increase of average assets per person.

Now, this point about the gap is a priori true. Even though we can put forward examples, it's simply logic that where there is no misallocation of wealth, there will be a growth in the gap, and also that the growth of the gap will help to alleviate the poverty of the poorest at the same time as it increases the fortunes of the richest.

But of course, not all wealth has been accumulated in a free-market way. Some wealth represents the proceeds of government misallocation. For instance, there are many rich businessmen in Brazil who have made mercantilist fortunes by alliance with the regulators.

Carlos Slim—the richest man in Mexico, and also the richest man in the world from 2010 to 2013—owes his wealth in part to free-market exchanges with the more advanced society in the United States and in part to his associations with governments.

However, in the absence of regulation, it is a priori true that enlargement of the gap means that someone is investing resources in the correct way. If the gap is reduced by regulation, you're taking away wealth that would otherwise be very well invested.

## *The law of the inverse of the gap*

This reveals the presence of a law. You can call it the "law of the inverse of the gap." This law states that where the gap is wide, the poor are less poor than where the gap is narrow. Similarly, where the gap is wide, the rich are more rich than where the gap is narrow. In other words, the wider the gap is, the better off both the rich and poor shall be.

There are two corollaries of this:

1. It is better to be poor in a rich country than to be poor in a poor country, and
2. It is better to be rich in a rich country than to be rich in a poor country.

What is the origin of the gap between the rich and the poor? This gap is caused by the nature of wealth in a dynamic mind-set. The gap is the natural outcome of wealth being dynamic.

Prosperity springs from the mind of the entrepreneur, who recognizes opportunity, making him rich. The more value that he creates and transforms into wealth, the richer he becomes and the greater the gap he (temporarily) creates between him and other persons. Thus, the gap is the direct effect of an act of creation, invention, and entrepreneurship.

However, according to a static-minded individual, the source of wealth cannot be unlimited. He believes wealth to be static and unchanging. It could not possibly grow. Therefore, it must be divided and shared according to some criteria.

Dividing and sharing is the only way for society to participate in static capital. For the static-minded individual, therefore, any growth in capital must be the result of the quantitative work of someone. In the mind of a static-minded person, such growth can only have been achieved through exploitation and abuse of the workers. (If the new wealth was gained in finance, there must necessarily have been usury.) For those with this mentality, it is only natural to assume that wealth is limited and therefore people must organize themselves to fight for it. Thus, we have the warlord mentality of old or the Marxist class struggle of modern times.

When wealth can only be divided, not multiplied, war and conflict are born. Violence is carried out by class-struggle militants, by dictator-states full of regulations and controls, and by mafias and delinquents of all sorts. All of these people share something: they believe they are unable to obtain wealth without taking it by force from someone else. Aggression is their essential way, not only of action, but also of thought and feeling.

Behind this way of thinking, acting, and feeling lurks an inferiority complex. These people regard themselves as unable to create. Each act of predation they commit affirms to them their ultimate inability to contribute to the value and wealth creation of man.

The opposite of this negative and destructive way of thinking and acting is the dynamic mind-set. In this mentality, value and wealth are seen as unlimited and renewable. They arise from an act of creation and entrepreneurship.

These two mind-sets give us the creators of wealth and value on one side and the predators of wealth and value on the other side. These two kinds of humans have their own sets of beliefs that result in specific spiritual, social, economic, and political outlooks.

The predator's way of looking at things is that one should reduce the gap between the rich and the poor, while the creator's outlook implies the opposite. We will now illustrate further what we mean by saying that we should be widening the gap between the rich and the poor. We shall use electricity in a metaphor to explain our viewpoint.

## THE ELECTRICITY METAPHOR

No one really knows what electricity is. The formulas that describe it are really just operators with which to predict its behavior. However, we can use the scientific model to describe electricity.

### *Two poles are needed to create a current*

In a metal, the electrons near the nucleus of each atom are called bound electrons. They are bound close to the atom's nucleus. The outer electrons, however, can abandon their particular atoms and flow through the metal. Thus, a metal is a *electrical conductor*.

Every electron has a negative charge. Electrons repel one another because like charges repel. Electrons are attracted to anything that is positively charged.

Consider an electrical circuit consisting of a battery with a metal wire connecting its two metal posts. The battery posts are called the *poles* of the circuit. The battery forces extra electrons into one of the poles (in spite of the fact that electrons repel one another and therefore resist concentrating together), and as a result that pole has a net negative charge. The battery also "pulls" electrons out of the other pole. As a result, that pole has a net positive charge (due to a shortage of electrons to balance out the positive charge of the protons in the nuclei of its atoms).

The pole of an electric circuit that has excess electrons is the *negative pole*. The pole with excess protons (i.e., a lack of electrons) is the *positive pole*.

Electricity, or electric current, is the movement of electrons. The strength of a current (the rate at which electrons pass through the conductor) is measured in amperes, so the strength of the current is sometimes called the *amperage*.

For the electrons to flow, producing a current (which can produce something useful for humans), there must be a potential (a sort of "electrical pressure," or "electric tension").

The potential is caused by the difference between the concentration of electrons in one pole and the concentration of electrons in the other pole. The positive pole exerts an attractive force on the electrons in the negative pole, a sort of "electric tension" tending to pull those electrons toward the positive pole. At the same time, the negative pole exerts a repulsive force on the electrons, a sort of "electric pressure" pushing the electrons away from the negative pole. So the electrons in the negative pole have a tendency to move away from the negative pole and towards the positive pole. The potential is this tendency. The strength of the potential is measured in volts, and is called the voltage.

In a car battery, for instance, the negative pole has excess electrons, and the positive pole has more protons than electrons. A voltage results from of the difference between the charges, positive and the negative, of the two poles, and voltage is what creates the current. The higher the difference between the two poles (which is the potential, or voltage), the greater will be the current, or amperage, the strength of the current that results.

(The potential, or voltage, is present even in the absence of a current, as when the wire between the two poles is disconnected—that is, the switch is "off.")

Imagine a water hose and the valve to let water flow into it. The current of water, the flow of water in the hose, can be regulated and measured. The measure of the rate at which water passes through the hose is the current (like the electrical current, or amperage, in an electrical circuit). At a higher speed, more water passes through the hose in a given time, and at less speed, less water passes through. Regulating the water pressure (which is like the voltage in an electrical circuit) enables us to regulate the amount of current (which is like the amperage).

The amperage times the voltage gives us the power, which is the rate at which the electricity can do work. Electric power can be used to illuminate light bulbs, to operate electric motors, and for many other purposes. It is what you pay your electric company for. Power is measured in watts.

But to produce this useful electrical power, you need the voltage. The voltage is only possible when two poles exist—a negative pole and a positive one. The greater the opposite strength of the two poles, the more energy is made available to do work when electrons cross the gap between them. Similarly, as we will see, the greater the gap between rich and poor, the stronger the force of movement from poor to rich will be.

Because there is a voltage between the two poles in a light bulb, the incandescent filament that connects them gives off light and heat. In an electric motor, electricity is converted to motion instead of light.

In other words, two poles are required to create energy that can accomplish work of some kind. What matters is the size of the difference, the gap, in wealth or in number of electrons, between the two poles.

To create a flow, we need two poles and this gap. The energy will be created by the flow that crosses the gap.

Another example of this involves a waterfall used to generate electricity. Here also we have two "poles," an upper pole and a lower pole. They will have a void or physical gap in between them.

In the case of the waterfall, this gap is the elevation difference, the distance between the top of the waterfall and the bottom of it. The greater this distance is, the greater will be the speed, and therefore the energy, of the water when it reaches the bottom and the greater will be the electrical energy generated.[33]

Electricity as a metaphor helps to illustrate the requirements for economic prosperity. There must be two poles, a gap between them, and something to flow across the gap, thereby creating energy. Now consider these four elements as the conditions of value creation.

The first pole is the one identified with value and wealth. Let us call it the Positive, Rich Pole. The second pole is the need for value and wealth. We'll call that pole the Negative, Poor Pole.

In between, we have a void or gap filled by the intermediate levels of value and wealth creation. We have the entire range from rich to poor and the circulation between the rich and poor. Circulation here is produced by the exchanges that create a flow of value and wealth.

## *The two poles for wealth creation*

This differential in the charge between the two poles of the rich and the poor is equivalent to the "voltage" of the electrons flowing from the negative pole to the positive pole. Voltage can be equated to desire, motivation, or enthusiasm for the acquisition of value and wealth.

Without a differential in charge, or economic "voltage," there would be no desire to obtain wealth and value. In our example, the difference between the rich and the poor is the cause of the desire for value and wealth, without which prosperity would never be attained. This gap is the cause of the motivation and enthusiasm that makes entrepreneurship possible.

It is the wealth gap that creates the movement toward wealth and prosperity—the less wealthy becoming wealthier, and the rich becoming richer.

---

[33] (We are assuming that none of the elevation differences are great enough for the falling water to reach terminal velocity.)

Economic "voltage" gives entrepreneurs, investors, and all people the motivation to act for their own benefit and the courage to take initiative to become wealthier and to contribute to value creation.

Let us assume that we eliminated this gap between rich and poor. What would be the result? We would have eliminated any desire to achieve more value and thereby contribute to general prosperity. Everyone would live in the same sort of house, eat the same sort of food, and wear the same sort of clothing. This would be a road to misery.[34]

When the rich become richer, it is natural for the poor to also become wealthier than they were before. What is unnatural is the opposite.

Many people assume that the richer the wealthy become, the poorer everyone else will be. Facts and logic prove the opposite.

The ratio of the average income of the richest 10 percent to the poorest 10 percent in any given country gives us a view of wealth and poverty in that place. For example, in Bolivia this ratio is 157.3 (CIA, year 2010), in Namibia 129 (CIA, year 2010) in Sri Lanka 36.1. Compare that to the ratios in richer countries. In the USA the ratio is 15 (2007 est.), in the UK it's 13.6 (1999 est.), Switzerland 8.9 (2000 est.), Israel 11.8 (2005 est.), France 8.3 (2004 est), Germany 6.9 (2000 est), and Canada 9.5 (2000 est).[35]

These numbers show that the advanced countries, where the wealthiest people live, are also the countries where the rest of the population is less poor. This proves that the wealth of some does not increase the poverty of the rest, but rather the opposite.

---

[34] In the Soviet Union, the brilliant promarket agricultural economist Nikolai Kondratiev, was arrested and convicted of being a "kulak-professor" in 1930. (A kulak was a wealthy peasant supposed to be the class enemy of poorer farmers.) For creating value with his influential theories of industrialization and business cycles, he received an eight-year prison sentence, which was ended by his death.

[35] *The World Factbook* (Washington, DC: Central Intelligence Agency, continually updated.) https://www.cia.gov/library/publications/the-world-factbook/.

## *The economic engine to generate wealth*

The first condition for a country's prosperity is that the country must install an economic engine that will be able to generate wealth. This engine or motor of prosperity has two poles that interact.

These two poles are the rich and the poor. The tension between them creates a flow of prosperity that is essential for the development of a country.

But this tension and the development that it generates are possible only in very specific conditions. There can be this tension only when there is a strong social fabric, when economic freedom rules, and when minds are inclined towards creativity, research, invention, and innovative enterprise.

A prosperous society has a goal. That goal is the creation of a society where the "ultra rich" and the "ordinary rich" coexist in dynamic tension. Such a society generates and builds wealth to its highest level.

A wealth-building society exists in opposition to the mentality that is the signature of third-world countries. In third-world countries, a spirit of pride, along with hatred and envy of rich countries, destroys creation and leads the country to poverty.

Poverty begins in the mind with hatred of success and ignorance of its cause.

## *The voltage and amperage of value and wealth*

Returning to our electrical metaphor, voltage is the equivalent of a "wealth differential." The greater the wealth differential is, the greater its voltage is, and the easier the creation of value and wealth are.

Now, as I mentioned earlier, the flow or current that circulates between the two poles is termed amperage. When we translate this to economics, we have investments and exchanges as the flow.

The power produced by the flow, which in electricity is expressed in watts, would be the productive power that those investments and exchanges must have to generate prosperity and wealth.

Here again, a current of prosperity and its productive power require a definite condition to function effectively. Another look at the electricity metaphor will help us to understand this point.

Electric current needs adequate conductivity to circulate efficiently. To have adequate conductivity, the resistance in the circuit must be weak. The weaker the resistance, the higher will be the conductivity.

In our metaphor, conductivity represents economic freedom. The more freedom we have, the higher the conductivity and the lower the resistance of the economic circuit. Thus, the way to prosperity is to have low resistance and high conductivity.

Here we see that bureaucracy and regulations are obstacles to economic conductivity. They hamper the circulation of wealth and create the resistance that blocks and finally chokes the economy. Above all, this resistance impedes the current that creates value. When the resistance is extreme, the economic current shuts down.

A lack of resistance in the economic circuit is the condition that enables wealth to run its full natural cycle of value creation, its conversion to wealth, and its dispersion outward that creates prosperity for all.

Let us now examine the same ideas from a different perspective.

## *The minority and the majority*

I have so far attempted to show the need for two poles in the generation of value and wealth. One of the poles is the abundance of value and wealth, whereas the other pole is its absence.

The gap between them is where value and wealth are generated and grow. The sole condition is that no obstacles should hinder the flow between the poles. If this condition is respected, prosperity will be achieved.

We can also discuss these poles in terms of the minority and the majority. The rich are the minority, while less-wealthy people are the majority. Similarly, the highly educated are a small minority, and the uneducated or less educated are the vast majority.

In each case, we have two vectors in opposite directions. One vector tends toward unity (the ultimate minority is, of course, the minority of one), while the other tends toward multiplicity.

The creators, discoverers, and inventors tend to be in the minority as compared to the rest of the people. Now, the more freedom there is to create and invent, and the greater the gap between creators and noncreators, the more the minority *will* create.

The ordinary people are numerous, but the minority of creators at the other pole are a magnet that attracts inventors and scientists and, with them, all the rest of us. The more genius the discoverer or inventor has, the better it is for all of society. So tending to the creators, the elite minority, is essential for success as a society.

Let us think about it another way. Here is a simple question. If you were to hire a manager, and you had two candidates at the same salary, which would you hire? Here are the candidates:

Manager A is highly intelligent and has a successful track record. However, manager B is the best manager ever in modern history. He has the highest recorded rate of success and also the highest IQ ever known for a human being.

Would you hire A, or B? Also, do you think that manager B's unique ability would be a good influence for all and that he would be able, not only to act efficiently, but also to teach his skills to the other people in your company?

Here is another example. If you had to choose between delivering mass education to the below-average majority and providing the best possible education to a small number of exceptional people, which option would you choose?

Remember whether the creators are in the majority or the minority. If education sides with the creators and focuses on educating an elite minority to the highest possible level, it will guarantee success for all. If we focus instead on giving a mediocre education to the majority, poverty will follow and prosperity will be delayed.

If instead of giving an above-average education to one person in ten—assuming that we can only give it to one—we give a mediocre or poor education to all, the result will be that no one will succeed, and the resources that we allocate to education will have been wasted. Indeed, a bad education is often worse than no education at all.

Even if only one person can have an outstanding education, this will be better for the rest, the majority.

However, this position is anathema to politicians. Why? Because, as explained in chapter 4, it doesn't attract enough votes.

A third example is that of allocating resources to enterprises. Would you allocate resources to nine companies that are losing money and have poor management teams or to one remaining company that makes money consistently and has a brilliant management team? You choose. (Remember, investing in the efficient company also makes it possible for that company to take over the inefficient ones and bring them under good and profitable management.)

This third example illustrates the waste of money and energy that is the outcome of allocating resources by government fiat and refusing to let the market take care of itself. Governments follow the way of the many, while the free market is always in search of the best one, the true minority.

Let us now consider economic differences.

## QUANTITATIVE AND QUALITATIVE ASPECTS OF ECONOMIC DIFFERENCES

We have explained the need for a gap between the rich and the poor as a condition for prosperity. Now we must add a cautionary note. The gap between the rich and the poor must not be thought of as being only quantitative, in terms of dollars owned, for instance.

If quantity of wealth were the only thing that mattered, the gap would not contain an active principle within itself. It would never be the source of an energy that is able to generate prosperity. The gap also has a qualitative dimension to it. It is this dimension that causes it to be dynamic instead of static.

Money is only the quantitative and visible sign of a qualitative and invisible reality. This invisible reality is what we call value. The gap in quantifiable wealth tells us about the qualitative differences between the rich and the poor.

What we call value here is an incorporeal reality. This incorporeal reality is what is found in discoveries and inventions; it is their potential usefulness for society. When this incorporeal potential gives rise to services that make a discovery or invention available at a cost, the meaning it holds for life in society will express its value in practice. When value is offered and accepted in this way, it changes to wealth.

## *From mind to matter*

The difference in value between the works of Pablo Picasso and an average artist is simply the difference in value between Picasso's talent and that of an inferior artist. This gap is a gap in minds that is reflected in matter.

A reflection in matter is the actual material embodiment of an idea. The gap between an Einstein or a Picasso and lesser minds is a gap in thought and creativity.

In other words, the gap that we are speaking about is the gap between creators and noncreators.

The source of prosperity is intellectual property. A country's prosperity can be measured by its amount and quality of intellectual property. Even the number of patents gives an idea of a country's potential for wealth.

Let us imagine for a moment what the world would be like without inventions or discoveries in science, technology, or the arts. Take a few seconds to look around you. Try to realize the effort and special conditions required to create and deliver the goods that you are enjoying or using at this instant. How many people whom you know could have invented at least one of the things that surround you now? How many of the things that surround you could you have invented yourself?

The tools that we use and the things that we enjoy are possible because of the minds of their creators. This is the story of intellectual property—having ideas and owning them for the benefit of all.

The computers that we use, the telephones, the radios, the light fixtures, and everything that we can think of in that line, are possible because of intellectual property. A mind created them and a mind owns them.

Rich societies are wealthy because of their ideas that have been converted into useful things. This idea wealth is manifested in patents, industrial secrets, trademarks, and copyrights. Intellectual wealth is the secret behind rich, first-world countries.

## THERE IS NO WEALTH EXCEPT IDEAS

Once we understand that ideas and the intellectual property that they generate are the source of value, we have the key to prosperity. When we recognize that ideas generate value, which in turn changes into wealth, we have the secret of prosperity.

The same can be said of money. Money is wealth that results from value conversion. Value can be converted into monetary wealth. When this happens, money becomes a condenser of potential energy.

Money is static. It is finite and nonrenewable. Its value depends on the ideas of its users. Money can be spent, and thus decline in quantity until it disappears from the hands that possessed it.

However, the opposite can also happen. Money can be used as capital and become the catalyst of new value creation and wealth conversion. For this to happen, ideas are needed. So, in the end, whether it is an idea for an anti-aging drug or for a breakthrough computer program, it is always an idea that gives life to money and makes it useful and available.

## *The infinitely renewable resource*

The generative power of ideas is inexhaustible and free. Ideas are behind the greatest fortunes made in our time.

It is ideas that make money useful as capital, for example by giving birth to new technologies, which require financing for their development and distribution.

Ideas do not eventually become exhausted, as does an iron mine or an oil field. The value of iron, for example, is due to the existence of technologies that need iron, as a building material or for motors, tools, and a multitude of other things.

Even today, many countries do not realize that their minerals and other resources are valuable only because a few thinkers in first-world countries had the genius to invent things that gave value to those resources.

Further, those resources could disappear even before their physical disappearance. If new technologies make iron or oil useless again—and it could very well happen—all the "wealth" of many third-world countries will disappear into nothingness.

Third-world countries should, above all, be thankful to the genius of the thinkers and creators who have given them indirectly the mineral resources from which they benefit today. All their wealth comes from the ideas of those creators.

## *The strange machine*

All wealth comes ultimately from ideas, so promoting the free birth of ideas is essential. Our material world, including our mineral resources and all that surrounds us, becomes valuable only because of ideas.

We live in a world of ideas that are invisible and give worth to the visible. The visible side is the less important one. It is only a fraction of reality.

Imagine that someone discovers a strange machine whose function he does not know or understand. He might not even recognize it as a machine at first. Only by discovering its similarities with other devices would he learn what it is.

Now, imagine that someone else figures out the use of the strange machine. He has an idea of its use and function and how to start it. That person's mind has given value to the strange structure by recognizing it and using it as a machine.

## *The true source of prosperity*

The wealth of countries is their wealth in ideas. The wealthy countries are those that had a Louis Pasteur, a Nikola Tesla, or an Albert Einstein.

The output of people such as those is what explains the wealth of rich countries. The absence of those kinds of people is why poor countries remain in such misery.

Therefore, we need to know how to foster or attract such idea-generating people. They will enable a country to develop value for itself and to convert it to intellectual property and then into wealth.

## *Synergy*

In solving the problem of how to foster idea generation and its conversion into wealth, we must also take into account the factor of synergy in invention. Discoveries and inventions of all kinds interact synergistically.

Synergy, as mentioned previously, is essential for the exponential explosion of technological and scientific advances. Below a given threshold of inventive activity, no advance will have sufficient momentum to cause further advances. Isolated inventions or discoveries that are not disseminated or acted upon by the community will not generate further refinements or inventions.

Rockets in sixteenth century China did not advance beyond their amusement value. Toy airplanes in the premodern Western world were not developed into transportation airplanes. Today, many third-world inventors are unknown or isolated, and their research dies with them.

Discovery and creativity do not operate in a vacuum. They need the appropriate conditions to generate synergy. In addition, synergy exists primarily among the minds of scientists, thinkers, and creators.

For this synergy to exist and for technological and scientific development to take place, there must be certain conditions. Without them, development and prosperity will not occur.

The primary condition is unregulated economic freedom. In particular, the wealth gap between rich and poor must be left to grow naturally. In addition, two other key elements must come into play.

These two elements are a *critical mass* and a *social fabric*. Both will guarantee the stock of discoverers and inventors, the fundamental human capital that makes up the wealth of countries.

Let us consider these concepts further.

# Chapter 6

# Social Fabric and Critical Mass

*If you stick me down in the middle of Bangladesh or Peru or someplace, you'll find out how much this talent is going to produce in the wrong kind of soil.*

— Warren Buffett, quoted in Warren Buffett Speaks: Wit and Wisdom from the World's Greatest Investor, 2007.

What we can call *social fabric* is the sum of all the aspects of a society that make it friendly or hostile to the creation of value and wealth. Social fabric defines a population's potential.

Many factors contribute to social fabric. They include the society's framework of legal rules, its general world view, educational level, and family structure. Although not all of the factors are always identified or known, the results of a given social fabric are easily perceived.

Guy Sorman gives an example of a Mexican peasant who owns a piece of land and does not work on it efficiently; he is lazy. [36]

---

[36] Guy Sorman, *La Nouvelle Richesse des Nations*, (Paris: Fayard, 1987).

When this Mexican worker crosses the border into the United States, things begin to change. He no longer is lazy. He works efficiently and soon has a better economic position than he had in his country of origin.

Sorman explains that the government regulations in Mexico suppressed all motivation for work. The peasant could not have earned any more in Mexico by working harder or better. So he did the minimum work possible, and faced a gloomy future.

When he crossed the US border, his work immediately came to be rewarded according to his effort and talent, and so he developed the habit of using them. What can be learned from this is that whatever social fabric an individual finds himself in causes him to modify his outlook and his action.

## SOCIAL FABRIC DEFINES SUCCESS

The social fabric can be likened to the environment in which a seed is planted. In good earth, the seed will eventually become a full-grown tree, but in poor soil it will become a stunted one. In a field of stones it will die. Each society has a kind of social "soil" that has many nutrients, some known and some unknown.

Our social environment, including the kind of human beings who surround us, will determine our future to a great extent. The differing social fabrics of different countries will define the futures of their inhabitants.

Scientists, inventors and entrepreneurs will locate where they are welcome. They are not found in every kind of society because the social fabrics of some societies are hostile to their presence.

This hostility is manifested in obstacles to entrepreneurship, invention, and scientific research. The reason for these obstacles is that the overall population and the society's leaders do not understand the true implications of knowledge, research, and their applications.

What they do not understand is that they need these creators to build dynamic wealth. Furthermore, although the leaders of such countries do not understand the real issues behind science and technology, they believe that they do, and that makes it even worse.

They do not understand that the issue is not one of preserving or understanding a technology that already exists, but of being able to create a new one. All that matters to them is being able to reproduce or copy. Creating something new is never considered, even though it is the solution. In the long run, a country that does not create or does not convert its creations into wealth cannot become prosperous.

Because creation is the act of free minds, it cannot be forced; it must be left to itself. Having politicians or bureaucrats direct matters of science and technology runs counter to providing the freedom required.

Real freedom requires an attitude of humility. It means accepting that reality may surprise us. One free country can create technology, while another might be better at applying its creativity to tourism or finance. It is not for us to decide. We must learn to respect freedom.

## *The interdependence of social fabric and critical mass*

Freedom builds and promotes the kind of social fabric that enables discoverers and creators to thrive. Those creators will find a community that welcomes their efforts and is ready to help them and to provide moral support for their actions.

The experience of the Wright brothers at Kitty Hawk was an example of community support. When the brothers experimented with their first airplane, the people of the surrounding area came to give them a hand. This solidarity was a characteristic of the social fabric in which they lived.

This social fabric, in turn, requires an initial critical mass of thinkers, creators, researchers, and inventor-entrepreneurs to enable it to form. Laws by themselves do not build society or its people; you need a critical mass of the right kind of people for laws to be useful.

The number of creative and inventive people in a society needs to attain a quantitative threshold, its critical mass. Below this threshold, modernity and development are impossible. Above it, prosperity and wealth grow explosively.

In third-world countries, the best, most modern-minded individuals—in the sense we have specified—are isolated from one another because the critical mass of modern-minded inventors, creators, or discoverers has not been reached.

That is why poverty pervades significant areas of the planet. An initial critical mass of people with a dynamic concept of value and wealth is necessary if those areas are to become prosperous.

### *Critical mass and the prosperity explosion*

An initial critical mass of creative people will progressively transform the social fabric of a country.

A social fabric that is properly developed thus receives its energy from the critical mass of creators, who will generate the economic tension, or wealth gap, needed for prosperity and growth. The noncreative population revolves around these creators and innovators. As soon as there is a critical mass within a population, there will be a burst of creativity and entrepreneurship; both will grow explosively. Prosperity will follow.

The question, then, is how to create such a critical mass and such a social fabric within a population in order to trigger the creativity-entrepreneurship effect that leads to prosperity.

Let us now return to our concepts of critical mass and social fabric to better understand how they operate. This time we will look to chemistry for answers and metaphors.

## THE CHEMISTRY OF PROSPERITY: THE EMULSION METAPHOR

Like attracts like. This concept will help us explain how the critical mass of creators in a society is initially formed and why it acts as it does.

The concept of *like attracts like* can be illustrated by the metaphor of an emulsion.

If you pour a bottle of oil into a pitcher of water, the two different elements will at first mix with one another, but they will not dissolve into each other. If you mix the two vigorously, you can obtain a homogeneous liquid for a short time. This is called an emulsion. But soon the two elements will separate.

The oil droplets come together and merge, progressively separating themselves from the water.

Something similar happens with populations. Similar people will tend to congregate. Just as oil droplets in water seek to come together, creating a single mass of oil, so do people who share interests, skills, or knowledge come together.

At the end of an often long process, similar minds will end up in the same geographical region. In a way, we can say that countries are the result of the merging of similar persons and groups.

The same thing happens with thinkers and creators. They tend to seek similar minds and to converge in the same place. To them, this means having access to the collective mind of their peers. Thus they become concentrated in a country where they find a favorable environment. They end up forming a critical mass in that country that will progressively permeate the population. This critical mass will influence the entire society and become a center of attraction for progress and prosperity.

Thus, a country's first step to prosperity is to achieve the critical mass of creators that will activate all of society.

## *Minds are not equal*

Minds differ. Not everyone is a creator, inventor, or discoverer. Some people are good at creating, others at organizing, and others at helping.

Minds are not equal. In all fields there are strata—different layers or levels—of ability, and those strata complement each other. The discoveries of Einstein must be taught by people who are themselves not discoverers.

To understand modernity and its formation, we must understand what is required to gather the best, most creative people together in the same place. These people—inventors, discoverers, researchers, thinkers, and entrepreneurs—are attracted to countries that provide the freedom, the tools, and the social environment in which they can work and create.

Without an environment that allows freedom of thought, safe working conditions, and optimal living conditions, such people cannot develop their talents or personalities. And they need a climate of freedom, honesty, and reliability to bring out their best.

This climate or atmosphere, the social fabric, should not be taken for granted. In fact, few regions of the world offer it.

## *The gravitational force and acceleration of minds in society*

To understand why these conditions should not be taken for granted, we merely need to look at third-world countries and their social fabrics.

Much as freedom, honesty, and reliability are traits of first-world countries, the opposite traits are found in third-world countries.

In third-world countries, corruption is not the exception but the rule. A sense of the importance of time is nonexistent in these countries, as is the recognition of the need to be truthful. Lying, stealing, wasting other people's time, and laziness are common.

Even the elite of those countries will tend to say what others want to hear and to be slightly devious. They are too frequently tardy, and they do not use time optimally. Of course, there are exceptions to this, but they are rare.

This means that the social fabric is one in which tardiness, corruption, laziness, and stealing are common. Even though there is a segment of the population that does not descend to this level, they are pulled down by these practices. It is difficult to achieve anything worthwhile in such an environment.

In a land of obstacles, it is difficult to develop a critical mass of creators and inventor-entrepreneurs. When you cannot have tools, books, or a free working environment, it is almost impossible to have scientific and technological development.

Most politicians of third-world countries like to use such fashionable terms as the "need to promote innovation" and "scientific research." However, no scientist or entrepreneur would ever willingly work where bureaucrats will benefit parasitically at his expense.

Few creative people are attracted to countries where the police look for any pretext to extort money from drivers; where judges do not provide justice, but merely sell judgments to the highest bidders; where bureaucrats require bribes to release imported tools that they have intercepted and held in the customs department; and where a positive critical mass will never be reached.

The only kind of critical mass in these countries is a critical mass of corruption, deceit, laziness, and depredation.

Because of such a negative environment, creators and inventor-entrepreneurs are not attracted to third-world countries to do their thinking, conduct their research, and lead their lives. Those creators prefer a social fabric that makes it easy for them to develop and share their abilities.

The social fabric will attract both the people of the same, creative kind and also people who differ. This means that a positive social fabric will tend to convert the negative outliers to its positive outlook.

Conversely, a negative social fabric will tend to pull down its positive outliers. The result is that the social fabric will tend to pull the society toward prosperity or toward poverty.

In the end, each society receives what it deserves.

## *Everything and everyone finds its natural place*

We must emphasize that to generate prosperity people need an environment which welcomes them and offers them the means to work, prosper, and be themselves.

Many creators flee their countries of origin in search of a milieu in which their creativity can thrive. In this context, we must mention another kind of obstacle that creative people encounter in third-world countries. This obstacle is the lack of persons with whom to exchange ideas. It is difficult for creative people to find creative minds at their level. Teamwork thus becomes impossible. The creator will become isolated, which will hinder the development and expression of his potential. In the end, he will have to decide whether to look for another environment or to accept the limitations of his present one.

A decision to stay usually implies losing an opportunity to generate value for his country and the world. Bureaucrats, politicians, and predators of all kind relish this scenario. They will try by every means at their disposal to convince the creator to stay in his country of origin.

If they do encourage him to leave, it will be under the condition that he later return to work and live in his own country. The politician or bureaucrat will appeal to the creator's sense of charity, patriotism, selflessness, altruism, and even religion.

With this attitude, these obstructors are blocking the road to prosperity and callously destroying many people's lives and futures. When someone is told by a politician that his country needs him, it is a warning. He should leave immediately.

The fact is that neither politicians nor anyone else are entitled to control other people's lives. These would-be controllers include any "altruistic" entities that have their own ideas of what others should do with their lives and resources. It is easy to decide for other people without their consent.

To be altruistic with other people's hard-earned money is bad enough—indeed, it typifies the predator who disguises himself in the cloak of an apparently noble cause. Nothing is easier than telling others what to do with their money.

Worse still is deciding what others should do with their minds. Predators constantly try to convince people to waste their minds.

Prosperity can only come when the individual discovers that he is the only one who is entitled to decide how to use his wealth and, more importantly, how to use his mind. When minds are finally freed, prosperity will come as a natural consequence.

## *Brains are not "draining"; they're regaining their freedom*

The simplest way to find a free environment where the mind can work in optimum conditions is to move from a bad place to a better one. Moving is an efficient way of recovering freedom, and it is what many third-world people do.

This fleeing to a better environment is often called "brain drain." This is the same as happens with capital. Brains, like capital, flee to more welcoming environments. Both investment dollars and intellectual talent will leave countries where their potential will be squandered.

This is a survival reaction, and one that is legitimate and benefits all. It benefits not only the country to which the brains flee but also the country that is left behind. Each mind that achieves its natural potential benefits humanity.

Not fleeing to a better environment entails paying a personal price and also retarding progress and prosperity for everyone. Here is an example:

In Peru at the end of the nineteenth century, there was an inventor named Pedro Paulet. He moved to Paris, and there he invented a space rocket and a jet plane. He was not a silly dreamer but a practical and brilliant man.[37]

Wermer von Braun, the father of rocket science, who was NASA's director of the Marshall Space Flight Center and architect of the Saturn V rocket, considered Paulet one of the "fathers of aeronautics."

When Paulet created the first working prototype of a liquid-fueled rocket engine in Paris in 1895, Henry Ford noticed his work. Ford suggested that Paulet give up his Peruvian nationality, and offered to give him employment in the United States—plus a million-dollar bonus. This was a considerable sum of money at the time—the equivalent of approximately $100 million in today's dollars.

However, Paulet refused the offer. He fell for an appeal to his sense of patriotism. He had not yet understood that the only true patriotism is the one that exists among like minds. He wanted his home country, Peru, to have his discoveries and inventions.

Unfortunately, what happened to him was what could be expected. To the Peruvian elites, an inventor was nothing more than a dreamer and a madman. The politicians of the time saw wealth and value deriving mainly from agriculture and mining. To their way of thinking, minds and their inventions had no real value or application. They thought that their country was rich because it had material resources.

So Paulet held throughout his life a series of unproductive jobs in the Peruvian government, and he died as an obscure bureaucrat. His brilliant mind received only academic recognition and menial scientific jobs. He never received financial support to build his prototype air- and spacecraft, despite requesting the money from the Peruvian government.

---

[37] Sara Madueño Paulet de Vásquez, "Pedro Paulet: Peruvian Space and Rocket Pioneer," *21st Century Science and Technology Magazine,* Winter 2001–2002, http://www.21stcenturysciencetech.com/articles/winter01/paulet.html.

If Pedro Paulet had accepted Ford's offer of work and a bonus of a million dollars, he would have had the funding he needed and he could have become the equal of Edison or Tesla. But he didn't, and because of his refusal, America lost a great mind and the prosperity it could bring — and so did the rest of the world.

The absence of a positive social fabric in Peru—and Paulet's choice to stay in that country—caused him to sink into inaction. Not one of his ideas ever saw light. They all remained, except for his Paris prototype spaceship, in the mind of their creator. What a loss!

Paulet is an example of why an exodus of brains from countries that do not offer them the environment they need should be encouraged and supported by all possible means.

A brain exodus will never be recognized or accepted by any politician or bureaucrat, whatever his nationality or his political affiliation. Bureaucrats and politicians belong to a higher order, where their national affiliation no longer matters. They belong to the ruling class of predators on wealth, minds, and lives. These kinds of people will use any argument or stratagem in hunting their prey.

It is sad to contemplate those passive beings who allow themselves to be hunted by the predators, and even offer themselves as sacrificial victims.

## *When minds find their optimal allocation: Victor Ochoa*

Victor Leaton Ochoa (1850–1945), born in Ojinaga, Mexico, became a United States citizen in 1889 after moving to Texas. He married Amanda Cole (granddaughter of Thomas Cole, the American famous for his painting "the Last of the Mohicans").

Ochoa resided in New York City and the area of Paterson, New Jersey, where he made several inventions. Among his inventions were an airplane, a reversible motor, a rail magnetic brake, a windmill to generate electrical power, and an adjustable wrench.

His first aircraft was a folding-wing glider. Later he invented the Ochoa plane, a true airplane with foldable wings, which became a reality in 1904 and was built by the International Airship Co. of Paterson.

In 1900 he sold his invention of a fountain pen to the Waterman Company. In 1907 he sold his patented electric brake for street cars to the American Brake Company. Also in that year he sold a patented pen and clip to the American Pen and Pencil Company.

His windmill was a forerunner of our clean-energy windmills. It was a combination of a windmill and a dynamo that converted wind power into electrical power. (His windmill was not circular but had four arms with shutters in each attached by hinges. The wind lifted two of the shutters while propelling the others in the direction of the wind; thus, each arm offered minimum wind resistance.)[38]

Here, by contrast with Pedro Paulet, we have a man who had the courage to emigrate to an environment favorable to his inventive mind. As a result, his many inventions benefited the whole world—something that would never have happened had he stayed in his country of birth.

## *Harnessing the movement of minds and capital*

Free countries are preferable to ones that are not free, so minds and capital naturally flow toward free countries.

Now, freedom has no need of its opposite to function. A country benefits from its own freedom even when other countries also are free. However, those free countries that are surrounded by countries that are less free also prosper from their neighbors' self-inflicted losses. Creativity and money will flee the restrictions of repressive countries and go to the free countries.

The right response to the phenomenon of "brain drain" is not to imprison people so that they won't flee their countries but, instead, to

[38] Victor L. Ochoa Papers, 1894–1945, Archives Center, National Museum of American History, Smithsonian Institution, Washington, D.C.

give them the freedom that enables them to remain without fear of having their money or minds preyed upon by white-collar thieves.

Capital and minds that do flee unfree countries not only benefit the countries of destination, but also the countries from which they flee, as paradoxical as this may seem. The benefits are many. For example, countries from which capital flees will necessarily multiply their exports. This is because, to flee, capital must change to a currency that will be accepted abroad. Exports are a way of "importing" such a currency.

The entrepreneur escaping with his capital will sell his business to someone who has the political influence to keep it running. In this sense, this departing capital creates exchanges that benefit everyone, even if it is for a bad reason (i.e., because the politicians are frightening capital away).

The departed capital will prosper and grow in its new home. The same capital can someday return, having grown in amount, to its country of origin. When conditions are favorable again for freedom and entrepreneurship, capital always returns, having increased as a result of having fled in the past. When capital does return to its country of origin, it can help to rebuild the country.

Chile provides an example. Capital took flight under Salvador Allende's communist regime. Later, capital returned to Chile when conditions changed and freedom returned to the country. And when capital did return, it came back in a far greater amount.

Capital returned because many of the obstacles to its free circulation had been abolished. Chile then became a world model of free enterprise, and the results spoke for themselves. Chile went from being a third-world country to being almost a first-world country in just a few years.

Chile is an example of how freedom and safety immediately attract capital and build prosperity. Its story also shows that it takes only a short time to obtain results. Chile showed the world the consequences of eliminating obstacles to capital and entrepreneurship.

These consequences imply prosperity. When we want an inflow of capital, we first must eliminate all that hinders its free circulation.

## *Creative minds are not equally distributed throughout the world*

The force of minds looking for welcoming environments should not be underestimated. Not only is the society of minds not equal in the sense that not all persons have the same level of intelligence, but also, because of the processes described above, the distribution of intelligence is not the same everywhere in the world.

Not all types of minds gather in the same geographical locations. The minds that populate MIT or NASA will not be found in a third-world country, because creators from such a country will go to environments that welcome them.

Thus, highly developed countries have more highly developed minds working for them than do less developed countries. We do not mean that there are no highly developed minds in the latter countries. There are, but those countries do not have the critical mass needed for those minds to deliver their full potential.

The heterogeneous distribution of minds is what makes the elimination of obstacles to the free circulation of minds urgent for every third-world country that wants to develop and prosper. Development and prosperity are the visible signs of invisible minds.

True prosperity is prosperity of the minds that populate a country. Its outward manifestation is a sign of the inner spirit of its inhabitants. Material prosperity and other outward factors are less meaningful than the underlying, inner factors that define a country's world view and attitude.

The wrong attitude and world view will generate obstacles of every kind. Not only will freedom be limited, but violence and corruption will also emerge as a warning of what is going on in the thoughts and inner lives of the population.

For example, the US government's answer to the 1980s Savings and Loan crisis was to introduce a new set of regulations via the 1989 Financial Institutions Reform, Recovery, and Enforcement Act (FIRREA). Those regulations helped to precipitate the 1990 recession by causing corruption and inefficiency, because regulators used "creative accounting" to hide their deficiencies.[39]

On the other hand, a dynamic mind-set that understands that resources are unlimited and mind-based will swiftly manifest itself as a free society where honesty, respect for other people's time, and freedom will emerge in a peaceful and safe environment.

## HETEROGENEITY MUST BE ACKNOWLEDGED

### *Are you unique?*

You are unique. There is no other like you. Furthermore, you are the ultimate reason for your existence. Everything in the universe has its specific purpose. You have yours. This purpose is in your case the enactment of freedom and free will. You are not a robot or a slave; you are a free mind with talent and purpose.

Talent and purpose must be acted upon. For this to occur, there must be a free market where individual initiative can be exercised. Freedom is what enables your uniqueness to be revealed. Indeed, freedom is the essential condition that gathers to it everything else needed for prosperity and happiness.

Freedom means an absence of obstacles to our rational choices, a state where all that can be, comes to be, because there is nothing to oppose it. A void of government obstacles attracts all possibilities and opportunities.

This void or vacuum generates entrepreneurship, creativity, and invention. Science and technology can then advance. Above all, the

---

[39] Dale Steinrich, "75 Years of Housing Fascism," *Mises Daily* July 9, 2009, http://mises.org/daily/3544.

individual can perfect his spirit, mind, and body—or, in other words, his life.

When individuals use their uniqueness and their specific talents, it will be reflected in their society. If a sufficient number of people can develop themselves in this void or vacuum resulting from lack of government intervention, a free society is born.

Every society will develop in the direction of its own critical mass of entrepreneurs and creators. In this sense, we can say that societies are also unique.

This means that neither creative people nor inventive and enterprising societies are homogeneous. This is because the main condition for the existence of such people and societies is freedom itself, and freedom leads to uniqueness—to heterogeneity.

This takes us to the relationship between freedom and equality.

## *Is homogeneity desirable?*

Freedom does not mean homogeneity. It means exactly the opposite. Freedom implies an absence of boundaries, and an acting out of different possibilities and perspectives. Equality and homogeneity kill the mind and all initiative.

In socialist regimes, equality and homogeneity are the rule. Anything that differs is suppressed. The people live in a prison of grayness and conformity. We have witnessed this in the Soviet Union and all other communist regimes.

When the threat of incarceration forces you to think like those who obey the regime, you cannot exchange ideas usefully. If you cannot think freely because someone will betray you and the government will confiscate what you have and imprison you, it is difficult to do your best.

Egalitarian thinking, acting, and owning not only kills the individual's mind, but also kills the country and prevents it from achieving its greatest destiny. This destiny has nothing to do with the heroic "national destinies" that politicians are so prone to give lip service to.

The real destiny of a country is the destiny of its free-thinking, free-acting, and free-living individuals—without government coercion of any kind. This destiny comes naturally.

The destiny of a country can be realized by setting each inhabitant free to be himself, develop his talents, create value, and exchange goods.

This kind of destiny, the one that characterizes the few free countries of the world, requires a special world view, and stamina. Most nations do not care about freedom, although they may pretend to.

## *The pole of progress and prosperity*

This suggests the existence of two poles. In one, freedom and its benefits, including individual uniqueness, are fully developed. In the other, there is unfreedom and its dire consequence, lawlessness.

In countries where there is a critical mass of creative people, invention and value creation can be found. Where the social fabric is permeated by such a critical mass, it becomes receptive to creativity and thought. These countries attract the builders of value—they are like magnets that gather creative minds around them.

This is why some regions of the globe have become centers of creativity. The critical mass of entrepreneurs and creators that enables value creation has been reached there. Only when the critical mass is achieved will an environment give creators the tools to build value and wealth continuously. What we call first-world, or developed, countries are characterized by having this creative critical mass.

But why have creators and value builders attained such a critical mass in some regions of the planet and not in others? Why are there such differences? To answer these questions, we must first learn why such a critical mass has developed in a given location.

The reasons for this are the same as those that create affluence in capital in some regions of the world instead of others. Capital and minds are linked at their roots.

Capital is value that has been converted to a kind of wealth that can enable the creation of more value in an ascending spiral.

Minds go where capital goes. The converse is also true. Capital flows to where minds gather. Minds and capital both seek freedom.

## *Capital and minds seek to preserve their energy*

Minds and capital move in the same direction. They flee danger and go where they can expand. They preserve their energy by escaping dangerous environments that would destroy them.

If their power is destroyed, everyone will lose. Minds and capital will do whatever they can to find havens of safety and opportunity. Rich, developed countries offer these.

Creative minds are on the lookout for freedom. Economic freedom and political freedom are the foundations of all creativity. Creators, thinkers, and entrepreneurs go where they will find the least number of obstacles to the development of their minds and resources.

These people will flee what we could call "obstacle states" and move to "freedom states," where individual talent is highly appreciated and supported.

The best way to bring together talented people is to create conditions of freedom for research and creative entrepreneurship. Helping talented people should be encouraged even to the point of persuading them to leave their countries in a search for better working and living conditions.

## *Capital and minds together bring the spark of wealth and prosperity*

Invoking patriotism to pressure talented people to remain in their countries of origin is a recipe for poverty. This is the same recipe for poverty that attempts to prevent capital from leaving. Capital and minds must go where they fare better. This is the law of nature.

A brain that flees a country to find a better environment is an intelligent brain. Any person who is awake wants to live where he can develop his abilities. The primordial capital is human talent. It is the origin of all wealth.

Human talent flourishing and fulfilling its potential is the only source of the wealth of countries.

Now it becomes easier to understand the difference between poor and wealthy countries. The wealthy countries are those where there is a critical mass of talent that is acted upon. Nothing else explains why those countries are prosperous.

The need for talent is why freedom to associate must be permitted without conditions. Talent can be easily frightened, and, without freedom, will feel and act in a fearful and limited way.

Let us now examine further the attempts to limit or restrict freedom through regulations, which hamper the development of an entrepreneurial social fabric and critical mass.

# Chapter 7

# Freedom versus Predation and Regulation

*There is always a cry for our leaders to do something, even though their understanding of the problem is probably not much better than ours. The most frequent solution—to take control by limiting the freedom of individuals—effectively limits the system's ability to find its own solution. Thus the "solution" often makes things worse.*

— Edgar E. Peters, *Patterns in the Dark*, 1999.

~

*Creativity requires freedom to act. Every constraint on freedom is a constraint on creative action.*

— Michael Strong, *Be the Solution: How Entrepreneurs and Conscious Capitalists Can Solve All the World's Problems*, 2009.

Regulations slow action. They can even stop it or make it impossible. Red tape and regulations not only render action inefficient but also discourage people. Even worse than this, regulations are the swamp in which corruption rules. Throughout history, the more regulated that economies and societies have been, the poorer and more corrupt they have been.

Politicians and bureaucrats endorse regulations (after all, they make a living from them). Businessmen may also endorse regulations if they want to use them to acquire a de facto monopoly or a quasi monopoly for their business. By encouraging government regulations, these businessmen manage to end or retard competition. Their profits are conducive, not to prosperity, but to poverty.

## ABOLISHING REGULATIONS

When we abolish regulations and encourage freedom, prosperity becomes possible. But here we need to be precise.

By regulations, we mean government regulations that have nothing to do with justice. Justice means the enactment of moral law in civil and criminal matters.

All regulations restricting free trade in any way should be abolished. All regulations limiting business in any way should be abolished. Markets should regulate themselves.

### *Aquinas and Rothbard on the nonaggression principle*

Self-regulation also applies to people. People should regulate themselves in what concerns their lives without attacking or transgressing on the lives of others. The first principle in trade and in life is the principle of nonaggression. Indeed, nonaggression by itself will suffice.

St. Thomas Aquinas states the principle of nonaggression when he says, "Human laws do not forbid all vices ... but only the more grievous vices, from which it is possible for the majority to abstain; and chiefly those that are to the hurt of others, without the prohibition of which human society could not be maintained: thus human law prohibits murder, theft and such like."[40]

This nonaggression principle belongs to the wisdom of the ages and is part of humanity's *philosophia perennis.*

In more recent times, Murray N. Rothbard, basing himself on Aquinas, has elaborated on this nonaggression principle. In his book *For a New Liberty: The Libertarian Manifesto*, Rothbard says that the nonaggression axiom is the core of libertarianism. It is the idea "that no man or group of men may aggress against the person or property of anyone else."

Rothbard follows in Bastiat's line of thought that government is not above the individual when he says, "In contrast to all other thinkers, left, right, or in-between, the libertarian refuses to give the State the moral sanction to commit actions that almost everyone agrees would be immoral, illegal, and criminal if committed by any person or group in society." And he adds that "if we look at the State naked, as it were, we see that it is universally allowed, and even encouraged, to commit all the acts which even non-libertarians concede are reprehensible crimes."

By simply not regulating, and by allowing the law of nonaggression to resolve all affairs between men, we can make freedom possible in all its facets. The first consequence will be the freeing of minds. And free minds in a free environment will create value by their initiative.

Prosperity can only result from value creation by free minds, and the free and unregulated conversion of that value to wealth.

Deregulation and the full enactment of freedom, based on the principle of nonaggression, is a proper, minimalist way of ruling. It is ruling in full accordance with human nature. The result cannot be anything but the exercise of man's full potential. And what else is that but the creation of value? Free and fully developed humans are the cause of all

---

[40] Thomas Aquinas, *Summa Theologica*, trans. Fathers of the English Dominican Province. (New York: Benziger Brothers, 1947), Question 96, Article 2, p. 1863.

value and wealth. When humans can achieve their potential without being hindered, they naturally become prosperous.

There is more. Regulations appear when law and justice disappear. Regulations banish and displace the proper sense of law; they push away the legitimate law.

Those regulations not only have nothing to do with true law, as such, but usually are unlawful. They are, for the most part, a pretext for bureaucrats to prey on society and control it by a simulacrum of justice.

There are still many other evils hidden under the banner of regulations.

## *Regulations misallocate resources*

Time and capital are lost in complying with regulations. Most compliance is useless, but the regulations must be heeded to avoid conflict. Bureaucratic red tape creates obstacles to enterprise. Having to invest in ways directed by governments will misallocate resources that the market would have used more efficiently.

Bureaucratic red tape is one of the chief obstacles that prevent the efficient circulation of capital and of minds. These bureaucratic barriers go hand in hand with corruption, which is the only reason for them to exist.

Useless regulations mean less profit for society. By sapping energy, time, mind, and ultimately life, they harm everyone. In the last analysis, time is life, and its depredation is a major crime.

Entrepreneurs should be free to start any business in an unregulated fashion. No one should need to comply with bureaucratic steps to create a business. It should not be up to the entrepreneur to ask permission from the government. It should be the other way round.

At the most, there could be a form to identify the business and its associates, but it should be the government's responsibility to complete it (and the government should use the form for information only). That is, if there must be some registration of a business, it should be government that discovers and acknowledges the existence of the businesses. No bureaucrat should ever be able to put an obstacle in the way of the creation of a company.

The only regulation needed is to enforce the law of nonaggression. Penalties for transgressing the rights of others should be enforced legally. The principle behind the law should be freedom.

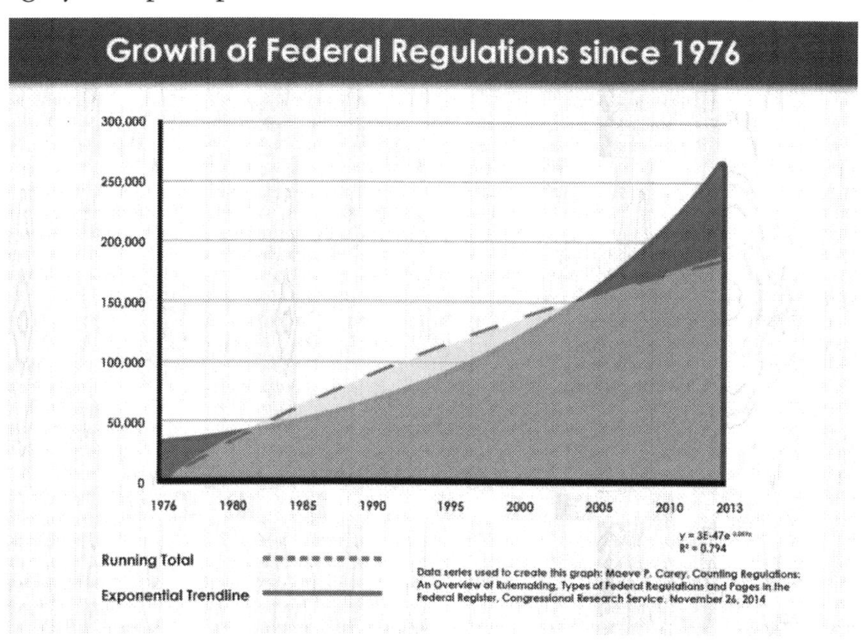


Figure 3. The growth of federal regulations since 1976

## *The inevitable growth of regulations*

Regulations, besides distorting the law, limiting freedom, and destroying prosperity, are also constantly expanding. Each bad regulation leads to a new one.

Why do regulations constantly seek to expand? Here, the mathematics of Kurt Gödel comes to our rescue.

Kurt Gödel (1906–1978) was an Austrian-American logician and mathematician who proved that every formal system that consisted of a finite set of rules was either incomplete or inconsistent.[41]

This "first incompleteness theorem" of Gödel has implications for government and society. The theorem is about the inherent limitations of every formal system of rules. According to Gödel, no consistent, finite set of rules is sufficiently complete to prove every true statement. This means that at least one true statement cannot be proved unless we add a new rule from outside the system.

For the new system that arises by adding a rule from outside the original system there will also be at least one statement that it will need another external rule to prove, and so on, ad infinitum. Always needing to add another external rule means that any initial system will begin a process of indefinite growth. The larger the system becomes as a result of this endless need to bring in a rule from outside, the greater the number of rules becomes. So however large a finite system becomes, it will never be complete; that is, it will never be sufficient to prove all true statements.

Governments and societies also have systems of rules that regulate human events. However, no set of social rules or laws is ever complete. Thus, we can multiply laws and regulations indefinitely. The more laws and regulations you have, the more you will need. Laws and regulations will grow exponentially from the initial impulse that proposed the first one, because no system of laws can ever be complete.

The growth occurs because the initial set of laws or regulations will not regulate all the behaviors that they are meant to regulate. So, sooner or later, it will be necessary to bring in new, outside regulations. As soon as this new and now-larger set of regulations begins to direct people's behavior of, new flaws will appear that show that at least one human

[41] See Ernest Nagel and James R. Newman, *Gödel's Proof* (New York: New York University Press, 2001).

event is not regulated by the new system. So, once again, a new set of rules is created by the addition of another regulation, and so on.

Mises, when discussing one interventionist scholar's admission that each intervention leads to a further intervention says that had this opponent taken the argument to its logical end, "he would necessarily have come to the conclusion that there are only two alternatives: either to abstain from all intervention, or, if this is not the intention, to add ever new interventions."[42]

To further understand this cycle of damaging regulations, we will look to another mathematical concept, degrees of freedom. This will help us to understand the relationship between regulations and financial crises.

## *Degrees of freedom*

The number of degrees of freedom in a calculation is the number of variables in the calculation that are free to vary.

For example if we know that two numbers must add up to 10, we have only one degree of freedom in that calculation, that is, one possible free choice. Let us say we freely choose 4 as the first number. We are then not free to choose the second number. We are forced, like it or not, to pick 6.

$4 + 6 = 10$.

The more degrees of freedom a system has, the greater its latitude of movement—i.e., the freer it is. But this is true only when those degrees of freedom are left undefined (i.e., unregulated). As soon as you begin to define each degree of freedom with specific content, the freedom of the system becomes restricted.

If someone regulates that single degree of freedom in our example by passing through Congress a regulation that, metaphorically speaking, forces every citizen to pick 4 as his first number, freedom has been

[42] Ludwig von Mises, *A Critique of Interventionism* (Auburn, AL: Mises Institute, 2011), p. 28.

hampered and the population enslaved. By having to pick a 4, each citizen is forced to pick the 6 as well.

Contrariwise, in an unregulated system each person is free to choose as his first number 1, 2, 3, 4, 5, 6, 7, 8, or 9. (For simplicity, this example uses only positive whole numbers.)

Of course, once we freely choose this first possibility, our freedom has been used up, and so we have no choice as to the second number.

Here is another example: if we are looking for three numbers that add up to 10, we have two degrees of freedom, because once the first two numbers are chosen the third is predetermined. If we chose 2 for the first number and 5 for the second, then of course the third number must be 3.

However, choosing even one of the three numbers in this example restricts the whole system. Let us say our first choice is an 8. The two next numbers must be 1 and 1. If our first pick is 3, the two next choices could be 1 and 6 or 2 and 5, but they could not be 1 and 1, or 4 and 2.

The greater the number of degrees of freedom that are used up in this way, the more rigid a system becomes. In real life, rigidity brings sluggishness. The smaller the number of degrees of freedom used, the greater the system's latitude of movement—that is, the freer it is.

This explanation takes us to the boundaries of freedom. At one extreme we have a clockwork mechanism. It can move only within a narrow range. At the opposite extreme, we have unbounded movement with absolutely no restrictions. In between the two extremes, we have an entire spectrum that ranges from pure mechanism to free will. The less mechanical something is, the fewer limiting conditions it has and the freer it becomes.

The concept of degrees of freedom can be applied to everything from atomic particles to human beings. The fewer the limiting conditions, the greater the freedom of action and the more possibilities there are.

## *Degrees of freedom, the incompleteness theorem, and financial crises*

A financial crisis is an example of these mathematical principles—Gödel's first incompleteness theorem and the concept of degrees of freedom—in action. Let us begin with the incompleteness theorem: the fact that any system of rules is necessarily incomplete.

Each financial crisis provokes the creation of new regulations. Once these new regulations have been enacted, a new future crisis shows that they not only were unable to solve all future crises, they even created new problems.

Once the new and unexpected crises occur, all the bureaucratic and political gurus clamor for a new system of regulations. They forget the uselessness of past regulations. So a new set of regulations is brought in while we wait for a new crisis, and so on indefinitely.

For instance, the crash of 1929 was a result of a wave of new credit that created a stock-market bubble in global equities. When that bubble burst, it destroyed the wealth of a decade. The US government, to prevent this from happening again, issued new regulations by passing the Glass-Steagall Act of 1933. In it, commercial-bank activities were separated from higher-risk speculative investments. However, these regulations didn't stop the creation of new bubbles, leading to the stock-market crashes of 1939, 1973, 1987, 2000, and 2008. Bankers managed to find loopholes, enabling them to engage in speculative activities by trading via subsidiaries. (In 1999 the Glass-Steagall Act, which was almost useless in practice, was finally repealed.)

The Glass-Steagall Act also didn't prevent the Savings and Loan crisis of the 1980s, in which 1043 out of 3234 savings-and-loan associations in the United States failed. As I mentioned earlier, the government responded to the Savings and Loan crisis by issuing a new set of complicated regulations, FIRREA. But that didn't prevent the 2007–2008 financial crisis, which arose from the housing bubble.

Furthermore, each set of regulations uses up our degrees of freedom. The more complex a system of rules is, the less effective it is. By consuming at every turn more degrees of freedom, the regulatory system limits the freedom of businesses and individuals to make decisions, and it eventually impedes prosperity and hinders living. It does not and cannot work.

So the system, due to its own complexity, actually hinders itself. Whatever the system was supposed to prevent (for instance, a financial crisis) is exactly what will occur again. The system is useless and becomes a hindrance and an obstacle in itself.

## *Why it is silly to try to regulate society*

Regulations exist due to government's obsession with control. Governments think that they can isolate factors and control them. They forget that society does not work like the trajectory of a projectile, which can be calculated in advance.

A projectile's actual trajectory usually fits the calculations exactly. However, in the case of "social engineering," failure of the engineers' predictions has always been the rule. The consequences of their tinkering have always been crisis and a slow economy.

Society cannot be controlled, because its motor is freedom itself. The primary agent of economic behavior is free human action.

Humans are not robots. All they think and do and feel depends ultimately, and only, on being free. Free choice is what gives value and legitimizes human action. Free choice is our ultimate destiny.

Whatever the result of our choices, their meaning comes from our freedom. For example, we condemn a criminal because he acted freely. No one would send a robot to prison, nor would they charge a tornado with vandalism for destroying a town.

The same holds for positive consequences. A company pays a bonus to its employees because they acted freely. No one gives bonuses to computers. The same can be said for any prize. When a car receives a prize for the best design, it is the designer who is honored.

Freedom is the motor, not only of all social economic activity, but also of our human actions and our life's meaning. We exist to be free and to develop all the possibilities that our freedom enables us to achieve in our specific circumstances.

Our inner freedom, combined with the outer world, enables us to create, to develop, and to be. No regulations and controls will ever create prosperity. On the contrary, they will always guarantee misery and poverty.

Because society is driven by free human action, its future cannot be predicted or controlled. The models of social engineers cannot describe future events. However, the engineers *can* appear to explain the past by retrofitting their explanations to the data after the fact, and thus creating an illusion of control.

This illusion makes us believe, wrongly, that the engineers' system will work in the future. This is what happens to the control freaks in government: their wishful thinking lures them into believing that controls and regulations work.

They fall victim to the illusion that past data fit the model. When the bureaucrats and politicians then fill the present full of regulations, they utterly fail to control the future.

The illusion that the data fits the engineers' models has created many failures, such as the five-year plans of the Soviet Union and Cuba, Raúl Prebisch's disastrous Argentinean import substitutions (see chapter 2), and countless other inefficient measures.

No, controls do not work. They do not work today, and they will not work tomorrow.

The philosophical reason why these artificial controls of freedom do not work is that regulations try to limit reality instead of opening it. They use up degrees of freedom. They nullify reality's dynamic nature and tie it to a fixed and static framework.

In truth, to accept reality one must embrace change. Indeed, what we call change is simply barriers and limits falling, progressively freeing reality to be itself. Reality is dynamic. It cannot be controlled or limited.

## *Away from regulation and toward freedom*

So, what is our way out of the conundrum of endless regulations? Let us consider the following.

First, laws and regulations have one purpose: to enable things to work smoothly and well. They should not create obstacles, but remove them. And we have seen that regulations and laws cannot legislate or regulate everything. Human action will always escape regulations. The more regulations there are, the more inflexible, inadaptable, and inefficient any system becomes. So, to avoid life-destroying inefficiencies, we must look in the opposite direction.

Laws and regulations are only signposts. Signposts ought to tell us the direction that we should take. Above all, they must be simple. Similarly, no map can account for every detail.

Laws and regulations should only be sufficiently complete to guide us. In themselves, maps are useless. Once we know how to go somewhere, we no longer need the map and can discard it. Similarly, regulations should be as limited as possible, because the goal is to not have them at all. Really, we need laws only to prevent us from being attacked and victimized by others against whom we cannot defend ourselves.

Basic moral codes must be enforced to preserve our freedom, so that no one will trample on our rights. We need minimal protection to preserve freedom. Most of the work of self-protection should be left to the individual. Only when the individual is powerless to legitimately defend himself should an external regulation come to his rescue. In almost every area of life, the individual can take care of himself.

The only way to have a working society is to move away from the indefinite multiplication of regulations. The fewer the regulations, the better the system. Laws should only enforce the basic norms of behavior, in case someone deviates from them to the detriment of his innocent neighbor.

The ideal is an unregulated society. The law of freedom and the principle of nonaggression should be the only laws. Even though we call these "laws," they are not restrictive. They enhance our action instead of restricting it. These laws are nothing more than "roads" or "ways" along which reason-enhancing freedom can flow.

Freedom is the goal. Freedom does not mean arbitrariness, but the opposite. Freedom means enlarging possibilities and opportunities—and leaving people to be what they want and to develop their talents, vocations, and lives.

## *Slave minds*

When freedom is exercised for the sake of inefficiency and control, freedom has been used against itself. People lose their freedom because they use their free will to do things that will result in the loss of their political freedom—and later even their free will itself.

The free individual may temporarily comply with regulations. However, he must know that it is important to do everything in his power to eradicate them. When he doesn't, his exercise of freedom will be further restricted.

Here we find a fundamental paradox of freedom. The first act of the free individual is to assume full responsibility for his life, thus accepting his personal freedom in full. However, he can also say no to the gift of freedom.

When he chooses this second alternative, he becomes a slave. He hands over his right to freedom, his birth as a free person, to someone else who will live for him. At that moment, he is expelled from paradise. Because of his laziness, he ceases to own his life. This abdication of freedom begins in the spirit and the mind and then materializes in outward reality. By abdicating his freedom and voluntarily becoming a slave of blind forces that will guide his life, he begins a downward spiral.

The loss of freedom of such slave-minded people grows and accelerates. Freedom is restricted more and more as regulations proliferate. Regulations, even up to the total loss of freedom, are the self-inflicted fate of slave-minded people in a slave-minded society. In such a society, the individual ceases to exist and becomes an embodiment of the collective mind.

The converse is also true. No regulations are possible within a society of free-minded individuals.

Slave minds are ready to abdicate their freedom to "solve" the problems of hunger, health, and education. As long as they are fed, they are willing to live mindlessly in slavery and fear.

Relinquishing freedom and thought is the easy way out. It is the way of least possible effort. When we take this way out, entropy wins.

If there is one cardinal sin, it is using one's freedom to choose in order to destroy freedom. Using freedom to destroy freedom is akin to suicide. It kills the core of life itself.

However, every day, bureaucrats and politicians ask the population to abdicate their freedom. Their argument is that people should be protected against themselves. This protection includes deciding whether you can drink or not, smoke or not, and drive or not, and whether you must save for your retirement or not. They believe everything should be regulated.

Thus, society is infantilized. Once this happens, people lose consciousness. They forget freedom and what it means and does. They enter into a dreamland where they become the puppets of politicians and bureaucrats, who can prey on them and exploit them at will. They willingly become victims and slaves, and they admire and support their enslavers.

Worse still, they believe that they are free.

## TAXES AND THEIR HIDDEN REASON FOR EXISTING

Taxes are a special kind of regulation. What we have said above about regulations in general (and the need to suppress them) also applies to taxes. Furthermore, studying taxation can tell us about the regulators themselves and the slave mind-set they try to create.

## *What should taxation be like?*

Taxes should favor value creation. The government should collect the minimum required to have a society of free individuals who function smoothly. Taxes should never become an obstacle to the free development of minds and capital. They should be as low as possible. Tax rates should attract entrepreneurs instead of frightening them away.

Refusal or failure to pay taxes should never be a crime. Anyone who does not pay taxes should simply no longer receive benefits.

This takes us to a second important concept: Taxes should deliver. We should be eager to pay them. Taxes should be like the membership fees paid to belong to a club and benefit from its services. They should be nothing more and nothing less.

Taxes should never carry any kind of moral connotation. They should simply be payment for the goods they purchase. That is all.

Helping the needy with welfare, or even protecting an individual who can protect himself, should never be a reason for taxes. Why? Because these taxes will lead to overregulation, complexity, and inefficiency. Above all, inconsistency with the true purpose of government would crowd in. It already has—almost everywhere.

Inconsistency is the key here. Welfare, antismoking laws, mandatory car insurance, and all kinds of "social-benefit" programs have nothing to do with the money needed to run the collective side of a society. All that a society needs is a minimum degree of safety and efficiency. It needs roads, cleanliness, and defense against physical aggression. An example of good working order can be found in the microsociety of a condominium.

In a condominium, someone must see that everything works. Elevators must function, the entrance and corridors must be clean, the lights must turn on, and the people who live there must be safe. Little else is required. If someone wants to pay for more, he can go elsewhere.

It is the same with a larger society. Little is needed to ensure its efficient functioning. Physical safety and basic material working order are all that a society needs from government. Individuals and entrepreneurs can provide all the rest; they will find in the society's unregulated but ordered freedom all the conditions necessary to satisfy the community.

## *Taxes feed the predators*

Why, then, are taxes so high that they frighten away people who would like to live in an environment of safety and peace of mind that enables them to live as they wish and to develop their lives, personalities, and talents?

This question takes us to the hidden reason for taxes. This reason is the same as that behind all regulations. It is a strictly personal reason disguised under moral and patriotic arguments: Taxes and their growth are what enable a group of people to live off the government. All those government people want their paychecks at the end of the month. They need that money as much as anyone else. Nothing except their paychecks matters much to them.

Bureaucrats live off bureaucracy. They need its expansion as a source of power and personal wealth for them and the subordinates who surround them. They are professional predators, experts in creating guilt to extract unmerited funds. Bureaucrats spend other people's money on projects that create and justify the existence of more bureaucrats. All they care about is legitimizing, in the eyes of the public, the need to confiscate other people's earnings "for a good cause."

Thus, the real purpose of taxes emerges. Taxes are the business of government people. Taxes are how government people make their money and their living. Taxes are their money.

To make money as a store owner, you need to sell merchandise. You must fill the store with goods and have a good profit margin.

The same applies to taxes and bureaucrats. Government is the store. It offers people such products as insurance, welfare, education for the less favored, protection against smog and against smoking, and anything else that they can invent to fill the store.

The more products government offers, the more taxes it can levy and the more profit it makes. Imagination is the only limit to what bureaucrats and politicians can find to tax. But of course, they still need a marketing strategy.

Their marketing strategy consists of persuading you by publicity and propaganda that you need what they are offering. Public opinion, therefore, is a government scam to make you believe that there is a collective will joyfully asking to be preyed upon. This is not so. Today, individuals are defenseless victims of a propaganda machine that has been created to wipe them out. The individual is voiceless; when they tax you as an individual, you cannot say no.

Taxes today are the result of predation by government people and their associates, mafioso businessmen who make money by helping government prey on innocent victims.

Taxes should never be this way. Instead, they should be voluntary contributions from people who freely choose the services given by a minimal government, just as you voluntarily pay your condominium fee or voluntarily agree to pay the bill after having dinner at a restaurant.

## *Creators or predators: choose your camp*

We must choose where we belong. Either we are with the predators and victimizers or we are with the victims and free men.

In the predators' camp, we have bureaucrats and politicians. They are experts at instilling guilt in the minds of free men: the workers, professionals, entrepreneurs, and creative individuals who build wealth through their own efforts.

They make entrepreneurs feel guilty for making money, for having money, for inheriting money, and for not "giving back" the money they have to society.

Their marketing headlines feature popular slogans, like "put human need before corporate greed," or US President Obama's famous "If you've got a business—you didn't build that."

They have excellent copywriting help.

Of course, these arguments and the new ones that they will find will always help them to be on the receiving end. The bureaucrats will get your money.

In addition, they will make you feel guilty. When you fight for your money, you are guilty of selfishness. When you give away your money, you are guilty of having guilty feelings. So by giving your money away, you prove that they were right.

This does not mean that you should not give money to causes that you find worthy. What I am saying is that you must avoid being made to feel guilty by a ploy that has been intentionally designed to prey on you.

Note that the key element of predation is conceptual. All arguments to make people unjustly part with their money are based on a misunderstanding of money and wealth.

Again, we are back at our divide between the static and dynamic concepts of wealth. The idea that money is an inert lump, so that you can provide wealth for your fellow men only by giving your money away, as well as the idea that having money is a reason for guilt, can only be true if one accepts a static concept of wealth and value.

The politician or bureaucrat who asks you to part with your money and who invokes a patriotic or altruistic argument of some kind is, in fact, thinking of himself. He knows better than anyone that predation, his job, produces no wealth.

As products of predation, politicians lack the spark that comes from true value creation. For them, making money means taking it from someone else. It is not the result of converting value into wealth.

People whose business is preying on someone else, directly or indirectly, can only conceive of value as something static. They think that wealth is bounded and finite.

They think that material reserves are limited and that all wealth is the result of extracting limited matter. They cannot conceive of wealth and value as a creation of unlimited thought.

They also have an obsession with catastrophe. They enjoy all sorts of disaster scenarios. The more catastrophes there are, the more regulations are needed to protect you and me against them.

They say these regulations are necessary because you and I, the taxpayers, are responsible for all natural evils, such as gas emissions or the destruction of the ozone layer.

The reason behind this approach to regulations is simple to understand: nature cannot be taxed or regulated. Imagine a politician or a bureaucrat fining a volcano that pollutes more than all industries combined — or taxing the atmosphere to protect the ozone layer. They cannot do this.

So, what do they do? They tax and regulate us—you and me. They can seize us, and we have the money with which to pay our ransoms. They can fine us and, if necessary, imprison us. There is little that we can do to stop them, unless we invent ways to rebel intelligently.

To avoid this predation, we must learn to choose. We must decide if we are going to be on the side of the predators or on the side of the heroic individuals who will oppose the confiscation of their freedom and their lives.

## *The greatest world conspiracy*

Choosing sides in this battle between free individuals and predators takes us to a delicate subject. Welcome to the subject of world conspiracies, in which a group of people have developed an invisible and secret power to rule the world.

There are many conspiracy theories. Each theory designates some group of people as those responsible for all world evils. Now, it is important to know whether these theories are right or wrong. It *is* true that a world conspiracy is at the root of all political and economic evils. However, it is not the kind of conspiracy that most people theorize about.

It is another kind of conspiracy, directed by another kind of conspirator. It is a deeper and more effective conspiracy. It is so effective that it almost cannot be stopped. It is so effective that it doesn't need to be concealed in order to remain secret.

This conspiracy, the most secret conspiracy that has ever existed, was born in the night of time, millennia ago. It was created by a group of people who, for many centuries, have ruled the world under cover.

They have hidden behind tribal chieftains, kings, emperors, dictators, and elected presidents. All countries of the earth have participated in their conspiracy, and their members are all united by the same secret oaths and recognize each other immediately by the same signs. They have based their success on a social law that has worked for them almost without fail. The principle is that of the open conspiracy. There is no better way of keeping a secret than keeping it *visible* to everyone. In this way, no one sees it, because everyone has become used to it.

Now this secret conspiracy can become the most visible conspiracy, once our attention is brought to it.

Can you guess what it is?

You probably can. The true world conspiracy is that of the bureaucrats. They live by preying on victims who are persuaded to believe that the bureaucrats actually serve them.

Here is where the real secret of the conspiracy enters. Almost no one sees a bureaucrat for what he really is, a predator. His disguise, like his name of "civil servant," makes him invisible to his victims.

Bureaucrats have existed since times immemorial. They have existed under all political regimes. They have always preyed on their innocent victims, but they have presented themselves as the victims' protectors and benefactors.

Politicians belong to the same breed. Politicians are, in fact, a subspecies of the bureaucrat—a kind of higher-level bureaucrat. And the bureaucrats have always taken the same form worldwide.

For example, when monarchies constituted the principal political system, the bureaucrats' power extended from Spain to China. Whatever you may think of monarchy, it was a bureaucracy. Each king had an army of bureaucrats in his service. The bureaucrats lived by preying on their defenseless victims and, *en passant*, protecting them. The protection was real to some extent, but so was the predation.

When the age of monarchies ended, the entire planet became covered by dictators, elected presidents, ministers, congressmen, and bureaucrats of every kind imaginable. From America to India, from the extreme west to the extreme east and from north to south, you still find presidents, congressmen, and bureaucrats who prey on their defenseless victims. They overtax them and overregulate them "for their own good."

These bureaucrats are members of a hierarchy that goes from the elected president of a mighty republic to the lowliest tax-collection clerk. They not only recognize each other as belonging to the same group, but engage in deals with one another.

Bureaucratic cooperation is a global phenomenon. An African bureaucrat and an American one see themselves as colleagues. They make deals together. For example, a favorite form of predation is foreign aid, or lending by government financial institutions to finance foreign government projects.

## REVOLUTION AND BUREAUCRACY

This takes us to the subject of revolutions promoted for the bureaucrats' benefit. Political revolutions promoted for the benefit of bureaucrats tend to mistake a political form for the real evil behind it. The political forms were only disguises. The true evil, which was concealed in the system's political form, was the bureaucrats.

### *The French Revolution*

For instance, contrary to popular belief, the reason for the French Revolution (1789–1799) was not the monarchy itself. The cause of the revolution was the existence of a class of bureaucrats, the tax collectors, who took a commission on every tax payment they collected.

France was so heavily taxed that agricultural products were put to the torch in the fields instead of being brought to the market for sale; it was cheaper for a farmer to destroy the product than to sell it and pay taxes on it. The economy of France became so depressed that the monarchy and all its tax collectors were overturned—sadly, by another group of bloody bureaucrats eager for power.

One particularly sad aspect of this story is that Antoine Lavoisier (1743–1794), one of the most important eighteenth-century scientists, who identified oxygen as an element and discovered the law of the conservation of matter, was one of the tax collectors and was beheaded during the French Revolution.

After the revolution, a new breed of bureaucrats took power in France, then in the rest of Europe, and later all over the world. The French Revolution was thus a parody of the American Revolution. The American Revolution was begun to secure freedom; the French Revolution existed for the sake of a new kind of bureaucratic tyranny.

## *Revolution and bureaucracy today*

Now that the conspiracy has been uncovered, we can see that bureaucrats have been the obstacles to progress, invention, and prosperity worldwide.

The only revolution that would be conducive to prosperity would be one to overthrow bureaucrats, all of them, and render them harmless. This would enable freedom to emerge worldwide.

Is such a revolution coming? Yes, it is, and at full speed. It is just around the corner.

Bureaucrats will soon be wiped away. A new technology, the computer, has begun a digital revolution that is destroying national boundaries and barriers.

Worldwide communications and computing capabilities, coupled with new transportation technology, such as planes that can fly across continents without refueling, make national boundaries obsolete. People can now leave unfavorable environments very easily. States have lost their grip on people.

Previously, populations were captives of geographical boundaries. As a result, they were the prey of politicians and their hordes of bureaucrats.

Today, governments know that people can easily take flight. Systems like the Soviet Union, which tried to keep people captive within territorial boundaries, have failed and crumbled.

Even within their governments' boundaries, people can do things to enhance their freedom and expose any abuses to the outside world. China is an example where freedom-seeking people now use the Internet to tell the outside world what is going on.

In short, an individual today has tools of freedom at his disposal that he could not have dreamed about previously. Governments fear this and know that in the long run they are lost.

## *Who wins in the end?*

Reality always wins. Although any technology can have a good or a bad use, its best use will prevail.

Each new technology is a human creation, an extension of the mind. These inventions have freed people from the boundaries of time and space. Of course, this freedom can be used for better or for worse.

However, those who use their freedom for good gain an edge over those who use their freedom for ill. More specifically, using one's freedom to further enhance freedom and creativity is more powerful than using one's freedom to limit and destroy and prey on others.

So, finally, free men will prevail over bureaucrats and socialists and collectivists of all kinds. The free men's victory will benefit us all, because freedom is the foundation of human beings and human action.

Because freedom is the essence of human nature, bureaucrats of any kind, however well organized, cannot win. Free people will always be more intelligent, able, and creative in the defense of their freedom than slave-minded people will be in defending their limitations.

Governments often appear to be more lenient today in persecuting free people. But they appear more lenient only because they can no longer contain their populations and to force them to do their will. In fact, governments are searching for new techniques of control to replace the old ones.

But each new method of government to restrict and control freedom is also bound to fail. Furthermore, any attempt to restrict technology and science is bound to fail.

## *The attempts to restrict freedom*

The goal of all the new methods of control is the same as that of previous ones. The goal is to restrict freedom by rendering the individual powerless and defenseless—and to convert every individual into a victim who will welcome the bureaucrats' predation.

For this to be accomplished, the individual must be atomized and disintegrated as much as possible. First comes the destruction of his mind, then comes the destruction of his social and family life and his savings and capital.

This destruction is accomplished by subtle acts of collectivization in the name of the public good.

To accomplish this, the individual must be made to lose all sense of what the law truly is. Legislation must be made to lose contact with reality. In addition, the proper vision of the world, anchored in the reality of things, must be destroyed piece by piece. To attain this goal, bureaucrats use the media to tell people what to believe.

They must turn all categories of thought upside down. They must make up into down and down into up. They must stimulate disorientation and disinformation.

Specifically, the key method for creating a passive population that will be easily manipulated by its political predators consists of breaking the link between law and nature. In order to break this link, governments attempt to place human-created law above nature.

One example is family, where laws created in the mind of the legislator will replace nature in defining what a family is.

Another example is that law, not nature, will come to define property. What this means is that property will become an act of toleration of the lawgiver, defined by his rules.

Society comes to be governed by arbitrary rules, and as they impose these rules, those in power will work them for their own benefit.

One writer who had a clear vision of this was Frédéric Bastiat, the nineteenth-century French economist, who in his essay *Propriété et Loi* warned against law defining human nature, instead of the reverse. He said that society, persons, and property existed before the law, and that the law existed because of them. In particular, he emphasized that property is not a consequence of legislation but a natural right that legislation should acknowledge. In other words, the law doesn't create property, it is property that creates the law. However, legislators seek to subvert this natural order so as to make the spoliation of populations easier.

This could not be more true. When people lose the idea of a natural order, "reality" becomes whatever the legislator decides it is. The individual then thinks what the legislator wants him to think. Whatever the legislator decides is true, the individual will deem to be true. As a result, the individual becomes defenseless—the ideal, passive victim of predators.

## *Collectivization*

When, for instance, the owner of a building cannot knock it down because the government considers it to be a property of historical value, law is taking precedence over nature.

Now, if the government believes that something has historical worth, it could offer to buy it from its legitimate owner, without preventing him from exercising the right to dispose of his legitimately owned property.

The same is true for gun possession. Every individual has the right to defend himself and is responsible for his acts. Limiting gun possession by law is an act of victimization of the people; it renders them defenseless.

Impeding gun possession takes from people the opportunity to defend themselves. It also removes from them their natural responsibility for self-defense. By taking away such responsibilities, society is collectivized, and, at the same time, the citizen is reduced to the status of a child.

Inheritance taxes, antismoking regulations, environmental regulations, capital-gains taxes, income taxes, and many other regulations represent the same method of collectivization.

The common result of all this is to make people unable to think for themselves and to subtly collectivize their minds and property, turning them into a defenseless and homogeneous mass of humanity. In all these cases, law replaces nature, enabling bureaucrats to rule at their whim.

## *"Public opinion"*

The thinking of this amorphous mass is what today is called "public opinion." Public opinion does not really exist. There is no such thing as "the public." What exists are people like you and me. However, when governments rule over an unthinking mass of slaves, they can decree what to think on a given subject.

Opinion can only be private and individual, although it may be publicly expressed. A teacher, or a lecturer, or a scientist who publishes a paper, or a writer who publishes a book or article, has an opinion that he makes public. However, he is far from being "the public."

"Public opinion" is the slavers' thought manifested as if it is the will of their slaves. It is a tool to direct events with an apparent consensus that no one will doubt.

Similarly, in a news broadcast, when the "public wants to know," it is, in fact, the media man speaking, interpreting the will of a nonexistent public. This interpretation is based on the pursuit of ratings and sales.

The ratings and sales result from an offer of information or entertainment that has been purposefully designed by the media. When their offer elicits the desired ratings and sales, we have "public opinion" expressing its will. This so-called will is nothing but the will of a mass responding automatically.

The masses respond automatically and unconsciously to the purposefully designed offer of the newsman. The result is that "public opinion" can be guided and manipulated to manifest the will of the newsmen.

The "public" is not a human being. Certain it is not us. In the end, you, the free individual will prevail over all those unidentified, faceless, and nameless entities known as the public. "The public" is just a mask that bureaucrats and politicians use to carry out their predatory actions.

## *Would you sacrifice your freedom for comfort?*

The real issue is whether you are prepared to sacrifice your freedom in exchange for limited comfort. Many people are ready to give up their freedom, so long as they are guaranteed a minimal living wage and comfortable slave work.

This kind of thinking is misguided, because life itself requires action and initiative. When a society does not want to accept responsibilities, but wishes to be completely taken care of, the road to poverty is open, and misery must sooner or later become the new reality.

For many, the bureaucratic mind-set is the only way of looking at life. They know no better. They think that it is only just and proper to be provided a minimum living and to be fully taken care of by government.

This welfare mentality makes the society a breeding ground for predators.

Humanity is lost when a society of slave-robots replaces a free society. Within this kind of society some people manage to survive, but they must put their minds and their lives at risk to preserve their individuality. If they are discovered, the Gulag will welcome them.

# Chapter 8

# Capitalism and Mathematics

*In nature and in social systems there are many processes that self-organize; that is, independent elements spontaneously begin cooperating and acting as one entity without an organizer. In the weather we see these processes as hurricanes or tornadoes. In social systems, they have been variously described as bull markets, the "invisible hand" of the free markets, or the madness of mobs. In the sciences, the study of complex systems has identified the characteristics of those natural processes that self-organize, evolve, and adapt to changes in their environment. Thus, if social systems are complex, the vestiges of self-organization will look like a conspiracy. The links are there, but there is no planner or mastermind behind the structure. What look like patterns are merely the shadows of complexity.*

— Edgar E. Peters, *Patterns in the Dark*, 1999

The new revolution in communications that is weakening predatory bureaucrats and freeing creative individuals comes from new computer technologies.

In turn, the advances in computers depend on a much older invention, the binary system, as the language of these machines. Binary is the simplest language possible, containing only one and zero, and yet it is the key to the intelligent machines that are changing our world.

## THE LEIBNIZ REVOLUTION

This language was foreseen first by Gottfried Wilhelm von Leibniz (1646–1716), a German philosopher and mathematician who dreamed of a universal language that would enable reasoning to be expressed in mathematical form. It was Leibniz who refined the binary number system into the form that computers use today.

Leibniz developed the binary system and contemplated a machine that would enable us to process thought. We could say that the information revolution in which we are living is the enactment of his ideas. Indeed, we can call our new revolution the Leibniz revolution.

### *Leibniz's yin and yang*

Leibniz drew much of his inspiration from the sixty-four hexagrams of the Chinese *I Ching*. Each of the hexagrams is composed of a set of six lines of two kinds. One kind is a two-part, segmented line and the other is a full line.[43]

These two types of lines represent the *yin* and *yang* principles. The principles themselves are derived from the unknowable and underlying way of everything, the *tao*. Yin is the passive pole and yang the active pole; one represents the full and the other the empty.

---

[43] See Gottfried Wilhelm Leibniz, "Explication de l'Arithmétique Binaire" in *Principes de la Nature et de la Grâce, Monadologie et autres textes 1703–1716* (Paris: Flammarion, 1996), pp. 70–75.

Leibniz understood those symbols and was an avid supporter of the binary system. Because binary, like the system of yin and yang, represents the fundamental polarity of reality (zero and one, yes and no, passive and active, empty and full), everything conceivable could be derived from it. For Leibniz, then, the binary number system became the ideal mathematical language.

According to mathematician Pierre-Simon Laplace (1749–1827), this language was the "image of creation" to Leibniz. For Leibniz, "one" was the image of God and "zero" was the image of the primal Void.

Leibniz said *omnibus ex nihil ducendis sufficit unum*. This means that the "One" is enough to derive all that is from nothing. The One and its opposite, the Void, then become the principles that enable us to understand all and say all. One and zero become the universal language.

The binary language, the fundamental essence of today's computers and microchips, was thus defined.[44]

## *Leibniz's calculator*

Leibniz also created a calculating machine, the "stepped reckoner," which relied on indented wheels of different sizes (now called Leibniz wheels). His machine could add, subtract, multiply, calculate square roots, and do other calculations.

[44] However, Leibniz's contribution to microprocessing does not end here. Leibniz developed calculus. This enables us to calculate rates of change and to study the movement of quantities.
The change of quantities as they moved with respect to one another was expressed in differential equations. As the name suggests, those equations measure differences in the rates of change among related quantities.
Physics, the science of the world, is the science of differential equations. This is because movement is the underlying law of all that exists in time and space. So Leibniz and Newton, who discovered calculus independently, gave us the tool to quantitatively study matter in motion.

Figure 4. Replica of Leibniz's stepped reckoner in the Deutsches Museum. Photo by Kolossos, via Wikipedia, CC BY-SA 3.0. https://en.wikipedia.org/wiki/Stepped_Reckoner#/media/File:Leibnitzrechenmaschine.jpg.

Leibniz demonstrated his machine in 1673 before the Royal Society of London, of which Newton was later president. For Leibniz, this calculating machine was the beginning of new ways of considering thought.

Leibniz went on to suggest that human thought could be mechanized. He understood that a language was needed for this mechanization to be effective. However, it had to be an ideal language that overcame the lack of rigor of a common language.

This ideal language had to be so precise that it would enable one to mechanize it and run it through a machine in such a way as to process syllogistic reasoning automatically and free it from errors. Leibniz was definitely ahead of his time. His achievements happened as a result of the synergy of scientific minds made possible by Gutenberg.

## *Leibniz, the microchip, and the computer revolution*

How big was Leibniz's contribution to the computer revolution? Huge.

First, he proposed binary counting and its polarity of one and zero, which is the foundation of all computers today.

Secondly, he created an actual calculating machine, the first that could do addition, subtraction, multiplication, and division. This was proof that at least some mathematical reasoning could be made to be automatic. The modern microchip had been anticipated, up to a point.

Thirdly and finally, Leibniz envisaged the need for a precise language that would enable thought processes to be mechanized; that is, he anticipated the need for programming languages.

Above all, his concept that machines, and not merely biological brains, could use language and mechanisms of a kind to process thoughts automatically and without error opened the door to the creation of our thought-processing devices, microchips.

The American inventors Jack Kilby and Robert Noyce developed the microchip (separately) in 1958 and 1959. This technology made possible our small, inexpensive, powerful computers, almost all of which have relied on binary.

The advent of the microchip has put into practice Leibniz's dreams of a thinking machine and a universal language for thought.

## *The best of all possible worlds*

This new technology is already transforming our economic and social landscape and giving rise to a new world. Let us hope, as Leibniz did, that it will be the best of worlds. One of Leibniz's fundamental philosophical tenets was that he was living in the best possible world.

This idea is relevant for the future of technology, science, and their effects on economics and on society's evolution. Leibniz's positive outlook is fully in accordance with a perspective affirming that value is dynamic and unlimited.

Two centuries later, another mathematician would continue in the line of Leibniz's though.

## *The hidden source of number science, or Cantor's secret*

The German mathematician Georg Ferdinand Ludwig Philipp Cantor (1845–1918), contributed ideas that laid the foundations for the dynamic concept of value.

Cantor studied infinite sets, and he postulated that there were different sizes of them. These different orders of infinity are themselves extant in unbounded quantity.

Cantor developed set theory. It is in his set theory that he developed his series of indefinites. These had a hierarchy according to their cardinal numbers. A set is a collection of entities or objects.

Cantor also developed a collection of symbols to operate on his sets. These symbols, such as the union symbol and the intersection symbol, became part of an effort to express mathematics in the language of logic.

All things could be considered to be sets, or elements of sets, and could be dealt with according to the rules of sets. Because of this, the language of programming became possible. In essence, Cantor helped us to translate the word into formal, mathematical terms, which is a precursor to today's computer revolution.

The creation of this language was also intimately linked to research on infinity.

Cantor, like Leibniz before him, was fascinated by infinity. Cantor studied philosophy and theology. Religion was important to him throughout his entire life. His set theory had, above all, a metaphysical foundation that was based on Platonism.

For Plato, the One was the origin of everything. This idea is essential to understanding Leibniz, who, as we have seen, developed the binary system from ones and zeroes. This Platonic One is truly infinite and boundless.

As it was boundless, Plato said that his One was beyond even the One and was not a one, but indefinable in any way. His One was the unbounded source of all. This same idea was the foundation of Leibniz's mathematical work, and of Cantor's.

Cantor, in a letter to the mathematician Richard Dedekind, stated that a set was akin to a Platonic eidos, or idea. The reason was that each set could be thought of as a One bounded by a law. In this sense, a One law bounded infinite infinities.[45]

In Cantor's work we find the thought that reality is unbounded and can be perceived as a series of infinites or, more precisely, indefinites. This suggests that ultimate reality, because it is limitless and unbounded, is also unknowable.

In fact, it *is* unknowable because there is too much to know, and its reality exceeds all knowledge. This has immediate practical applications and consequences, and this is also why the ideas of Leibniz and Cantor paved the way to a new conception of the world.

This new conception could come to life due to the Gutenberg revolution, and it is continuing to expand to higher levels due to the Leibniz revolution, which finds its main agent in the microchip.

When reality is considered to be unbounded and when mathematics has a foundation in infinity, a new kind of freedom emerges. It is not by accident that Kurt Gödel proved that a set of propositions within a system could not be fully proved.

---

[45] Cantor wrote to Richard Dedekind in 1883 telling him that a "manifold or a set" was "every Many that can be thought of as a One" because its elements "can be bound up into a whole through a law." In the same paragraph, Cantor adds that, by defining a set, he believed that he was defining "something that is akin to the Platonic eidos or idea." Loren Graham and Jean Michel Kantor, *Naming Infinity: A True Story of Religious Mysticism and Mathematical Creativity* (Cambridge Massachusetts: Belknap Press of Harvard University Press, 2009), p. 26.

What Gödel's and Cantor's ideas show is that reality has an escape hatch.

The same can be said of Leibniz's universal language. Such a language could not prove all of its propositions. Nevertheless, it exists as long as a universal logical operator can be used functionally, precisely, and successfully.

All that was needed was a practical universal logical language. The binary system became the perfect number system to express the rules of that language. Ultimate simplicity.

Microchips (specifically, the computer microchips called microprocessors) became the material support for that language. They enable us to calculate and, beyond that, to process and think through information in a fraction of the time that a human being once required.

By "think," we do not refer here to conscious thought. "Thinking," in this context, means processing a specified collection of data according to certain rules to obtain the solution to a specific problem, such as the best next move in a chess game.

The mathematical ideas about infinity helped us to recognize that reality is unbounded. This becomes true also of our world and its resources. The practical consequence of this in economics is that we realize that value creation is an infinite source of value.

This infinite source of value can then be converted to wealth. All new technologies come from this single foundation, the idea that resources are unlimited.

This implies a dynamic concept of value and wealth that, as we stated in earlier chapters, is conducive to prosperity and a happy life. The opposite of this is a static, nondynamic concept of value and wealth, which is conducive to poverty and unhappiness.

This leads us to emphasize that our success in life, as individuals and as a society, depend on our perspective and attitude towards the nature of ultimate reality. Here we are confronted by only two possibilities, and our free choice will define our destiny.

## *The two possibilities*

One possibility is to believe that reality is limited and bounded. If we believe this, poverty and failure will follow, and we will increase the army of predators. Alternatively, we can believe that reality is ultimately unbounded. This leads us to exercise our creativity and live a life of prosperity and happiness.

Returning to the differences in wealth among countries, we must remember that it is the dynamic concept of value and wealth, originating in the unbounded concept of reality, that has made some countries of the earth rich.

Like Leibniz, I believe that we live in the best of worlds. The world is always the best of worlds. It cannot be any other way. However, as time passes, we can confirm this philosophical conclusion empirically by reviewing what has taken place. A laptop is definitely better than a mechanical typewriter and its ink ribbon. Ask anyone who writes, and he will tell you this.

So progress does take place along specific lines of thought and action. In this sense, the world that is coming will almost certainly be better. How do I know? I don't, but let me explain. I'll begin with Socrates.

## *A Socratic digression*

One of Socrates's most important discoveries was one about the practical use of "ignorance." He went against the current of prevailing opinion, and his thinking still does. While many attempted to know everything, he attempted to know nothing. This method is not only simple, but easy and fast. All you have to do is acknowledge your own ignorance in all fields. If someone asks you something, you will always have the perfect answer with, "I don't know. Do you?"

This second, back-end question is the key to the method. It was used extensively by Socrates to question other people who were quick to challenge his ignorance. In the process, he demolished their weak arguments. This Socratic "ignorance" makes us think of Kurt Gödel. Not everything can be demonstrated in a system of rules. However, this is not the true point. The point is that reality is beyond whatever we think about it. All that we think is only provisional.

This does not mean there is no truth or that truth is relative. No, truth is absolute and that is why we must not attempt to reduce it to words. This does not mean we must deny the validity of our own words and definitions. We must use them to approximate this ever-fleeting truth.

Now, applying the Socratic method of ignorance, we can say that we do not know what the future, which this revolution precipitated by the microchip brings, will look like. This is equivalent to saying that the future will transcend all that we can imagine.

We can try to say something about it, but from a foundation of ignorance. So, after this digression on the Socratic method of "ignorance" as a tool for daily life, let us return to why I think a better world will appear from this computing revolution.

## *The prophets of doom are doomed to error*

The only reason that I have for such a belief is that all prophets of doom of all ages have always failed catastrophically in their predictions. The world should have ended long ago, and frequently, if the prophets of doom had been right. The prophets appear in all guises. They play upon the irrational fears of their victims in a subtle way. This may be called the art of fake prophecy.

We have prophets who announce the end of the world *tout court*. Other prophets specialize in financial crises, apocalyptic wars, epidemics, and planetary conflagrations. As you can see, the prophesying of doom has many specialties. But in all cases, the underlying tenet is that you are a sinner and you must repent.

In the beginning of the industrial era, the prophets of doom announced that the consequences of using machines would be misery and poverty. People would lose their jobs. Exactly the opposite happened. New jobs were created and multiplied.

Never in all of human history have there been so many opportunities for job and wealth creation. This can be attributed to the fact that machines have accelerated the process of value creation and its conversion to wealth.

By creating entirely new fields of value and wealth, machines created entirely new fields of work and opportunities for inventors. So the prophets of doom were themselves doomed.

At the end of the twentieth century, the American economic theorist Jeremy Rifkin prophesied the same thing that the early opponents of mechanization had prophesied at the beginning of the industrial era. The only difference was that Rifkin specialized in computers and their applications.[46]

For Rifkin, the loss of jobs was the inevitable consequence of these machines. Like all prophets of doom, he worshipped the past as a golden era that was forever lost. New technologies were to him new evils that were soon to doom humans.

Like the industrial machines before them, computers did the opposite of what the doomsayers expected. They multiplied opportunities in every sense. Jobs multiplied as never before, and a new era of prosperity was unleashed before the eyes of all the new prophets of doom.

As this new era began, the Reagan era of changing monetary policy and economics was in full blossom, the Berlin Wall fell, the Soviet Union collapsed, and thus freedom was given a boost. With all of this came new jobs and opportunities.

Strangely enough, or perhaps not strangely at all, a prophet of doom named Ravi Batra announced the crash of 1990 just when the stock market was beginning the greatest bull market of its history.[47] The bull

[46] For Jeremy Rifkin, computers will create worldwide unemployment. See Jeremy Rifkin, *The End of Work: The Decline of the Global Labor Force and the Dawn of the Post-Market Era* (New York: G.P. Putnam's Sons, 1996).

[47] Ravi Batra, *The Great Depression* of 1990 (New York: Dell, 1988).

market began timidly in 1982 and climbed to cruising speed in 1994, when it really began to pick up strength. It did not end until 2001.

Batra's predictions for 1990 were dire and catastrophic. Luckily, however, his predictions failed to materialize in reality.

When prophets of doom announce their unhappy predictions, it is usually just the opposite that takes place. This, of course, does not mean that some prophets of doom aren't occasionally right.

If a prophet does prove to be right, it usually is a result of his persistence. If, every year he announces that a huge stock market crash or depression is lurking around the corner, sooner or later he will be right.

However, history has not especially favored the prophets of doom No one is master of the future, and all that we can do with relative safety is to merely observe what has happened in the past.

If the microchip revolution changes the world as previous technologies did, we can expect more prosperity, more jobs, and unexpected answers to problems that seem unsolvable today.

This perspective and way of thinking about the future, which agrees with Leibniz's idea that we live in the best of all possible worlds, derives from a dynamic concept of value. A dynamic concept of value implies that value and wealth have intelligence as their only source.

Intelligence, by definition, adapts, solves, and enhances things. Everything that is created by intelligence and intended for its development goes in the direction of life, happiness, and simplicity.

If our goal is the mastery of space and time, we must make better use of our intelligence with our available resources. This is what technology is for. If technology were used against freedom and life, it would be working against itself and depleting its only source of existence, freely inventing minds.

Free, inventing minds are the source of prosperity and wealth for individuals and countries alike. This is what capitalism is about.

## *Capitalism, the tool of freedom and prosperity*

Thanks to capitalism, the world's prosperity is rising, and this rise is accelerating. We are leaving the static concept of value and the prophets of doom behind.

The new dynamic mind-set, helped by mathematics, logic, and technology, has freed us from static resources and static methods of acquiring value and wealth. It has caused the widespread realization that value and wealth actually come from the mind, and that matter is a plastic element that the mind molds to its will.

Of course, the task of transforming matter is not easy. The mind's job is to find new paths in the structure and organization of matter at every level of its existence in space and time.

Mind must find or create the right forms to achieve its goals. By rendering value creation more dynamic (i.e., more mind-dependent), the mind also makes the creation of prosperity and wealth more efficient.

Mind shows that nothing material is static and bounded; material resources can be substituted for one another. A building, for instance, can be made of wood or concrete or metal, or any number of combinations of the three. Thus, there are many ways to achieve prosperity and wealth by applying mind to matter. Mind can arrange and rearrange the material world like a LEGO® construction set.

However, the manipulation of matter by mind needs freedom as its fundamental condition. Capitalism is the social environment in which the mind is most free to roam and thrive. Freedom itself will help to find new avenues of value creation and its practical applications.

Capitalism is rising to a new level today, a level on which we are becoming even freer of material forms, such as land, mineral resources, and even genetic codes. Mind is taking over matter more strongly.

Capital creation needs intelligent humans. The more intelligent they are, the more capital they will create, and the more valuable that capital will become. Technology and all sciences are ways in which the mind can work on itself to better itself.

Each new discovery and invention in turn implies an increase in intelligence and the practical exercise of it. New discoveries and inventions are the outwardly visible signs of inner progress and an increase in intelligence itself.

This makes capital itself more valuable. Capital's potential to create new value and wealth grows as new inventions and ideas arise. Money acquires its real value when the mind is applied to it to find its most profitable uses.[48]

Not only does a given quantity of money acquire its value depending on society's technological level, but the same is true of the value of things other than money. For example, Leibniz's binary system and Cantor's work on set theory and the development of the microchip gained added value from their confluence.

Values interrelate among themselves. The acceleration of capitalism in the Leibniz revolution has enabled values to integrate in new and unexpected ways and has enhanced traditional capitalism.

## *Ricardo's nemesis, or the source of capitalism*

As I mentioned in chapter 2, the British economist David Ricardo believed that the value of a thing depended only on the amount of time spent to produce it. This concept was purely quantitative and mechanical. Consequently, it was also static and did not accord with the proper, dynamic concept of value, which always escaped Ricardo.

Under Ricardo's assumption that *work* is the source of value, all money earned by a business should be measured simply by the amount of work that each staff member provides.

---

[48] Here, we must make a distinction between real profit and nominal profit. Real profit means any benefit that someone obtains. For example, it is profitable for me to learn languages. This is not necessarily a nominal profit in dollars. See chapter 9 for a more thorough explanation.

However, his premise is wrong. The source of value is not work—as Ricardo thought, and as his intellectual descendents, the Marxists and socialists, still think today—but the mind. The sole source of the value of a good is in the incorporeal qualities of that good, that is, in its form and function. Matter is only the support for the mind, which can give matter its function.

In other words, it is the usefulness of ideas that defines their value. The writer of a bestseller that brings in millions of dollars has contributed more to the value of his book than the person who typed it. By making things useful, ideas create value around them. The value of a material thing is never in the thing itself.

An engineer who can understand an industry fully and efficiently and bring profits to it contributes more value than the person who sweeps the floors of the company's offices.

Although Ricardo proposed that work should be the unit of value, he knew that something was wrong with his theory. For instance, he tried unsuccessfully to explain why antique furniture had more value than modern furniture.

What escaped Ricardo's notice was that value has an intellectual source, and it is therefore dynamic. Static units, such as material quantities and hours of work, cannot account for value.

Value is given by a thing's meaning or form, or by an understanding of it that will cause it to function. When you buy an antique, you are not paying for the working hours that the artisan devoted to it, just as you would not expect to pay for a Picasso by paying for the artist's time at a modest hourly or daily rate.

What you pay for is the value that the thing represents to you. You will pay more for things that mean more to you because they are more useful or desirable to you and because the service that makes such things available is worth its price. You and I never pay for the thing, but for the service. The true source of capital is value, and value is incorporeal, not quantitative.

### *When capital becomes knowledge and mastery*

Capital's value depends on abstract knowledge and practical mastery. With these two keys, capital can be opened like a treasure chest that will deliver its riches. Without the keys, the capital will erode, whether slowly or quickly. (Even in this case, however, it will fall naturally into hands that will value it.)

The same amount of money can make a fortune for one person or be the source of destruction for someone else. Capital is a tool that depends on the ability of the user.

Above all, capital originates in the mind and tends to increase the mind's power. The intelligence of inventors, especially, uses capital to further develop the intelligence of society and the individual. In this way, intelligence has the power to develop itself.

Capital is not in things, but in the intelligence to render the services that make things available. Capital is the aggregate of services condensed in the things possessed, of which money is only a representation.

Capital helps us to discover, understand, create, solve, and better adapt ourselves to our environment.

Capital's value depends on its user's abstract knowledge of a field or a market. Knowledge will enable capital's optimum use. For example, if I am a researcher, my knowledge will enable me to obtain and buy the best tools to attain my goals.

If I am a businessman, and know my field, I will be able to better understand the opportunities that it presents, and my working capital will have, by this fact, more value.

However, this knowledge must be completed by practical mastery. If I know what to do, I must also know how to do it efficiently. The value of capital is enhanced when it is in the hands of someone who is masterful at using it.

Ray Kroc, who created McDonald's, is an example. He had abstract knowledge coupled with practical mastery. He observed and studied his market intelligently and acted efficiently, eventually creating a worldwide chain of successful restaurant franchises.

So, in the end, the value of capital is incorporeal. It is in the mind, its ultimate source. Capital is dynamic. It has no definite boundaries and can intelligently adapt itself to any need or circumstance.

Capitalism is the dynamic mind-set par excellence.

Now let us examine how the Leibniz revolution has transformed money and the world.

# Chapter 9

# Computer Science and Money

The evolution of money over the millennia has followed technology and is an expression of man's creative intelligence. Let us explore money's evolution as an area where the information revolutions of the printing press and the microchip have had an important impact.

We are now living in what we shall call the fourth monetary revolution.

The first monetary revolution was the advent of barter. People simply exchanged things. The physical object was the exchange medium and the repository of value. For example, you could trade some nuts for some mammoth meat, or, if you wanted to store the value of the nuts, you simply stashed them in your cave.

The second monetary revolution came with the appearance of metallic currency. The first metal coins appeared in the seventh century BC under King Pheidon of Argos. The use of coins as an exchange medium and a repository of value freed us from requiring the physical good.

Barter works when goods are few and are being exchanged within a small group, but it doesn't work in large and complex societies.

This is when coins become useful, freeing people from direct barter. Suppose, for instance, that an animal skin had a higher value than the spear you wanted to trade it for. If the owner of the spear accepted the skin, he would have to give you "change," and to do so he would have to find items to give you that would make up the difference in value. Or suppose the spear's owner was willing to swap his spear for something, but he didn't need an animal skin. Then you would have to go to the extra trouble of first exchanging your animal skin with someone else for something the spear owner wanted, or else hope the spear owner was willing to accept the skin and trade it later for something he wanted.

With coins you instead have a uniform exchange medium and the possibility to agree upon precise and unequal values for your skin and his spear.

Metallic currency came with writing. Coins carried inscriptions saying who the issuer was. They also often carried an image of the ruler, along with a notation or message about him or the kingdom.

The third revolution came with the rise of account, or scriptural, money. This involved having a banker who held your money deposits and wrote you a receipt of some kind. Having this receipt freed a man from having to carry gold or coins around.

A cuneiform tablet from ancient Egypt attests to the early use of letters of credit. These same negotiable instruments were used in Ancient Greece and Rome. According to Nicholas Ferguson, "the basics of the system—financial accounts, drafts, contracts, letters of credit, credit money…were mentioned on clay tablets dating back to 3000 BC."[49] However, the third monetary revolution did not become fully realized and provide its complete benefits to commerce until the rise of European banking systems in the Renaissance.

---

[49] Quoted in Agasha Mugasha, *The Law of Letters of Credit and Bank Guarantees* (Sydney: Federation Press, 2003), p. 39.

## THE FOURTH MONETARY REVOLUTION

The fourth revolution, digital currency, has freed money from space and time. This revolution has not eradicated the three previous ones; instead, it has enhanced them. It gives instant access to money wherever you are in the world.

Each one of these four revolutions has increased the power of exchange. They have done so by increasing the dynamism and speed of trade, thereby reducing the energy loss between exchanges within the economic circuit. Today, exchanges have become so efficient that one of the fourth revolution's visible effects has been a previously unequaled growth of worldwide wealth. Capital is now being created on a planetary scale not previously thought possible.

How has this occurred?

### *The hidden cause of the new money*

The reason for the rise of this new digital money and the resultant multiplication of exchanges and growth of capital lies in the new microchip and computer technologies. Their speed of calculating and processing enables them to operate automatically and at high speed.

As a result of microchips, stock quotations are sent instantly all over the world. This technology also enables financial calculations that, in the past, took entire teams of highly qualified professionals considerable time, to be performed cheaply, quickly, and automatically.

In the past, stock-market price charts were prepared by hand and delivered by mail. A ticker delivered real-time prices. The ticker is now a relic of the past; the computer monitor has replaced it.

Not only is stock-market financial information instantly tabulated or charted by computer software, but that software can also analyze the same information to plot an indicator, and it can use that indicator to give "buy" or "sell" signals.

After the computer software finishes analyzing the information, it can show the results in spreadsheets, tables, charts, or any other type of display on your screen.

## *The acceleration of time*

The microchip alone has created a sudden transformation. The first consequence of this change has been an acceleration of human events. What used to take years or decades to do now takes days or months.

As I suggested before, we are at the inception of the greatest social and economic revolution since Gutenberg.

More specifically, the fourth monetary revolution has changed the relationship between money and time. Digital money can travel almost instantaneously and is not limited by spatial boundaries. Thus, it has enabled a creation of wealth unknown in the past.

Any two persons at opposite extremes of the earth can now exchange money almost instantaneously. Because of this new efficiency of money transactions, and therefore of work in general, people and businesses need less money and less time than before to produce goods.

Digital money is high-acceleration money. Through it, money has freed itself of material requirements. As a result, commercial exchanges have freed themselves from their space-time boundaries.

The same thing occurs to digital money in relation to space.

## *The contraction of space*

Digital money needs less space or, rather, almost no space. There is no need for someone at a window to give you cash. There is no need to go to the bank to make a deposit, and no need to telephone your broker. Money can be stored as ones and zeroes inside a computer.

As a result of this new technology, many old financial institutions are likely to change in relative importance. For example, we could see face-to-face banking disappear altogether. Online banking is already very competitive.

Also, other institutions, such as large retail stores and pension funds, can now offer many of the services that only banks previously provided, such as credit cards and financing. So, for many people there is no need to visit a bank.

Also, there are big companies that have their own electronic pools of money. These pools enable such companies to fund themselves without having to pay expensive bank fees. Because we are no longer dependent on account money, in which we need to have a deposit in a secure physical bank, traditional banks may soon become obsolete.

Even currency as we know it could disappear one day and be replaced by new, more efficient currencies that are independent of central banks. That day would mark the end of central banks.

That this can happen is shown by the rise of the digital currency called Bitcoin. In 2009 an unknown developer using the pseudonym Satoshi Nakamoto created this virtual currency and payments network.

Bitcoin and other digital currencies like it are going to have a huge impact, because they cannot be manipulated by government. They are not issued or controlled by any central bank. So the bureaucrats cannot play with Bitcoin as they do with the euro or the dollar or almost any other currency.

In this way, currency is now becoming independent of government.

## FIAT CURRENCIES: THE WORST OF REGULATIONS!

Fiat currencies are a subtle form of socialism. Governments confiscate your monetary assets by forbidding you the use of real money, and then they give you instead a promissory note (i.e., fiat currency) they will never repay at full value.

Money must be an intrinsic store of value, a unit of account, and a medium of exchange. If one of those three conditions is missing we do not have money.

Modern fiat currencies, created by central banks, do not actually store value. The value of these currencies diminishes over time until they end up almost worthless due to inflation. For instance, the US dollar has lost 95% of its value due to inflation since 1913.

Thus, fiat currencies are not money. They are only promissory notes by which the issuer promises to pay a debt.

Governments forces the use of the IOUs they call currencies upon their citizens. This is why governments do not recognize real money (like gold or silver) as legal tender today.

This enables the government to keep the actual money, which *is* a store of value, for itself. And in return, the government gives us a promise to repay the debt. Governments' next step is to dilute the debt so as not to have to pay it. We call that dilution inflation.

The avowed goal of central banks is to have minimum inflation (i.e., minimum dilution of debt). They do not want runaway inflation that would cause the rejection of their currency. Instead, they want slow inflation, so as to be able to borrow the maximum real wealth over time from the unaware recipients of their currency.

In short, governments transfer the wealth from taxpayers to politicians and bureaucrats by diluting the value of their currency through debt. The pretext for this distribution is reducing the gap between the rich and the poor by wealth transfers to the needy. In fact what happens is that wealth is redistributed to bureaucrats and politicians who manage costly projects which misallocate resources in the name of welfare.

The day may come when governments will be liable to their citizens for not paying their currency debts. If your employer told you he was going to reduce your salary's purchasing power by 2% per year, would you consider it normal? Definitely not!

When the chairman of a central bank tells you he has an inflation goal of 2% its exactly the same thing; but most people accept this even though their earnings are losing value in time. This is money governments owe you. Even if you are unaware of it, we are lending government our purchasing power. They should pay it back!

## *The death of money*

Fiat currencies inevitably lose value until they become worthless or almost worthless. But this cannot really be called "the death of money," because fiat currencies were never really money in the first place!

The phrase "the death of money" instead properly refers to the earlier government prohibition of using real money as legal tender. Money died in each country the day currencies stopped being real money, because the currencies could not be converted to real assets anymore, and were replaced by IOUs.

This was the case, for example, of the US dollar. In decades past, US citizens could redeem their paper dollars for gold. But the American government stopped giving gold for dollars to its citizens in 1933 and stopped doing so for foreign official holders of US dollars in 1971. Thus, in America, money has been dead for over 40 years.

Why do we call fiat currencies and the control of money supply the worst of regulations? Every organization, profit or nonprofit, needs a source of funding and revenue. The governments, politicians and bureaucrats of the world finance themselves with fiat money. It enables them to incur a debt and never pay it back in full. All the other regulations come after, as a consequence of government having the money to finance its regulations and its power machinery.

So, the end of fiat money would also mean the end of many regulations that exist at present, simply because there would no longer be enough money to keep them going.

## *The IMF, the World Bank, and the Bank of International Settlements*

The IMF uses taxpayers' money to bail out failed governments. The recipient governments never repay these loans in full, and each bailout is only a step toward a new bailout. This was the case for all IMF bailouts —think of Mexico, Argentina, Brazil, and more recently Cyprus and Greece.

It was the IMF that helped the US government convince the rest of the world to sever the links between their currencies and gold when in 1971 Nixon abolished the conversion of the US dollar into gold.

For their lending and bailouts, the IMF uses a special kind of fiat currency called SDRs (Special Drawing Rights). It's defined by the IMF as a "basket of currencies" consisting "of the euro, Japanese yen, pound sterling, and US dollar." The value of the SDR basket in terms of the US dollar is updated daily in the IMF's website.

IMF members receive a quota of SDRs that is a "potential claim" on the usable currencies of IMF members. This means a member can exchange his quota for these currencies.

The IMF, called the "lender of last resort," transfers wealth from the taxpayers of rich countries to the bureaucrats and politicians of third world countries, or countries with problems. This money goes to pay loans used in bailouts or in World Bank–backed government projects on infrastructure, agriculture, or education. Most of these projects fail, but politicians, bureaucrats, and technicians become rich along the way.[50]

The IMF does its lending through the World Bank, the BIS (Bank of International Settlements) and the commercial banks. Each member country of the IMF has a SDR quota that is a credit. This credit means that if the issuers of the loans cannot collect back their debt, the governments guarantee the repayment, meaning that the taxpayers will

[50] "In 2000, the joint Economic Committee of the US Congress found a failure rate of 55–60% for all World Bank–sponsored projects. In Africa, the failure rate reached 73%." *New Internationalist Magazine*, issue 365, March 2004.

pay in the end. For example, if the IMF through the World Bank or a commercial bank lends to Argentina, and the Argentinean government doesn't pay it back, US citizens will end up paying. This is why commercial banks are so eager to lend to governments.

The guarantee given by IMF member governments enables the SDR credit quotas to be converted into reserves and the reserves into assets.

When the recipient countries' governments cannot pay back, they blame the monstrous capitalist imperialists of the IMF. The reason for this is that the IMF demands austerity measures forcing the taxpayers of the recipient countries to pay the debt incurred by their governments — debt the taxpayers didn't ask for in the first place. But accusing the IMF of pushing austerity measures actually helps the IMFs' bureaucrats and the recipient governments' bureaucrats to engineer new bailouts and loans.

And again, if the recipient countries' taxpayers cannot pay, which is usually the case, the rich countries tax payers end up by picking the bill.

The consequence of all this is the ongoing printing of fiat currencies, which produces inflation on a global scale and contributes to the spiraling poverty of the countries whose governments are the loan recipients as well as lowering the standard of living in the issuer countries. This destroys wealth by transferring it from responsible producers to irresponsible governments.

The goal is to confiscate the wealth and savings of productive citizens worldwide and transfer it into the hands of the politicians, the bureaucrats, and their mercantilist business allies.

But the newest monetary revolution of digital money has the possibility to liberate us from dependence on the fiat money system.

## *The economic results when technology breaks the boundaries of space and time*

High speed digital information technology has freed money from the boundaries of time and space. Distances no longer matter much. Nor are there long delays; transactions are all nearly instantaneous.

A person can receive on his screen information from miles away, or withdraw cash from a machine a continent away from home. All of this happens in almost no time and with no limitations imposed by distance. As a result, all kinds of work can be performed more efficiently with quicker results, producing greater value and more wealth.

Work is changing with the changes in monetary technology. We can imagine the effects of computers with their lightning speed of calculation doing in seconds what armies of workers did before. Thus, digital transactions and the new environment of a digital economy may seem dangerous to many people.

Prophets of doom like Jeremy Rifkin have imagined that legions of workers will be thrown out of work, with growing unemployment and poverty for the whole world. Well, nothing of the sort has happened so far or will happen. Prosperity is bound to continue to grow, and the microchip will create more and more jobs.

The reason is the freeing of energy. Prosperity will probably continue to grow to newer highs. Machines during the industrial revolution freed a new energy, without which the wealth required today for the survival of our planet's seven billion inhabitants would not have been possible.

We could well say that the new digital revolution is a new survival strategy for our species.

We see a job revolution today in which new technologies have enabled the creation of new products and services of all kinds that open up opportunities. We also observe a synergy among these new possibilities.

New markets and new job opportunities open up every day. On one day there is an Amazon, on another a Google, and then thousands of new online services and activities. At the same time, many people have, for the first time, an opportunity to work at home. The costs of doing business are lower every day. Today, many more people create their own businesses and leave their conventional jobs.

Corporations today need fewer people at their headquarters than before. Much of the work can be delocalized or outsourced. These are consequences of this new freedom from time and space. Being able to work anywhere and at any time means that workers and professionals will be less and less attached to a society within a geographic boundary.

Workers' offers will take over. The job market will be wherever the workforce that provides the best advantages for employers is. For example, China has a growing job market today because its workforce beats those of other areas in its low wages. Other countries can beat their competition in quality of output rather than low wages.

In the past, there was no possibility of choosing where to hire and where to work. Now, workers will become more independent. Unions will become less and less powerful and relevant. Corporations will seek to hire wherever the terms of employment are best for them. We see this happening in India, which offers its services worldwide in fields ranging from high-tech to clerical jobs.

Entrepreneurs will seek the areas or countries that offer them the best investing conditions and the most advantageous wages. Countries where unions do not place obstacles in the way of employment opportunities will become wealthier than other countries.

These worldwide and instantaneous job opportunities affect prices. Cheaper products at rising levels of quality will inundate the market. We already see this happening in China. This tendency will not only continue there, but will grow.

As a result, we are in an era of deflation. We are living in a worldwide deflation that will result in a true distribution of wealth through the ever-increasing competition for new opportunities and new markets.

There is an accelerating search for new products to offer at lower and lower prices while, at the same time, new technologies are reducing costs even further. As a result, the same amount of money today can buy better things at lower prices than yesterday. From computers to cars to private jets, prices are coming down. Life is becoming better and better in terms of enjoying the products of technology.

More and more people can afford today what only the wealthy could afford in years past.[51] For example, your computer today has hundreds of times more power than the first computer that IBM built, which cost $400,000.

So you are wealthier today from the standpoint of what money can buy. Today, you can have what only a privileged few could afford in the past.

We are at the beginning of the most competitive era ever in all areas of life—from technology and science to business, religion, arts, and charities. Competition will make life better worldwide, and it will make this improvement without government intervention.

## *A second industrial revolution*

The first industrial revolution enabled millions of people to live, rather than to starve and die. The growing European population, which could not survive on agriculture alone, was saved by industry.

Today we are witnessing another increase in the quality of life like the increase that began with the first industrial revolution—despite governments, which have hampered it and placed obstacles in its way.

The quality of work has increased too. This means producing a higher quality of output in less time. This is because the worker who uses a machine uses its "leverage" to perform his work. The machine not only enables the worker to do something he could not have done without, but also creates a job opportunity for him that was not there before.

[51] This is true even despite governments' debasement of currencies.

It is the existence of the new machine that creates the new job opportunity. Take the example of a person who has a job using a specific kind of graphic-design software on a computer to create advertisements. Without the computer and the software, his job would not exist.

As I said earlier, the machine gives the worker leverage. Software and computers make possible a level of output that could not be imagined in the precomputer era.

The worker obtains this leverage from the intelligence of the creators of the software and the computer.

He is therefore indebted to the minds of the geniuses who invented the equipment he uses. Without them, the worker's job would not exist. In fact, he and we will never be able to repay what the inventor's minds have given us.

In short, the economic environment has changed radically, and it will continue to change, due to the microchip revolution. We are witnessing the birth of a new world.

## *Magic as the art of materializing*

Real magic does exist. For a child, magic occurs when the seemingly impossible happens in front of his eyes: the magician pulls a rabbit from a hat.

If magic must be defined, it should be called the art of creating something from nothing. And this is exactly what the mind does when it creates. It draws down from the realm of the mind things that are invisible and incorporeal, and it changes these invisible ideas into something material and tangible.

Mental achievements and technological advancements are made from abstract concepts, such as 1 + 1 = 2, or A = A, or the chemical formula for aspirin, or the idea of a new airplane.

What matters is the ability of a creator to use and embody this abstract concept in matter. When the first three-axis-controlled airplane was built, it flew because it had been materialized in wood, tissue, and metal. Its inventors, the Wright brothers, performed the magic that called it forth. Before that, the airplane was only the possibility of a project. It did not exist as anything tangible. It was, in that sense, nothing.

The same happened with the computer and the microchip. People had thought of the computer, but it did not exist in concrete reality until its creators incarnated it in a machine. Similarly, the microchip did not exist until it was incarnated in a piece of silicon.

Creating something from nothing is the essence of value creation and its ultimate conversion to wealth. Creating value and converting that value into wealth is the magical act by which developed countries have become developed.

In that sense, magic does exist.

## THE MEANING OF PROFIT

The word "profit" has a negative connotation for many. It is associated with greed and injustice. Many people feel guilty when they admit that they want to make a profit. Indeed, many businessmen excuse themselves for making a profit by saying that this was not their motive, but merely an unavoidable consequence of pursuing other, nobler goals.

Such an excuse shows ignorance and weakness. In other words, it is evidence of a lack of mind and a lack of character. It shows ignorance because it misrepresents the true nature of profit. It shows lack of character because of the reluctance to admit the true motive for one's actions.

We must make a distinction between real profits and nominal profits in dollars. Real profit means any benefit that someone obtains. For example, it is profitable for me to learn languages. This is not necessarily a nominal profit in dollars.

## *The profit motive*

Profit is good, in itself, and it is worth seeking. The profit motive is a virtuous motive. For example, when you exercise, your muscles profit from their exertion. That profiting of your muscles is not bad. On the contrary, it is good.

When you want to learn mathematics or any other discipline, you will *profit* from having good teachers and good books on the subject. You will obtain a profit in knowledge—and obtaining that profit is good.

The same holds true for money. As long as you do not attack the property of someone else, cheat him, or steal from him, making money is good. Obtaining a monetary profit is beneficial for all.

However, money, in itself, has value only as a sign of the services or goods that you can exchange it for. Thinking in terms of money alone misrepresents the true nature of profit. The real profit is what money enables you to have, because the function of money is in fact to represent barter as an exchange of services. Indeed, barter is always the end result, despite all the monetary revolutions. Each revolution has changed the nature of money as an exchange vehicle, but barter, the original form of exchange, is always behind these modern methods of exchange. Money has simply freed barter from its space-time limits.

Profit is the result of services rendered that are exchanged for other services. Money as "profit" is only the exchange medium that you possess because of services that you have rendered to others. That money allows you, in turn, to purchase more services from still other people. Money conceals the fact that what is exchanged is a service for a service. Your profit is not the money, but what you can exchange it for.

Now, the goal and motive of a business is not to serve people selflessly. The goal of a business is to make a profit. When the profit motive is not the goal, inefficiency creeps in, and the business will go broke. Profit is one reason why the private sector is more efficient than the government sector.

To better understand the profit motive, let us reverse our positions. Let us place ourselves in the customer's shoes.

### *Purchasing a parachute*

Suppose, for the sake of argument, that you want to buy a parachute because you want to practice the sport of skydiving. Now, if that is the case, which parachute would you buy? Assume that you have a choice of two parachute makers.

The first parachute maker is a group of selfless people who work only to serve, and who hate the profit motive. They make parachutes because they think that society has the right to be served parachutes for free. They give away the parachutes at cost, including the workers' salaries.

They work for minimum wage, and their CEO is also paid the minimum wage. Because they detest money, they live in conditions that are the worst that money can buy. They take public transport, they eat cheap foods, and they live in the least expensive neighborhoods.

The second company is one in which the workers and the staff at all levels, including management, have among the highest salaries in town. Further, the company's stated goal is to make the best, safest parachutes in the world.

In addition, the company makes it a point of honor to make the most expensive parachutes available in the entire market. The workers and executives claim to make the Rolls-Royce of parachutes.

This company is by far the most profitable company in its field. Workers at the company are wealthy—and happy to be so.

Now, again, from which company would you prefer to buy your parachute? Remember that your life is at stake here.

Do you need to answer? No, unless you are suicidal we agree; you will buy from the second company. Now, let us continue to explore the profit motive.

## *Who wants to be a millionaire?*

Even if you want to achieve monetary profit, this does not ensure that you will. Most people are not millionaires, and this is not because they don't want to be.

Why? Because having a profit motive is not enough. You must be able to deliver the value that will change into wealth for you.

When your primary motivation is monetary profit, you must also want to create value for your customers. Unless you want *both* of these things, you will not deliver value with quality, and so you will not make a profit.

## *The enemies of profit*

As a stratagem to separate you from your money and leave you with a feeling of guilt and shame, politicians and bureaucrats denigrate the profit motive. You must definitely say no to people who try to dissuade you from having a profit motive. Generating profit is the best thing you can do for yourself, your family, your business, and your society at large.

If you want to contribute to society, try to reinstate the prestige of the profit motive. It is important for people to understand that profit can appear only when value is delivered.

No profit is possible without value that converts to wealth. Value and wealth benefit everyone. Furthermore, wealth used as capital enables the creation of new value. The more that wealth and profit increase, the more value and wealth are created and the more prosperous society becomes.

The power of free minds to create is the sole source of the prosperity and wealth of our times—and it's all because of those people who seek that ugly thing, profit.

# Chapter 10

# The End of a World

*The whole Revolution turned upon, asserted, and in theory, established the right of every man, at his discretion, to release himself from the support of the government under which he lived.*

— Lysander Spooner, *No Treason, No. 1*, 1867

Government has a duty to deliver goods to society—goods that have been paid for. The goods that government must deliver are the rule of law, security, and a minimal material structure for the country to function, to the extent that private individuals or businesses cannot provide it.

Adam Smith was basically right in listing a government's functions. Roads, national security, and the rule of law are all that is needed.[52] They are not free and must be paid for by whoever receives the benefits.[53]

---

[52] Adam Smith, *The Wealth of Nations* (New York: Modern Library, 1965 [1776]) pp. 734–35.

[53] According to Frédéric Bastiat, Adam Smith is far from perfect. Even though Smith understood free economics as the foundation of prosperity, he still

But in fact, even transportation infrastructure like roads can be better provided by entrepreneurs than by governments. Before the US federal government began financing highways, that role belonged in large part to private entrepreneurs.

---

missed the point concerning the relationship between value and matter. For Adam Smith, Bastiat tells us, value was "incorporated in matter," whereas, for Bastiat, value has its foundation in the "free appreciation of services." Bastiat emphasizes that "between value and matter there is no possible relationship." Bastiat goes on to tell us that "Smith had, because of it, prepared the error of modern socialists." So, for Bastiat, not only Ricardo but also his predecessor Adam Smith unwittingly paved the way for socialism, or communism, two names for the same underlying behavior that Bastiat singles out in one word, "spoliation." See Frédéric Bastiat, *Harmonies Economiques* (Paris: Guillaumin, 1850), p. 102.

By the way, Bastiat believed in God and was a follower of Leibniz's philosophy, adhering to his vision of Infinity as different from the indefinite. This is a key to understanding Bastiat's free economics. For him, "providential laws are in harmony because they act freely, without which they would not be in harmony" (*Harmonies Economiques*, p. 19).

He thinks, as Leibniz does, that we live in the best of possible of worlds and that reality tends towards the better. He tells us, "I think that Evil ends in the Good and propels to it while the Good cannot end up as Evil, from which it follows that the Good ends up by dominating." Immediately after, he tells us that the "invincible social tendency" is towards an elevation and progress of man and humanity (*Harmonies Economiques*, p. 22).

For Bastiat, eternal wisdom guides social mechanics to which is inherent "universal thought" so that an "extraordinary phenomenon" takes place — "that each atom is a living being, a thinking entity, provided of a marvelous energy, of this principle of all morality, of all dignity, of all progress, an attribute that belongs only to man, FREEDOM" (In capitals in the text) (*Harmonies Economiques*, p. 51).

Bastiat distinguishes between true Infinity and what is usually called infinite, but is, in fact, indefinite. He tells us, "Infinity admits no limits." (*Harmonies Economiques*, p. 75) He always uses the word "indefinite" when he refers to what is usually called infinite, such as a series of numbers or a series of possibilities. He tells us, "I say indefinite and not at all infinite because nothing that belongs to man is infinite."

For him, "indefinite" things, such as the "development of our faculties" are things that "have no assignable limits, even though they have absolute limits" (*Harmonies Economiques*, p. 91). The philosophy of Leibniz is at the heart of Bastiat's economic thought.

## WHO WILL BUILD THE ROADS?

In the nineteenth century there were 2,500 companies operating turnpikes, the total length of which was around 30,000 miles. The companies sold their stock to local citizens. No government financing was used, except in Ohio, Pennsylvania, and Virginia, where there were some state subsidies.

According to the US Constitution, article 1, section 8, Congress has power "to establish Post Offices and post Roads," but the spirit of this text was as a limitation to prevent government interfering with private ownership, private entrepreneurship, and freedom.

This is why President James Madison in 1817 vetoed a bill that would have enabled the federal government to construct roads and canals. Indeed, Presidents Monroe, Jackson, Tyler, Polk, Pierce, and Buchanan all vetoed transportation bills. Their reason: transportation bills were unconstitutional.

In the twentieth century, however, the US government abolished the private ownership of roads and began subsidizing free, state-owned roads. This made roads very expensive and unprofitable, and created one of the greatest misallocations of capital in US history. Also, it stifled private entrepreneurs' initiative, creating an artificial void that government filled by its own fiat, regardless of market needs.

One of the main reasons to promote government-sponsored roads was the idea Progressive politicians had that cars, not trains, were the future of transportation. The Progressives thought of the railroad owners as greedy capitalists. In 1916, they convinced the federal government that the road infrastructure for automobiles should be totally free to users and paid for with taxes, thus penalizing railway transport, which was more efficient. The modern federal highway policy thus began in 1916.

This policy orientation also had an effect on other countries within the US sphere of influence—for example, Peru. The example of US policy encouraged governments to provide toll-free roads for cars in such places, and thus stunted the growth of these countries' much-needed railroad infrastructure. This rail infrastructure is almost nonexistent even today in much of South America, and that fact has significantly retarded the region's development. Of course, government-built roads are an unending source of money for corrupt politicians and their mercantilist business associates.[54]

## *Society must rule government*

Government was not established to give away free, unpaid goods.

Free, unpaid goods can be given voluntarily by individuals or charities, but never by government. When government does so, it becomes a predator stealing from people in the name of altruism.

No one should ransack or plunder my property for the sake of welfare. We are not saying that charitable giving is bad. We are saying that government welfare depends on stealing the individual's legitimate property.

True giving can never be forced. Dictatorships always begin in that way.

Society must rule government, not vice versa. By society, we mean the free, producing individuals, who pay for government from their pockets. They ought to pay government for doing what they want and not what government wants.

But this is not what happens today. Governments take money from people and businesses at the point of a gun. This is not simply a metaphor. Government will put you in prison, literally at the point of a gun, if you fail to comply with its predatory taxes and other regulations.

What matters is not what you can do for government, but what government can do for you. Nothing gives government a right to go beyond what you are paying it to do for you.

---

[54] Gabriel Roth, "Federal Highway Funding," Cato Institute, June 2010, www.downsizinggovernment.org/transportation/highway-funding. Mark David Ledbetter, *America's Forgotten History. Part Two: Rupture* (Raleigh, NC: Lulu, 2010).

When government takes on projects that exceed what the free-thinking, paying population wants, government is usurping powers illegitimately.

We don't say the foregoing in the vain hope that governments will reverse their quasi-dictatorial trend. Although it is possible for a government to reverse its course and move away from illegitimate expansion, it is highly unlikely that it will do so.

However, governments' refusal to change their present course will lead to their demise. Governments, because they are no longer true governments, are on a road to oblivion. And the demise of governments will come because of microprocessing technology.

In other words, computers will spell the end of today's governments just as the printing press destroyed absolute monarchs. The reason for this is that governments worldwide no longer serve society as they should, and the new computer technology has eroded their foundations in a definite and final way, despite current appearances to the contrary.

## *The world's states are a vanishing dream*

The world's governments are losing their strength and their ability to cope with crises. The reason is regulation. True governments are not there to regulate our lives, but to enforce the rule of law.

Enforcing the rule of law differs completely from creating regulations in a bureaucrat's office. Enforcing the rule of law means letting the courts decide judicial matters freely and independently.

True government will enforce the rule of law and the property rights and family rights that form the basic structure of society. If these foundations erode away, the bureaucrats can easily enslave the population.

Now, enslavement will not fully succeed. Perhaps it could happen to some degree in the short run, but never over the long run. Remember the Soviet Union? It crumbled and disappeared. Today's Russia is on its way to becoming something else. The Soviet Union disappeared because its system did not work. However, just before disappearing, it seemed stronger than ever, with worldwide influence.

The same thing will happen to governments as such. National governments will not endure forever. The Leibniz revolution that made possible the recent advent of the microchip will erase them all, just as the printing press destroyed the monarchies of the past.

Monarchies disappeared worldwide. The same will happen to today's governments.

What will take their place? Perhaps a kind of direct democracy which will direct the government's primary functions, such as taxes and budgets, with each citizen voicing his opinion and placing his vote through his computer keyboard to ensure that he obtains what he pays for. I say this only as a thought and not as a prediction.

In the end, technology will decide, because it will continue to transform society. More precisely, the minds behind technology will use it to transform the world again. The change will be for the better. As for now, what may seem to be an increase in the power of governments to control their citizens' lives is in fact governments' last battle—a sign of their fatal weakness. Efforts to maintain control are at their greatest just before the end.

All governments, as we know them today, will soon be dead.

From their ashes will arise a new, living society that is happier and more prosperous. Leibniz's best-of-worlds dictum will continue to be true.

## THE END OF DICTATORSHIPS

Politicians, especially third-world politicians, hold their positions because they can't subsist anywhere else. There are few talented politicians who have a vocation and the aptitude to properly manage a state.

The proof of the above is that most governments are mediocre at their best. Good governments are the exceptions to the rule.

A politician essentially exists to satisfy his self-interest and egotism. He is ready to lie or do anything that he must to achieve his goals. This is a necessary condition of politics itself.

Politics is all about votes. Votes are the energy that the politician needs to accumulate to achieve power. No politician will sacrifice votes for ideas or principles. If he did, he would be contradicting his own purpose. No one enters politics to lose. Politicians are there to win, not to propose ideas for ideas' own sake.

To believe otherwise would be contrary to reason. A politician proposes ideas because of their potential to win votes.

A politician is not a tenured teacher whose goal is to educate people about the truth by means of reason. Suppose that you are a politician and you know that proposal A, which is based on lies, will bring you double the number of votes that proposal B, which is truthful, will bring. What will you do? You will not sabotage yourself, will you?

The politician will say anything to win and will sacrifice anything or anyone to his most immediate goals. Once you know this, you can to some extent avoid being a gullible victim.

What reason and logic also tells us is that you cannot trust someone who subordinates his ideas to his power objectives. Reason also tells us that this kind of person cannot really have ideas that he truly believes in. Ideas for him are mere tools. When a politician tells the truth, it is because it is temporarily convenient for him to do so in order to promote himself.[55]

---

[55] Thomas E. Woods Jr. explains in his book *Meltdown* (Washington, D.C.: Regnery, 2009) how George Bush and Barack Obama have the same policy of throwing good money after bad and misallocating the taxpayers' resources. Whether it is about Bush's checks and bailouts or Obama's massive infrastructure programs and bailouts or John McCain's proposal to buy up troubled mortgages, the end result, Woods points out, is "stimulus" spending by the government, increasing debt, and misallocation of resources.(p. 142).

## *Politicians are enslavers*

The politician is basically a predator. He is there to abuse people and to benefit himself and his gang. Abusing people does not exclude the possibility that, because it is convenient for his own goals, the politician may occasionally propose something that is reasonable.

It does not even exclude good government or not-so-bad government from time to time. However, providing good government is not the politician's goal, even when he does provide benefits. The politician's unspoken goal is to enslave people for the government's ends.

The government's end is simply whatever the politician and his clique have in mind. After all, they are humans—and they happen to be the worst of humans.

To the politician, people are fuel for his power. The politician is interested in votes that will put him into positions of power. However, securing votes is only the first step. The next step, once he is in power, is to use his position to prey on the people.

This second step is not as easy. It is possible to be elected using lies. The difficult part for the politician is to gain public acceptance for his predatory acts, such as forced regulations and taxes.

For this, the politician must render people passive and malleable. There is basically one method: do everything possible to weaken people's minds. He must suppress rationality until the public cannot distinguish good from evil or reality from appearance.

The politician appeals to emotion in every guise in order to eliminate any rational thought in his unsuspecting public. To do so, he will endorse and cheer for what he would never approve of in his private

---

In the end, even conservative politicians are conservative only apparently, in some of their words but not in the actions that truly would matter. Woods tells us that "the two major party candidates for president in 2008...agreed on the bailout package" and that "John McCain, 'the fiscal conservative,' even proposed that the federal government buy up troubled mortgages to the potential tune of trillions of dollars" (p. 59). The bottom line is that all politicians are the same, worldwide!

life. The politician subordinates himself to the feelings of his voters so that he can better enslave them later.

His demeanor is a kind of artifice to render his message pleasing.

## *Politicians, education, and the mass media*

However, when things get serious is when the politicians use education and mass media to distort reality. Bureaucrats and politicians know that when people are no longer reasonable they will be lost and become easy prey. The public will accept faithfully any opinion that the politician needs to articulate in order to secure power and enact his programs.

Let us think about regulations for a moment. Many people think that all kinds of regulations are required, because they hear professors, authors, or journalists say so.

Many people cannot explain why these regulations are needed. They will support any opinion, only to change it later when those same professors, authors, and journalists change their opinions, and they do not even realize that they have changed their minds.

The fewer anchors to reality the people have, the more passive and susceptible to propaganda they become. Propaganda never appears to be propaganda. It always is presented as science, or social progress, or altruism, or moral obligation.

Behind this appearance of legitimacy, propaganda achieves its goal of destroying reason and the public's sense of reality. The public loses its grounding and becomes ready to accept anything. There are immediate practical implications of having a gullible public.

For example, today the public thinks that an increase in banking regulation is reasonable and acceptable. And today, opening a bank account has become even more difficult and regulated than buying a gun.

Half a century ago, this would have caused any bank official to become indignant. Today, it is the opposite. In many countries, a bank official today will become angry if his customer refuses to complete the forms indicating the source of each cent in his account. The clerk has been trained to think and feel that way. He or she attends employee seminars and reads articles in the press and watches and listens to the media, all endorsing his or her belief.

However, when political policy eventually changes and banks must change their procedures, the same clerk will reverse his thoughts and feelings. And he will be as convinced of his new opinion as he was of his old one.

Such a person has no ability to think for himself; he is ready to think as he is told. He is the ideal prey for bureaucrats and politicians. He is the politician's perfect slave.

By destroying all natural social institutions and behavior and replacing them with institutions and behaviors that originate in the arbitrary orders or sanctions of politicians, governments can bring about an irrational state of society. Therefore, what the bureaucrat wants to do is replace natural institutions with artificial ones that he has created and can mold in order to prey on the population more efficiently.

By destroying the family, destroying property, destroying rational beliefs and traditions, destroying science and technology, and, in summary, destroying rationality, the politician becomes the master of an army of slaves whom he can prey on at will. There's a Latin saying, *divide et imperat*, which means "divide and rule." It is appropriate here.

However, these efforts to confuse, isolate, and disempower the people will not succeed, despite appearances to the contrary. Reality always wins.

## *Technology has knocked down the prison walls of modern nations*

Modern transportation and communications technologies have altered how we live and travel. Of course, this has brought problems, such as uncontrolled immigration. These problems show governments fighting their last battles before their ultimate demise, brought about by technological changes and government's own predation.

Government regulations will not solve illegal immigration. Government regulations cause it.

Transportation technology has suppressed geographical barriers for the world's population. No government dictate can change this.

What each government does not want you to know is the truth behind its anti-immigration policies. In fact, government bureaucrats and politicians do not care a whit about immigration. Politicians and bureaucrats use anti-immigration ideology simply to gain support from their native populations.

The real reason for anti-immigration laws is that welfare programs are too expensive. Many people immigrate in order to benefit from government's oppression of the productive citizens and to receive something for nothing. Today, large sectors of the population are receiving a free ride. It is not illegal immigration itself that worries the politicians, but having to pay for that immigration. Welfare has its limits. Its secret goal is to secure votes and enable more bureaucrats to make money.

So bureaucrats carefully craft measures to admit only the number of predatory immigrants that they can afford (in exchange for those immigrants' political support). As the deficits grow, the politicians have less and less money with which to enlarge their pool of predators, and so they must increase immigration restrictions. When someone walks into the country unannounced and asks for his share of what, in fact, was created as a propaganda stunt, government is not happy.

The best solution is to allow free immigration, without providing any government welfare to immigrants. However, this goes counter to bureaucrats' agendas.

If governments truly cared about immigration, all they would need to do is to deregulate it and suppress the advantages that immigrants seek from government. Then the only immigrants would be those who are able to support themselves and contribute to prosperity as free, working individuals without becoming an expense to society.

Immigration policies show, on one side, the government's imminent demise, and on the other side they show the power of technology to change the world.[56]

Governments are losing control over their territories and over their populations' freedom to travel beyond their national boundaries. Nothing will give governments back that control. Their end is near, and a new world order will soon come to be.

## THE END OF FALSE DEMOCRACIES

Democracy was for a long time the perfect cover for the politician. By falsifying democracy's true purpose, he distorted it to serve his corrupt agenda. However, television and the Internet have now rendered the politicians' intentions visible to everyone. The politician can no longer hide. Information about his doings circulates at the speed of light.

### *The politicians have lost all credibility*

The result is that almost no one believes in politicians nowadays. In third-world countries, where democracy has been especially distorted, the politicians' loss of credibility is complete.

For instance, many third-world countries imprison the regime's political enemies without proof of wrongdoing, and condemn them in courts that are travesties of justice. For the politicians and bureaucrats behind those acts, democracy was, for a long time, the perfect cover. But it is clear now to everyone that politicians use "democracy" to imprison their enemies and benefit their friends in absolute contempt

[56] David Osterfeld (*Prosperity Versus Planning* pp. 194, 195) explains that if trade and migration barriers were abolished, capital and labor would cease to migrate once they were equalized. Restricting migration creates an economic distortion that results in lower productivity of human labor and "a reduction in the supply of goods at the disposal of mankind."

for the law. The politicians cannot hide from the new media technologies.

True democracy is intended for creative and free minds. It is not meant for cliques of the powerful in land-based or material-resource-based countries. Democracy does not, and cannot, accomplish its end for those kinds of countries, so it necessarily fails.

Today in politics, what you see is what you get. Today everyone sees politicians and bureaucrats deceiving voters and later preying on them. False democracy has been deleted.

Democracy works poorly in third-world countries because it is unnatural to the population and the leaders, who have known only tyranny at worst or a bogus democracy at best. Thus, democracy must be enforced in these places at the point of a gun, as we see today in Iraq and Afghanistan. If those countries had a techno-scientific, dynamic outlook, they would already have democracies that worked efficiently.

## *True democracy is already emerging, even if it is still invisible to us*

Monarchy's obsolescence was due to a technology that changed the world by giving the human mind an opportunity to build a techno-scientific society. A change of the same kind is now occurring with the appearance of the microchip.

The first step in this revolution will be the dissolution of national boundaries as a result of new systems of communications and new technologies of transport. National borders will disappear. In the age of the transoceanic jet and maglev trains, borders and distances will collapse. Today, no politician can succeed in preventing the free migration of people.

The second step will be the use of new technologies to sidestep government regulations in general. This will enrage governments, because it will make them less and less able to prey on people.

The reduction in government power will not be due to a reduction in the number of regulations, but to the ingenuity of some individuals, who will evade those regulations. In fact, the number of regulations is actually being increased today; governments panic when they see their victims slipping through their net by means of modern data and transport technology.

Eventually, the new technologies may enable the citizens to decide matters directly. I discuss one possible scenario for this in chapter 11.

## *The new republic is already here*

These changes could come tomorrow, because the individual already has in his hands the tools for freedom. By freeing him from the boundaries of space and time, technology has enabled him to sidestep government at an individual level.

We cannot yet sidestep government at a collective level, as a society, because this will require the new form of government to replace the present one. However, sidestepping government is already possible for you as an individual.

Sidestepping government enables you to act freely, using your free mind not only to create, think, and live, but also to circumvent unnecessary regulations.

Freedom and its conditions that you as an individual may apply today are already here as a model that can inspire and guide your actions. However, first you need to have appropriate mental models. Plato was the forerunner of mathematical models and mental models of every kind. In this, he was well ahead of his time.

Remember, models are not reality. They are meant to guide behaviors or procedures, whether in one's personal life, business, or the sciences of any kind. Models are only guides; no model describes reality as such.

In this sense, the free individual must have rules that guide his acts. The rules that he will enact, with or without government approval, are like those that we find in the US Bill of Rights.

We mention this document as a model because it provides a functional and efficient way of understanding how a free individual can act.

## *Being a part of the new republic*

Now, here is a question: Are you a citizen of the new republic?

You are already providing an answer to this question. That answer is *yes* when you behave and act in a certain way. It is *no* when you do not. Some key behaviors will provide a clue to the ideal model that guides your thinking, acting, and life.

If you think that you deserve to be happy, then you may be a qualified citizen of the new republic. Happiness means developing your talents and your qualities to become an accomplished human being.

But more importantly, becoming a complete human being implies freedom of thought. Freedom is what makes you different from automatic or involuntary mechanisms and organisms. Valuing your freedom above all is what qualifies you as a human being. Freedom gives you choice. In a larger sense, freedom is also what enables you to overcome your limitations. Thus, the citizen of the new republic seeks to be free to do what he wants, as long as he harms no one and respects the rights of others to do the same. In other words, the only rule is the rule of freedom to be who you are.

This rule, the rule of nonaggression, is enough to enable everyone to develop his or her talents to the best of his or her abilities. The rule of freedom is the cornerstone of prosperity for any society. People, when left to themselves, find the best ways to use their freedom.

All of the rest derives from this fundamental law, the law of freedom.

A republic of freedom is made up of individuals who form a society simply by being free. This republic needs no government, no written laws, and no parliament or congress. All it needs are individuals living their freedom to the utmost.

Our new republic knows no national frontiers or boundaries. Its members are free minds living as free individuals anywhere in the world. Freedom of mind and action is the only passport required. It is a virtual republic in full harmony with our digital world.

Such a republic shares an essential idea with Plato's ideal republic. Plato's republic is ideal in the sense that it can be embodied only partly in the material realm—in our world of time and space. The republic can be embodied to various degrees and in various aspects, but it cannot be embodied fully. The ideal is there, but only as an ideal—and its embodiment is there, but only as a reflection of the ideal.

The same will be true for our republic of freedom. Freedom cannot be embodied perfectly. It is all a matter of degrees. Some countries will be freer than others. Some people will live more freely than others.

Plato had a keen insight of ideas as the source of reality. We do not want to enter into a discussion of the long-standing philosophical debate as to whether Plato's republic was socialist or not.

Our focus is on Plato's discovery of the gap between the material world and an ideal world. Our goal here is to provide a practical illustration of how the embodiment of an entity that has theoretical perfection is itself necessarily imperfect.

Returning to our subject of freedom, what matters is to be as free as possible—and to live a life of freedom in thought and freedom in action. Also, it is important to try to extend our possibilities to their fullest.

And let us not forget that freedom is not given, but must be taken. You must fight to obtain it. The best battle for freedom is the one that consists of living, thinking, and acting as freely as possible and letting no one hinder your legitimately won freedom.

Now we'll look at the advantages of such freedom and the kind of world in which it operates.

# Chapter 11

# The New Earth

*If the World were perfect, it wouldn't be.*
— Yogi Berra, *The Yogi Book*, 1998

Let us examine freedom in more detail. "Freedom" can be understood here in two main ways.

The first is understanding freedom as an absolute. Absolute freedom would be equivalent to having no limits or boundaries of any kind. In other words, it would mean being free of all restrictions.

This kind of freedom may be useful sometimes as an ultimate standard against which to measure our actual freedom. Imagine, for instance, being free of space and time and any of their conditions and not having to suffer them as limitations in any way. Or imagine having no limits to intelligence, to beauty, to truth, and to all else.

However, this kind of freedom is not within our grasp. For our purpose, it is freedom in its second meaning that interests us: freedom in a relative sense. This is the condition that enables you to decide for yourself without imposition from outside.

This freedom to decide is practical rather than abstract. In our daily life, we make free decisions every day.

This freedom is relative rather than absolute because when you choose, you have limited options—drinking coffee or tea, reading an Ayn Rand novel or a calculus book, etc.

Your choices are limited. You have, say, two options, and you have to choose one or none of them. You are free to choose only relative to those options.

## TOWARD A NEW FREEDOM

However, even though these boundaries exist, they can be vanquished through intellectual progress. All the boundaries to our freedom can fall progressively, but only because we are constantly fighting against them.

So, your decision to be free, to control these choices and to overcome these boundaries, is everything.

It is all that matters.

### *You are free of spatial limits*

Your practical freedom exists first in space. This is the foundational free choice. It means simply being able to move at will.

Furthermore, in a moral sense, as long as you do not invade other people's property without their consent, you are free to go wherever you want in any way you decide. As long as you do not damage someone else or his property, you can walk or use a bicycle, car, plane, or any other means of transportation.

Today, this essential freedom to move is being restricted more and more by government bureaucrats. This is dangerous, because the freedom to move is also the freedom to find opportunity. By restricting our space, governments restrict our lives.

The first type of regulations that limit our use of space is regulations that prohibit people from leaving their countries. Examples of countries with such regulations include the Soviet Union in the past and Cuba today. The prohibition against emigration enables governments to enslave their populations and abuse them.

The second type of regulation to limit our use of space is the reverse of the first. Instead of forbidding people to leave a country, bureaucrats can forbid them to enter it. For this, bureaucrats have invented complex visa and residence regulations.

The bureaucrats' excuse is that they are serving the nationals who are eligible to live in their own country. Bureaucrats subtly play the cards of nationalism and racial discrimination, even though outwardly they appear to be against these things.

Socialist bureaucrats thrive when nationalists rail against immigrants. One example is found in France. Racism and nationalism cause a great number of nationals to detest immigrants. They would like to see them taken by force to the country's border and expelled.

The bureaucrats will never stop those whose beliefs cause them to play the bureaucrats' game. Bureaucrats have a clear reason to stop immigration and they need public opinion to support them.

As explained in chapter 10, the reason that the bureaucrats are against immigration is that their welfare programs are used to oppress the productive minority in favor of the unproductive majority. These programs pay for all those who do nothing, but they make life and business very expensive for the productive minority.

What must be done is to respect and enforce the first fundamental freedom, which enables any individual to use space as he wants, so long as he respects other people's use of space.

Two other ways of restricting the freedom to use space are by limiting the free export and import of goods, property, and capital. Bureaucrats always justify these restrictions in the name of the public good or patriotism.

Bureaucrats and politicians often use the argument that capital should be forced to stay within some national border because it is unpatriotic to invest in one country and then remove the capital to another. For these people, your money should be captive for a time, if not forever, within their national borders.

But in truth, your property is an extension of yourself. You are the only one who has a right to decide where your capital should go and for how long. Your property has the same right to circulate freely as you have.

### *You are free of limits on the use of your time*

You have the right to decide how to use your time. Time is your most important asset. In fact, it is your life. It is up to you to decide how much time you will allocate to work or to leisure. You are the one who must decide, according to your needs and circumstances.

Your free use of time enables you to use it efficiently and to make the most of it. When anyone steals your time, he is stealing your life. You are the only rightful owner of your time.

However, people will try to steal time from you in countless ways. One major characteristic of third-world countries is a poor, lazy, and negligent use of time. What is more amazing is that some people believe that this is an advantage.

For example, people in such countries arrive late to meetings and show no concern in making others wait for hours. What this indicates is a sacrificial view of the world, in which one person is ready to sacrifice other people's lives on an arbitrary and irrational whim.

Yet the inhabitants of many third-world countries consider this negligence and failure to respect the energy, time, and life of others as a sign of a resistance to the capitalistic attitude, with its supposed robotic efficiency.

They will tell you that life is not only about work and business, but about leisure and learning to "take your time." However, this could mean standing in line at the post office all morning to receive a simple package that has been held up by customs.

Some years ago, before the advent of cloud storage on the Internet, I was in Lima, Peru, and needed a copy of the financial software I used to do my work in Paris. I contacted the vendor, who immediately sent me the software overnight.

But when I tried to get my package from the overnight courier service, I had to provide them with (among other documents) the registration number of my Peruvian business. Of course, I was unable to provide a Peruvian registration number—I didn't have one, because I lived and worked in *Paris.*

These bureaucratic hassles caused by government regulations threatened to make me wait days or even weeks to get my package. Finally, I contacted the software vendor, who retrieved my package from the "express" courier service and then uploaded it and gave me a download link. So I received the software in the end only by bypassing the bureaucrats and their hindrances.

Time abuse is a fact of life for the average inhabitant of a third-world country because of government and its bureaucratic hassles, which force citizens to lose countless hours standing in line to liberate a book from the customs department—or filling forms of no value that were created merely to give meaningless jobs to ineffective people.

Another form of time theft is taking hard-earned money from people by taxes. By stealing money through unjust taxes, unjust regulations, or unjust procedures, bureaucrats and politicians in effect steal the time that people spent working to save the money.

What you ultimately buy with money is time. By buying time, you are buying life. When someone steals your money, he is stealing your time, and thus stealing your life. Money is time and time is life—your life.

By abolishing taxes and regulations, a government can give you back much more than money. It can give back your time, and thus give you back your life.

Let us explore another fundamental practical freedom.

## *You are free of your government*

Freedom from government? Yes. You are free of government. That is why government should exist: so that you can be free of it. Let us consider the following.

Government is your employee and works for you. It is there to serve you and not for you to serve it.

Government is there to do what you pay it to do. This means that you delegate the management of your safety, infrastructure, and justice to it. Your freedom from government is what gives government its efficiency and its reason to exist.

Government is there to ensure your freedom from predation, to make sure others respect your freedom. When others violate your freedom by stealing your property, you go to court to seek redress.

When another country initiates violence against a peaceful country, the latter's army is there to defend its citizens.

A government should only take action when some free individuals give their consent to it. It is your freedom that gives rise to a proper government in order to protect it.

## *You are free to decide your actions*

The ultimate freedom is your freedom, the individual's freedom. Freedom cannot be collective. Collectivities may have individuals within them who are either more or less free, and either more or less eager to defend their freedom.

Freedom can be achieved in prison or even in death. Socrates was an example of a man who preferred to die rather than to abdicate his freedom.[57] The Soviet Gulag witnessed the deaths of many free spirits.

---

[57] Plato's dialogue *The Apology* is about his master's defense when he is sentenced to death because of his teaching.

Socrates is accused of corrupting the youth when, in fact, he teaches them to think for themselves by using the laws of reason. When given a choice of his sentence, he chose death because abdicating reason was abdicating life. He was judged and condemned by politicos because reason and logic were the chief obstacles to their predatory exercise of power.

*The Apology* of Plato is full of teachings about the millennia-long divide between politicians and scientists (for us, supporters of the rule of logic and reason, covering the spectra of all disciplines).

For instance, Plato warns us in his dialogue, through the voice of his master, about the dangers of politics. In the dialogue, he states that anyone who goes into politics endangers his life: "Now do you really imagine that I could have survived all these years, if I had led a public life, supposing that, like a good man, I had always maintained the right and had made justice, as I ought, the first thing? No indeed, men of Athens, neither I nor any other man." Plato, "Apology," in *The Dialogues of Plato*, vol. 2, trans. Benjamin Jowett (Oxford: Oxford University Press, 1892).

The meaning is clear. Truth and science rarely go hand in hand with politics and politicians. For Socrates, going into politics is a big No for the "good man"! In the same dialogue, Socrates explains why he prefers by far to be a private entrepreneur in the field of education, instead of a political adviser. He says: "Someone may wonder why I go about in private giving advice and busying myself with the concerns of others, but do not venture to come forward in public and advise the state. I will tell you why....This is what deters me from being a politician. And rightly, as I think, for I am certain, O men of Athens, that if I engaged in politics, I should have perished long ago, and done no good either to you or to myself. And do not be offended at my telling you the truth, for the truth is that no man who goes to war with you or any other multitude, honestly striving against the many lawless and unrighteous deeds, which are done in a state, will save his life. He who will fight for the right, if he would live even for a brief space, must have a private station and not a public one."

The message could not be more straightforward. Socrates tells us to stay away from politics and to be private entrepreneurs. This is the secret message of the "Apology" never highlighted by academics or politicians. Socrates unveils the most secret conspiracy of all times, the conspiracy by the predatory politicos and bureaucrats who condemned him to death.

For Socrates, politicians try to turn their victims into their accomplices in their crimes. In the same dialogue, he says, "This was a specimen of the sort of commands, which they were always giving with the view of implicating as many as possible in their crimes." Then, as today, politicians wanted to be endorsed by their defenseless victims while preying on them!

For a contemporary and enlightening view of the horrors of depredator politicians and terror regimes oppressing free minds, see Aleksandr I. Solzhenitsyn, *The Gulag Archipelago, 1918–1956: An Experiment in Literary*

Let us now examine the new world order that is emerging from freedom—a world order whose key trait is flexibility

## THE NEW ORDER OF THE INVISIBLE MONARCHY

Our era is typified by the advent of the scientist, the discoverer, and the inventor. Their primary functions are to create ideas that have value and then to convert that value into wealth.

### *The scientist and inventor as the new man of wisdom*

The scientist, discoverer, and inventor embody a wisdom that tells us about the core of reality itself. This wisdom tells us that reality is boundless and is not limited to what we think it to be.

In fact, all names that we give to things in reality, like "tree" and "gravity" are just labels we use to serve our own functions for our existence as humans. That is, the actual reality of a "tree" and of "gravity" are far beyond our concepts of them.

This truth is evidenced in the procedures of science. The scientific method is one of creating hypotheses and considering them as valid simply because they work for us. When a new fact contradicts a theory, a new hypothesis must be formulated to account for the new fact.

We must never confuse our thoughts with what is. Words such as "gravity" or even "reality" are only words—approximations, practical tools—to use in moving around and living. Reality itself is unbounded. It is not up to us to arbitrarily set limits on it.

This underlying concept of a reality without frontiers is what enables today's science to advance. Science does not limit itself to one way of thinking by confusing its constructed images of reality with reality itself.

---

*Investigation, Books I-II,* trans. Thomas P. Whitney (New York: Harper & Row, 1973).

This understanding of reality itself as free is also what underlies modern economics and entrepreneurship. It leads us to a dynamic concept of value and wealth, and thus leads us out of a static and limited world.

## *The new politician as entrepreneur*

The entrepreneur is the backbone of our new society. Each entrepreneur is an independent node for the conversion of value to wealth. These nodes, although independent, create a harmonious whole.

As a comparison, we can consider our bodies. We have cells that work independently, but their actions develop into a whole that functions harmoniously. Any friction or discord arises from a malfunction and is not intrinsic to the whole.

Through this comparison we can foresee our social future—a future of independent entrepreneurial nodes building a new political foundation.

Here is a possible scenario. We already have technologies via online forums and polls that could enable direct voting and the immediate and efficient processing of the votes cast.

If such technologies could be used to give voters the power to resolve important questions directly, the politician of the past would disappear, because he would have nothing to offer. The politician would become a simple clerk who executes general instructions for the daily management of society.

Each individual could decide everything of importance that goes beyond the level of general management. For instance, the individual would decide directly whether to raise taxes or abolish them.

(Although all individuals would have the same decision-making power, it would likely be the entrepreneurs who set the tone unofficially, by setting an example that most would willingly follow.)

In other words, the politicians and the bureaucrats would be progressively pushed aside. Because of this, and because of the prominent role of the entrepreneurs, there would be a tendency toward more freedom and free decisions in society.

In such a society, every member would be a potential entrepreneur. When people are free to decide about their lives and to keep the products of their work, everyone can convert value into wealth according to his or her abilities and areas of expertise.

In this society, government would not give anyone something for nothing. Welfare would be a private, charitable affair of helping those who are in need.

Government would be effective because of its reduced size. This kind of government would only need to ensure that it does not interfere with the natural actions of society.

All this is just a possible scenario, showing in broad strokes what the new technologies may enable. Of course, reality is not as simple as this, and the real future will differ from our imagined and simplified version. Let us not confuse reality with our projections about it.

## *When "defense" means "defense" and not "aggression"*

A word must be said about defense. Every society needs to be protected from outside aggression. This role has traditionally been in the hands of the army. But the provision of an army is just another kind of entrepreneurial activity.

Defense is a science, a technique, and an art. Like everything else, defense is properly the area of entrepreneurs—in this case, entrepreneurs who specialize in providing defense and everything pertaining to it. It is only when defense loses its rationality that it becomes the tool of aggressors who attack innocent victims. The true role of defense is to defend against aggression and never to initiate aggression.

For example if someone enters your home to rob you, it is legitimate to shoot him. His transgression of your home is of course an aggression initiated by him, not you.

You cannot be expected to risk your life to wait and see whether the robber only means to steal your television or whether he means to do violence to your body as well. So it is legitimate for you to shoot him to forestall the possibility of his harming you (or your family).

Another point that is important in connection with this is the right to own weapons to defend yourself and your country. As the Second Amendment of the US Constitution says, personal self-defense forms only part of the reason for the right to own weapons. The other part is to provide for national self-defense by a trained, armed, and organized citizen militia against a foreign invader.

A proper army, therefore, would thus be one to which you voluntarily *delegate* your right to defend yourself and your country.

An army is, therefore, an enterprise, and the people who lead it should be entrepreneurially minded. Only entrepreneurs will have the creativity to invent new and more efficient, peaceful, and lifesaving methods of defense.

The role of an army is not only to defend, but to search for ways of doing this in the least damaging way. At the same time, the army must seek to be as dissuasive as possible so that aggressors will never attempt to victimize an innocent society.

Value creation is what makes the army an enterprise and its leaders entrepreneurs.

One of the greatest examples was the attitude and entrepreneurial spirit of Winston Churchill. He fully understood the risks and rewards of defense and courage. He could summon in a creative and inventive way the defensive resources of the entire country.

The result was success against all odds.

Armies may be public or private. In a free society, traditionally it has been the function of government to oversee matters of defense. An army works under government decisions and supervision. In addition to assuring internal safety, government has the responsibility of deciding whether to retaliate against an aggressor.

Armies work like corporations that provide defense and security to governments.

## *Old-style politicians as present and future pariahs*

Old-style politician will gradually disappear into a formless shade. We see daily in the media the politicians' gradual loss of the control that they were once able to exert over society. Each year that passes, fewer and fewer people believe in politicians or take them seriously. Politicians' words mean little nowadays, whatever their political leanings or party ideologies may be.

As they lose control, politicians act irrationally and say things that time will show to be untrue. There is nothing that they can do about their loss of authority, just as the French absolute monarchs could do nothing to avoid the revolution and the birth of the Republic.

The advent of the Republic did not mean that the monarchy was bad. It meant that its time had ended. Society's paradigm had changed, beneath the surface of events , as it were, due to the dynamic concept of value.

When a system no longer works, it begins to fail at several points at the same time. Then people begin to lose faith in it. Today, government is not working as it should. It hinders free initiative. People find it more and more difficult to comply with its regulations.

The result is that more and more people attempt to escape from the government. Government is still there, but has a grip on only part of the population. Many people today have found a means of avoiding succumbing to government predation.

An example is the increasing number of people and businesses who emigrate physically or economically in order to escape the grip of governments that prey on their hard work and creative initiative.

As a result, many countries, perceiving this depredation, discover that they have a market. They understand that they can become prosperous by becoming havens for people who escape their predatory pursuers.

These countries, especially those that offer minimal regulations and a full working infrastructure for creative, free-minded entrepreneurs, will become the future poles of discovery, invention, progress, and prosperity.

## THE DIGITAL ERA AND THE LAST FRONTIER

It all comes back to knowledge. Knowledge is the key to politics and economics. Knowledge is what brings meaning and prosperity to human life, individually and collectively.

### *The last frontier is knowledge*

For a country to prosper, all that it needs is knowledge developed freely. Knowledge brings everything else—discoveries, inventions, and creativity of all kinds. Above all, it brings humanity, the respect for what freedom is, the essence of what we are.

Knowledgeable people in all fields are found at the highest levels in first-world countries.

When knowledge is free and all the tools to enhance it are available, prosperity results, and with it come social harmony and peace. Failing to understand this means taking the opposite way.

This is the direction in which the third-world countries have moved. They have taken the way of ignorance, which has left them in a state of poverty and deprivation. The poverty of these countries is mainly poverty of knowledge.

Ignorance and underdevelopment go together. By ignorance, we don't mean the ignorance of the general population, but primarily that of its leaders. Despite their words to the contrary, knowledge is not valued in the third world as much as in first-world countries.

Simply having access to books is an almost-impossible achievement in some countries. In such countries, everything works against the acquisition of knowledge, instead of for it.

As long as this doesn't change, poverty and inner chaos will be the daily routine for these countries. But these obstacles can easily be eliminated, and one day they will be.

# Chapter 12

# The Capitalist as the Quintessential Anarchist

*I am too high-born to be propertied*
*To be a secondary at control*
*Or useful serving-man and instrument*
*To any sovereign state throughout the world.*

— Lewis, in Shakespeare's *King John*, Act V, Scene 2

~

*Optimistic creators such as Apple's Steve Jobs and Google founders Sergey Brin and Larry Page have produced billions of dollars of wealth and immeasurable happiness and well-being that would not have existed had they not founded the businesses they and their teams created.*

— Michael Strong, *Be the Solution: How Entrepreneurs and Conscious Capitalists Can Solve All the World's Problems*, 2009.

Wealth creation depends on value creation. When incorporeal value is created and is accepted by society, it changes to tangible wealth. The person who is responsible for converting value to wealth is the entrepreneur.

The key entrepreneurial element is risk. When the entrepreneur discovers value and thinks others will welcome it and buy it from him, he is at the start of an adventure. When he is right in his perception, he can succeed. When he is not right, his enterprise will fail. That is the price of seeking success, and he knows it. Entrepreneurs face risk as a way of life. Both their capital and their time are at stake.

## TAKING RESPONSIBILITY FOR SOCIETY

Risk sharpens the entrepreneur's perceptiveness of an idea's value and of people's need for it. Entrepreneurs, as a group, know and feel the needs of society. They know how and when to convert value into an offer that will generate wealth.

Also, the entrepreneur, by offering a good or a service that he thinks is needed, begins a process of trial and error. In this process, error has no staying power and is immediately punished, while success brings what can turn out to be long-lasting wealth. This mechanism enables society to use and allocate resources optimally. No entrepreneur can afford to put money, time, and life into an unsuccessful enterprise.

If he does, he will be punished by a failure that will knock him off the road and enable others to take his place. Through the risk taking of entrepreneurs, society feels its way toward prosperity and learns to allocate its resources efficiently.

### *Optimal allocation*

Entrepreneurial asset allocation is the opposite of government asset allocation. The bureaucrats who determine government allocation have nothing to lose and are ready to let society bleed until misery and violence become the norm.

Think, for example, of all the failures and ineffective bureaucratic agencies of the former Soviet Union, which existed for decades, economically strangling people and preventing them from leading prosperous lives, when all that the people needed was the freedom to take risks and to live.

Stop for a second to think of the misery in Cuba, with its enslaved people, who live a daily life of despair. Cuba exemplifies the kind of world where politicians and bureaucrats rule the land and entrepreneurs are banned or bullied.

Only an entrepreneurial society honors freedom and builds the way to prosperity. A free society, where entrepreneurs can do their jobs at their own risk, is one in which resources will be optimally allocated, producing wealth for all.

A responsible society does not flee risk but faces it. Risk and freedom converge in an efficient allocation of resources, using creativity, seeking value, and converting it to wealth.

## *Optimal creation and invention*

Freedom enables the entrepreneur to discover, invent, and create. Freedom and the risk that it implies make trial and error possible

Freedom goes with ignorance of the future. Freedom means that we are not robots who follow some predetermined and fixed path. Life is an adventure. Freedom is the ability to try different paths and to wait for the outcome, which may be a surprise. Freedom is what enables men to create lives out of nothing. Humans who abandon risk for safety are inhuman. Nothing separates them from soulless machines.

Ignorance of the future is where reality shows its true nature. If reality were not free, all would be known beforehand and nothing would be left to chance; life would become meaningless, or in other words lifeless.

Our lives have meaning because of our intrinsic freedom. Practically, this means that we can try new things and, in doing so, discover value and convert it to wealth. Society and the world at large are a stage for our exercise of freedom. By exercising freedom, we create meaning in our lives. This is another way of saying that we endow our lives with value, for meaning and value are the same.

So freedom is the source of all value, and value is the source of all wealth, including the wealth that appears as money.

Now, freedom is based on our not knowing the future, which in turn comes because reality is unbounded and does not allow itself to be grasped in one formula or held within limits of any kind.

In fact, the unboundedness of reality is the unlimited source of all value, all creation, and all inventive action.

Freedom is what makes the entrepreneur an anarchist. Here we use anarchy in its ancient meaning, that used by the philosophers of ancient times. The word is *an arche*, "not principled," in the sense of being beyond bounds.

If reality is free and not determined in advance, the full use of our human freedom to discover, create, invent, and offer those actions, converting them to wealth, makes anarchists of entrepreneurs.

Anarchy does not mean being irrational, but exactly the opposite. It means having a positioning above reason as its foundation. Reason depends on principles, and has as the goal of abolishing boundaries or limits. Reason is a tool for freedom. However, freedom itself is the way of the ultimate un"principled" and unbounded reality, which goes beyond the grasp of reason.

Reality's boundlessness or anarcheness is what gives the entrepreneur and his enterprises a reason to exist. To discover, create, or invent, he must rely on the fact that our world is not bounded to what currently exists, and that therefore new things can come into being.

Freedom is the door through which new value and wealth can enter the world.

## *The rule of talent*

Above all, entrepreneurship is a game of the mind. The talented entrepreneur is motivated by an idea or dream and does what is needed to make it come true. Each entrepreneur works in the field where he is best able to accomplish something. Using his strengths enhances his probability of success.

But success is only possible because the entrepreneur lives in a free society. In such a society, anyone can choose his line of business. In such an environment, creativity and entrepreneurship can spread from our inner persons to our outer world; no bureaucrat dictates the path to follow.

Because a free society enables each of us to follow what we feel, we become the best that we can be. This is the rule of talent: a free society allocates its talents optimally.

Talent, entrepreneurship, and freedom go together.

The scientist, the inventor, and the creator, artist, or writer are entrepreneurs, just like those who make value accessible to society at large. When their actions are the result of free choice in a free world, their talents combine in the best possible ways.

## *Generosity and its meaning*

Entrepreneurship and freedom are linked to generosity. By discovering or creating value and converting it to wealth, the entrepreneur makes something out of nothing. From the immaterial mind, something comes into existence in the world.

*Generating* is what generosity is all about. Generosity means giving to others what we generate with our work or talent.

Discoverers, creators, inventors, and entrepreneurs are born generators. They contribute the inner generosity at the heart of society's prosperity. Their ability to generate has its foundation in their freedom to generate.

Freedom to generate—to create—arises in societies that do not put obstacles and barriers in the way of entrepreneurship.

Free societies are generous societies, and generous societies are prosperous societies. The contrapositive is also true. Poor societies are the least generous and the least free. For an example of this, we have free, first-world countries that not only produce almost all the wealth of the planet, but also are the countries where a generous attitude is most developed.

The best thing that anyone can do, for himself and for humanity, is to exercise his or her talents to their utmost. The exercise of talent is the best formula for generosity. The best allocation of resources is to follow your own talents. If, instead of studying physics, Einstein had devoted himself to charities in third-world countries, the world would have lost its greatest advances in physics.

So the best thing that talented people can do for society is to develop their talents and gain rewards for using them. The more they are rewarded, the more resources they will have with which to further develop their dreams, and the more prosperous society will become.

The same can be said of entrepreneurs and enterprises. The best thing that they can do is to maximize their efficiency in doing what they are proficient at.

This does not mean that charity should not exist. We should not exclude giving to others when we think a need should be filled. However, this also involves the exercise of a talent. Not everyone can do this efficiently.

Many charities are inefficient wastes, created by people who have discovered ways of depredating the wealthy by playing on their guilty consciences. Care must be exercised in this area. It's better to first help people near us who both need our help and will put it to good use. Another excellent way to exercise charity is to fund research in fields that you believe will benefit all of us.

Furthermore, charity must always be a private affair. Its efficiency depends on the free choice of free individuals in deciding where to allocate their giving. Government welfare and foreign-aid programs are inefficient and predatory.

Anyway, don't forget that the first recipient of your giving should always be yourself, especially if you care about others.

## THE ROLE OF THE INDIVIDUAL

Freedom is the ultimate foundation of human nature. Freedom is the ultimate foundation of economics and politics. Freedom is the ultimate foundation of science, technology, the arts, and indeed all human actions.

### *God as the archetype of the individual*

Freedom is equivalent to the boundless side of reality, to the openness of all that is. We can say with the philosophers of old that freedom is the God spark in us and in the world.

Imagine a flint. A piece of flint needs another stone to generate a spark.

Our cities, art, science, technology, philosophies, religions, and political systems all come from the spark that arises when we and the world come together under freedom. Reality—inner and outer, human and natural—is not constrained or bounded in its ultimate core. In other words, reality is ultimately free, and so are you. It is in this sense that philosophers of all times have identified men's freedom with a godlike spark.

For instance, Saint Augustine, a fourth-century Christian philosopher, believed that freedom was what made man godlike. Freedom of choice means an inner boundlessness and unconditioned state.

God is not merely free. God is freedom itself—an unconditioned and boundless state that contains in its unity all possibilities.

Many people would like to live in a predetermined world. Such slave-minded people rejoice in the thought that they are not free, that everything is predetermined, and that free action does not really exist. They think this way because it is how they avoid assuming responsibility for their lives and justify enslaving others.

But the truth is that reality is open to many possibilities and is not determined beforehand. This is why the slaves' mind-set is bound to fail. Slave-minded people end up by finding that what they thought was a secure and predetermined world crumbles and disappears.

The free mind is aware that freedom is the only rule—that is, that there is no rule at all. God, the archetype of ultimate and absolute freedom is, in this sense, the role model for the individual. God is the ultimate individual. This means that God is indivisible and not enslaved to anything existent.

Every individual is ultimately seeking that absolute freedom whose archetype we call God. This takes us to Leibniz and his monad.

## *Leibniz's monad*

Leibniz's monad is a model of the individual. Monads for Leibniz are units that contain the whole of the universe within their perspective. Each monad contains all possibilities, although it is an individual.[58]

Each individual is a monad that contains unbounded possibilities, but in the perspective or point of view of its own individuality. By containing all possibilities and an unconditioned state, each individual is free to choose his or her destiny.

Freedom is the essence of all human beings and what makes us individuals. However, this also means that, as individuals, we can contemplate all reality outside our individuality.

In this sense, all outer reality is within us, because by being able to perceive it, we make it part of ourselves. All this outer reality then enhances our being and opens new possibilities of creation and discovery.

---

[58] Gottfried Wilhelm Leibniz, *The Monadology*, transl. Robert Latta (London: Forgotten Books, 2008).

The simple fact of our being able to observe the stars makes them part of us and enables us to build telescopes and construct theories to explain them. Everything that we integrate with ourselves by understanding or acting on it enlarges our possibilities.

By understanding light, Einstein made it part of himself. By doing so, he discovered relativity and created the basis for releasing atomic energy and its power for practical uses.

Einstein was an individual who, by reflecting nature in his mind like a mirror, made it part of himself. In doing so, he released a new power that had unique consequences in the development of science and technology. Einstein did what he did because he was free. His freedom opened new and previously unknown possibilities to mankind.

## *Bastiat: economist extraordinaire*

Bastiat is the model for all capitalist economists. His thinking was far ahead of his time. He was the first to anchor the principles of economics upon a true understanding of reality.

For this, he used Leibniz as his foundation.

Bastiat believed that God was the model for the individual, following Leibniz's idea that each individual is a monad and that each individual monad is a reflection of the first monad: God, or infinity.

For Bastiat, as for Leibniz, infinity or God is unlimited and unbounded; that is, absolutely free. It is from this absolute freedom that harmony in nature and society comes. Freedom is the source of harmony.

Bastiat distinguishes between true infinity and what is usually called infinite but is, in fact, only indefinite—"for," as he puts it "the infinite admits of no limits."[59] He always uses the word "indefinite" when he refers to what is usually called infinite, such as a series of numbers or a

---

[59] Claude Frédéric Bastiat, *The Bastiat Collection*, 2nd ed. (Auburn, AL: Mises Institute, 2007), p. 489.

series of possibilities. He tells us, "I say indefinite, not infinite, for nothing connected with man is infinite."[60]

The world's resources are indefinite, and thus unlimited in their possibilities, and this is because reality, at its core, is infinite. Indefinite, unlimited possibilities are the worldly mirror image of infinity.

Bastiat sees a world of unlimited or indefinite resources whose foundation is the true infinity that is beyond man.

True infinity works its unlimited, indefinite designs through freedom.

In this sense, only free economics can work. Bastiat was the first and only economist to delve into the source and origin of laissez-faire and the invisible hand. For Bastiat, the "invisible hand," as Adam Smith called it, was none other than the hand of God operating through free human action. This is the reason why man should not interfere with the law of God, or in other words interfere with individual freedom by putting obstacles in the way of it.

For Bastiat, "If the laws of Providence are harmonious, it is when they act with freedom, without which there is not harmony."[61]

For Bastiat, eternal wisdom guides social mechanics to an inherent "universal intelligence," so that an "extraordinary phenomenon" takes place—"that every atom of which it is composed is an animated thinking being, endowed with marvelous energy, and with that principle of all morality, all dignity, all progress, the exclusive attribute of man, LIBERTY."[62]

In Bastiat's view, each individual was a monad, and freedom reconciled the multiplicity of human actions, making them result in harmony.

He thinks, as Leibniz did, that we live in the best of all possible worlds and that reality tends toward improvement. He tells us, "I believe that Evil tends to Good, and calls it forth, whilst Good cannot tend to Evil; whence it follows that Good must in the end predominate."

---

[60] Ibid., p. 499.
[61] Ibid., p. 447.
[62] Ibid., p. 469.

Immediately after, he tells us that the "invincible social tendency is a constant approximation of men toward a common moral, intellectual, and physical level, with, at the same time, a progressive and indefinite elevation of that level."[63]

Bastiat takes free economics to its ultimate consequences.

According to Frédéric Bastiat, Adam Smith, who many consider the father of free economics and capitalism, was far from perfect. Even though he understood free economics as the foundation of prosperity, he misunderstood the relationship between value and matter.

For Adam Smith, Bastiat tells us, "made value to reside in matter"[64] whereas, for Bastiat, value has its foundation in the "the appreciation of services exchanged."[65]

Bastiat emphasizes that "between Matter and Value there is no possible relation." He goes on to tell us that Smith "thus prepared the way for the modern error of the socialists."[66]

So, in Bastiat's opinion, not only Ricardo but also his predecessor Adam Smith unwittingly paved the way for socialism or communism (which are just two names for the same underlying behavior, which Bastiat singles out in one word, "spoliation").

In sum, for Bastiat, freedom is the way of the infinite to create harmony, and only free human action can create prosperity and wealth; furthermore, society cannot but progress towards its own good and ultimate wealth.

Bastiat is the model economist of a bright future and a promising present.

He is the ultimate thinker of capitalism, freedom, and our coming new world.

---

[63] Ibid., p. 449.
[64] Ibid., p. 582.
[65] Ibid., p. 592.
[66] Ibid., pp. 506, 507.

## *The root of freedom for all*

Value creation stems from freedom, as we have already seen. Freedom itself originates from the fact that reality has no bounds. Having no bounds, reality cannot be defined.

Our definition of it is only practical and functional. No one can define what is unbounded, and no word or name does justice to its nature. For our practical purposes, however, the words that we use, words such as "infinite" or "absolute" or "one," are sufficient.

Plotinus, a Greek philosopher of the third century AD, was very wise when he told his pupils to forget the One and not lose time thinking about it. Thought cannot catch it. We have better uses for our time.[67]

However, we must not lose awareness of our own limitations on the one side and the unlimitedness of reality on the other. This awareness is the practical point of departure for all discovery, invention, and entrepreneurship.

# FREEDOM AND ITS SECRET

Freedom, the source of all being and the foundation of value and wealth, has one origin, you. The external freedom of the outer world and your own inner freedom are only known and experienced through you.

## *You are the source of all value*

In this sense, each human being is a monad. You contain the potential of the whole universe in your specific individual perspective. This gives

[67] Plotinus in his *Enneads* says that one should turn away from the One and not think about it—meaning that all thought is limited and will distance us from the One instead of leading us to it. "[The soul] must not even know that it is itself that is applying itself to contemplation of the One." Plotinus, *The Essential Plotinus*, trans. Elmer O'brien, (New York: New American Library, 1964), p. 83.
This paradox, a kind of platonist koan, helps us to understand the difference between conceptual knowledge and real live knowledge.

you unlimited potential for the discovery of both the outer world and your inner realm.

Without a free mind that belongs to our inner reality, no discoveries, nor inventions, nor value creation, nor meaning of any kind would be possible. However, mind also needs the freedom of possibilities and dynamic nature of the outer world.

Therefore, the mind and the world constitute the meeting point of freedom. Consciousness and the world are two sides of the same coin. They are indivisible. Perception is the intersection between them.

## *All power is in us*

So, the value of the material world and all the power that matter can summon comes from our minds. All power is, in this sense, in us. We are the power source that fuels the world and gives energy to society.

All material and spiritual resources come from mind. Mind creates material resources by giving them their purpose and function. Mind also creates spiritual resources by discovering, or unveiling, the universal and invisible principles behind all that is.

In mind, the inner and the outer worlds meld into one resource, the origin of energy, power, and knowledge.

Both the outer and the inner worlds are needed to express the possibilities of man to their fullest. Both were needed to discover the uses of oil, to invent alternating current, to invent calculus, to create the space shuttle, to paint Van Gogh's *Sunflowers,* and to write *Moby Dick*.

Both the mind and the world work only when the mind is free. Freedom enhances human action in all directions. Freedom is what enables obstacles to be bypassed and things to be developed to their full potential.

### *Limits versus no limits*

A person cannot do wrong by having no limits or obstacles and by enjoying full freedom. A common argument against freedom is the fear of having no limits. Such a fear of freedom is based on the faulty belief that freedom can be damaging if it is not controlled.

The opponents of freedom may mention the need for regulations to protect people against themselves and their freedom. For instance, gun-control advocates wish to limit freedom just as drug-control advocates or financial-control advocates do.

Such limiting acts go against freedom, and they are a bad use of the regulator's own free will. Someone who uses his freedom to cause harm to his neighbor is limiting himself. His act is the result, not of freedom, but of an absence of it.

No wrongdoer is truly free. Even if he acted freely, his evil action was contrary to nature and showed inner regulations and obstacles to his inner freedom.

Although every human is free, the development of freedom is not equal for all. Even if, in the eyes of the law and society, we are all equally free, some use their freedom to develop their possibilities, while others use their freedom to restrict them.

Those who do not cultivate their freedom end up losing it. This is what happens to criminals who have been judged guilty and imprisoned. However, this also happens inwardly to people who do not prize their freedom, and thus self-destruct.

For example a person who does not seek to enlarge his knowledge in a given field ends up by losing the ability to make good and informed decisions. He becomes a victim of things he could know about but doesn't, as is the case of a surgeon who does not stay at the cutting edge of his medical field.

Another example would be a person who becomes a victim of his own vices, such as alcoholism, thus losing his mental faculties and his ability to think rationally.

People who limit their freedom do so, not because of their freedom, but because of an inner limitation that pushes them to act against their own freedom. As Socrates rightly said, "All wrongdoing is done in ignorance, for everyone desires only what is good."[68] (This ignorance, of course, is the opposite of the wise ignorance that comes from recognizing reality as boundless. The ignorance that pushes one to wrongdoing comes from not knowing things that are knowable and should be known.)

Since the kind of ignorance behind wrongdoing is a limitation and not a possibility, people who act wrongly do so because of this limit and for no other reason. This means not only that freedom is good, but also that freedom can be used only for good.

Third-world countries are examples of the link between poverty, corruption, government regulations, and lack of freedom.

There is an inverse relation between freedom on the one hand and corruption, misery, bureaucracy, and regulations on the other. Such an inverse relation shows that limits and not freedom are the causes of poverty, both spiritual and material.

Freedom is the basis of capitalism, because freedom is the ultimate capital and first source of all resources, natural and human. All prosperity and wealth are contained in freedom, and freedom is within us.

## *Know thyself*

So, we are back to the source of it all, ourselves. The wisdom of the Socratic dictum "Know thyself" has never been more evident. Only self-knowledge creates prosperity.

Knowledge begins with freedom as our inner core. The more knowledgeable the people of a country are, the wealthier is the country. Human capital is the source of all value.

---

[68] (Protagoras 352 a–c; Gorgias 46b; Meno 77c–78b) *The Complete Works of Plato*, Benjamin Jowett (Translator).

So, self-knowledge of our own freedom is our ultimate capital, the source of our outer and inner worlds. Capital, ultimately, is self-knowledge in action. From here stems all prosperity, individual and collective.

These thoughts take us to the core of government.

# Chapter 13

# Fire Your Government

*You probably know people who run their lives like socialists. They have their lives planned out: whom they will marry, when they will marry, how many children they will have, when they will become a corporate vice president, when they will take over as president, what colleges their children will attend, when they will retire. Such people are almost always disappointed. Something always interferes with their plans. These people think in a linear fashion. They are not resilient to changes in their environment. Neither were the communists.*

— Edgar E. Peters, *Patterns in the Dark*, 1999

We are the true source of political power. The reason is that political power has only one proper function: to guarantee freedom under all circumstances. Social life, as well as individual life, succeeds only when freedom exists.

The magic of the principle of freedom lies in its simplicity. Freedom itself organizes life in a more intelligent way than any regulations could. The concept of the invisible hand has withstood the test of time.[69]

All attempts to destroy freedom have ultimately failed. Freedom always ends with the best answer, the best way. All that we need to do is to let human nature follow its own course.

## ALL POLITICAL POWER COMES FROM YOU

Social freedom is based on individual freedom. There is no freedom other than yours and mine. Once you understand this and enact it in practice, you will discover where the source of all power resides.

Freedom is not abstract, but practical. It means simply that you and I are free to live as we wish, as long as we do not attack and victimize others. The function of law is to enact justice, and justice is intended to preserve freedom.

This means that you are the measure of freedom and society. All you can defend is your own freedom. Even when you think that you are fighting for someone else's freedom, you really are fighting for your own.

---

[69] "The invisible hand of the market" is a term coined by Adam Smith, and used in his *Wealth of Nations* to mean a force that is larger than the force of the individual and his self interest, and that is unleashed when individuals act freely and without coercion.
We could say that a higher and more powerful intelligence is brought into play by the invisible forces of a free market whose action is the composite action of all of its freely acting members when looking for their self interests without harming others in doing so.
We can add that reality has an intelligence of its own that will work for the good of all when left to itself without obstacles.
For Adam Smith, the Invisible Hand was, above all, benevolent. Once more we find a way of thinking in the line of Leibniz and his affirmation that we live in the best of worlds because our world is the best possible that a world can be. Reality tends towards the good!

When you understand or value someone else's freedom, you are understanding or valuing it through the experience of your own freedom. So if freedom for you is anchored in your freedom, and the function of government is to defend freedom, then government can do so above all by defending your freedom. It is you who legitimizes and endorses a government.

## *Fire your government!*

You are the one who gives support to government. You, as an individual, are aware of something called government, which exists out there. However, "out there" is actually within your sphere of consciousness and is thus part of you. Everything that surrounds us, including government, is part of ourselves. Further, you are the one who gives government its power to exist. And the government's existence is important only if it exists for you.

Once you remove government's power to exist, you have dismissed government, and it ceases to exist as far as you are concerned. This is similar to an employee in your business whom you fire because of his inefficiency. He ceases to exist as far as your business is concerned.

So, when your government does not do for you what you, as the master of your freedom, expect it to do, fire it immediately. Fire your government! It will cease to exist.

The consequence of this action is that you will make the world a better place for yourself. However, by firing your government, you will also be providing a service to society and the world. Nothing is easier than firing your government. All that is needed is an infinitesimal shift of consciousness.

No, firing your government has nothing to do with elections. By accepting elections, you are accepting government's conditions. You must not be lured into thinking that you can fire your government through its own procedures. That is exactly what a predatory government wants you to think.

No, firing your government is purely an act of will. It is saying no to government deep within yourself. It has nothing to do with elections or an absence of elections. It is an action from a higher standpoint. "Firing your government" means personally refusing its manipulations, lies, and regulations.

Firing your government is a "no," a refusal of government that comes from deep in the heart. Once you have done it, your thoughts, feelings, and actions will follow. The inner refusal, the first "no," is the strongest power to overturn a government—any government.

Your "no" to government is just the beginning. From then on, you will investigate and find the most intelligent and efficient ways to preserve your freedom and to no longer be enslaved by governments that exist for the sole purpose of preying on you.

Once a single individual frees himself from government, society can free itself too. All that is needed is for you to become free.

This brings us to the strategy and tactics of freedom.

## *The Atlas Shrugged strategy*

Ayn Rand's *Atlas Shrugged* is a science-fiction novel in which the leaders of creative entrepreneurship in the world go on strike. They decide to stop being preyed upon, victimized, and morally blackmailed by government, and simply withdraw from the world, abandoning the "looters" to themselves.

John Galt, the organizer of this strike, is a philosopher, physicist, and engineer who has invented a motor that can work using the static electricity of the air as its energy source. When the company he works for decides to run the factory according to collectivist principles, he abandons his motor and the company.

Galt organizes his strike so as to "stop the motor of the world," bringing the collapse of the bureaucratic society. Galt then manages to work incognito as a laborer for Taggart Transcontinental railroad with the purpose of traveling to contact and recruit key entrepreneurs to join him in his strike.

Galt's two main associates and friends are the entrepreneurs Francisco d'Anconia and Ragnar Danneskjôld.

In a Colorado valley the striking entrepreneurs create a secret enclave, "Galt's Gulch," from which the world can be rebuilt after the collapse of the incompetent government and its bureaucrats—which have lost the sustaining energy of the creative entrepreneurs they once took for granted and looted.

There is a lesson for us in this. Withdrawing from any form of "official" political participation is a way to remove government's main strength. The last thing a government wants is for its citizenry to withdraw, for instance, to abstain from voting, thereby showing a lack of support. Government doesn't mind what your political ideas are, as long as you play their game.

Firing your government through this personal refusal is a nonviolent and nonaggressive method of getting away from government's game.

This idea is the opposite of that used by socialists of all kinds, for whom class struggle is the foundation of society and the instrument of change. Their idea is based on a static concept of value and wealth—a concept of predation, violence, and aggression. The left wing always uses violence, however well disguised it may be. The primary violence consists in preying on the producer to take away his wealth. By doing so, government takes away the producer's fundamental means of defending his own freedom.

If he resists, the government will threaten him at the point of a gun.

All bureaucrats fall into this way of thinking. Their vision and attitude are aggressive and violent, which is typical of the nonproducers, the bullies of society, who extort resources from innocent, well-disposed people.

The roots of this violence are envy and greed—the real motivations hidden behind the clamors for equality. Envy is the sign of people who don't assume responsibility for themselves and who always depend on someone else's work—yours. Greed is what makes them want something for nothing. These are the distinguishing marks of a predator.

These kinds of predators love to ask you what you can do for your country (i.e., for them). The real producer is an independent mind who asks for nothing from anyone, except to be left in peace to achieve his life's goals.

Withdrawal from politics is the anti-predator position, the anti-victim position. It is a responsible, independent attitude. When a game is rigged, you cannot win by playing. Instead, the proper strategy is to withdraw from politics and thus take away the ground on which the politicians stand.

Getting away in a non-violent, Gandhi-like way is the strongest position. It challenges the argument that politicians always work for your individual good. When they do not, you must implement your individual retreat.

A clamor of voices may oppose this plan, saying that if everyone acted like you on behalf of your ideas, some frightening "opposition" would occupy the arena. In Greece, for instance, the most recent bogeymen are the neo-Nazis of the Golden Dawn political party. Much ink has been spilled over how to prevent them from seizing control of society.

But to dwell on the fear of such a political opposition assumes that we have a neutral society that is like a car that some thief can jump into and drive away with.

In fact, you are the car. If you withdraw, your own energy will be spent on more efficient ways of preserving your freedom. Furthermore, the politicians would self-destruct in the long run if entrepreneurs and other able people withdrew from politics to exert their power in other ways.

Withdrawing is the opposite of a passive response. It is an active response. You can take the work of politicians into your hands and do it privately on your own. For example, instead of paying silly taxes, you can contribute an even larger amount to perfect your own business and to finance the causes that you deem to be useful and just.

For instance, you could finance private research on freedom, or finance defense or education, or help students and researchers or artists. Whatever you do with your money, it will be better than what government does with it.

Once you embark on this path, you demonstrate what generosity is all about. You generate value and wealth, while helping others.

## *You can make government disappear*

If you want to have an advantage over government—and you should if you want a life of logic and reason—you must protect yourself by all lawful means available against government predation. By doing so, you help create the conditions in which government will disappear. The government will become weaker as its victims discover ways to avoid being prey in the politicians' hunting ground.

As governments become weaker for lack of victims, they will become harsher and more violent. In this time, we may think that government has regained its force and is even stronger than in the past. However, this will be an illusion. Destruction comes at the apogee, when all signs seem to indicate that things will never change. Reversals are abrupt and come unexpectedly. Just before the Soviet Union fell, it seemed to its inhabitants that nothing would ever change.

Our contemporary form of government will follow the same kind of sudden reversal. Absolute monarchies were destroyed by the printing press. Today, the microchip revolution is destroying national governments.

We must expect big things to happen. A new world will materialize at any moment and in the least expected way. A new religious, political, and financial order will arise, built on the new information technologies.

The reason for the downfall of the old world is because it has not adapted to the new technological level, which, in turn, is the outward side of a new level of intellectual achievement. The new technology will become your tool of liberation. Of course, it will not liberate you by itself, because it is only a tool (although a powerful one that drives new ways of thinking and actions).

This tool will enable you to propel ideas that advance freedom. Society is composed of individuals like yourself. The more you do to preserve your freedom and theirs, the freer and more prosperous you and your society will become.

Do not delegate the preservation of freedom to politicians. Do it yourself.

### *Wake up. It is only a dream.*

The world around you is, in a way, a dream of your consciousness. All you see and perceive is a reflection of who you are. You have educated yourself to perceive the world in a given way.

You, the individual, ultimately create all knowledge and the limits of knowledge. Everything you believe about the world stems from your own consciousness.

Consciousness and freedom are equivalent and directly proportional. The more freedom you have, the more conscious you are. Preserving your individual freedom is preserving your consciousness, your reason, and your logical thinking. Failing to preserve them will lead to your decay—mental, physical, and social.

Your freedom is the ultimate human, social, and economic capital. Your freedom is the primal value on which all else rests. When your freedom is not preserved, neither your neighbors' freedom nor your country's freedom will be preserved.

Therefore, your first task, for yourself and humanity, is to preserve your freedom. You must awaken from the dream that you ought to serve your government, or your country, to the detriment of your freedom.

The only task of society—through government or other means—is to preserve your freedom as an individual. Society is the collection of those free individuals. The interaction and synergy among its members are intended, not to serve society, but to serve individuality—to serve you.

Your first task is to be yourself. Wake up to the real you, to the free individual waiting to deploy all of his or her possibilities. He needs no government to tell him what to do. Instead, he reminds government of his true goals.

Free yourself from government as much as you can, in all areas of your life. In doing so, you will help government to acquire its proper dimension according to its nature.

The proper form of government is a small, efficient government that does not meddle in your life. You have a mission, if you value your freedom, of helping this kind of government to come about. To do this, you must refuse all government intervention that encroaches beyond simply protecting your freedom.

## THE COLLECTIVE MIND

The power of the individual is constantly increasing. This may seem to be a paradox in these times, when governments are tightening all controls. But these increasing restrictions come only as retaliation against the power accrued by the individual.

### *You are not alone*

The individual's power grows as the number of individuals who are conscious of their role and mission becomes larger. This mission consists of protecting individuality for themselves. Steps in this direction are what most helps other individuals too.

Technology enables you to sidestep government controls in many ways. It is easier to communicate today because of the Internet. It is also easier than ever before to travel and to move your business or yourself.

Educational and economic resources have never been so abundant. Self-employment opportunities abound. All of this means that you can escape government control while complying with the laws of your country. You can discover how to become free of the hindrances of government's illegitimate controls.

Government, not the individual, is the first to break the law, and it has done so for the benefit of power- and money-hungry bureaucrats. Many American regulations, for instance, infringe on the individual's legitimate rights as defined in the Bill of Rights.

All that free individuals like you are asking from government is that it be lawful and comply with its limited, legitimate function. Government should not be a tool of depredation.

## *They rely on us*

When government preys on an individual who chooses to become its sacrificial victim, it does so with the victim's consent. All sacrifices are based on consent. Indeed, sacrifice itself is the first predatory act.

Government relies on you to give your consent to be sacrificed and victimized. You are asked to sacrifice your work and your money and your talent for the benefit of a mafia that has created the myth of the public good.

The "public good" is the god you will be sacrificed to. The public good is a euphemism for *them*, those who ask for your money and invoke your moral duty to the state. When you cast a vote, you are giving your consent to be depredated. Each vote is your tithe to the priests whose gods will soon ask for your blood. When you consent to give your blood and your life too, the sacrificial circle will be complete.

However, things could be different. Let us see how.

## *Depredation works when you allow it*

Imagine that you are a regular customer of a restaurant. One day, the food is not as good as on the previous occasion. You decide to give the place another chance and continue to visit it. Alas, on every following visit, the food becomes worse. Finally, you have had enough. You stop frequenting that restaurant.

Other customers leave too. They do so, not because you have told them to, but on their own initiative and because of their own bad experiences. A few months later, the restaurant has a new owner. He changes the menu and quickly recovers the restaurant's old customers.

The previous owner is bankrupt.

Now imagine if instead you make the opposite choice. You continue to frequent that dreadful restaurant, because it is close to your home and you are too tired to travel farther. The owner will thrive on your captivity and will further lower the quality of the food.

It is the same with government and the state. When they give you poor and expensive service, you should not accept it. You should leave. A new owner will come and make things better. However, if you stay and accept the poor and expensive service, you can bet that things will get even worse.

A government is like any other business. It should deliver what you pay for, and you should pay when you deem its offer worthy of your money.

However, politicians want to persuade you to accept a different viewpoint. They tell you that it is your duty to accept ever-lower quality. Their chief argument is that things could be worse. However, you should never accept mediocrity. If you negotiate your way into mediocrity, you will be lost, and everyone else will be too.

So, do not accept bad quality, which is how depredation begins. Whenever you cast your vote, you are giving away your power to decide. And it doesn't stop there. You are also giving your support and endorsement along with your life and your time.

This gesture of support and giving of your time should pay off for you, or else you should withhold it. The day when citizens don't vote, governments will change or go bankrupt. Governments need customers, as every business does.

The primary argument made for voting is that it is your responsibility as a citizen. This is true. It is your responsibility to vote, in return for good service. In the same way, it is your responsibility as a father to send your child to school, but you aren't going to pay for bad teachers.

Your responsibility also is the reason to *not* vote. It is irresponsible as a citizen to vote for mediocre politicians because of the argument that without them things will become worse. Remember, there is an army of willing, would-be politicians lining up to give you what you want.

When politicians discover that you are no longer a willing victim, they will change. Changing their political views and actions will be the only way in which they can continue to make a living from government.

Now, there may be some reason to vote if you find it useful in your individual situation. For instance, if you wish to cast your vote for the least predatory candidate or party, you can. There are many strategies and tactics, and we must not be dogmatic. However, always remember that sometimes it is better not to endorse anyone.

Your choice to give or withhold public support by voting or not voting is, however, a secondary (if not irrelevant) action compared to your mission as a free individual. All of your actions to support your own freedom must take priority.

When you help with education or publishing or any activity to make people understand what it means to be free and to have an entrepreneurial spirit, you are acting politically in the real sense of the word. And when you legally avoid paying money for government predation, even at the price of relocating, it will be more effective than casting or not casting a vote. The important thing is your individual action.

Remember, the main tenet of a free individual is that he does not prey on anyone or lean on anyone. He is self-sufficient in the sense that he begins action within his own sphere. There is nothing more powerful than a team of self-sufficient individuals.

Freeing yourself is the first and fundamental political act. Do it now.

All it takes is turning your mind in the right direction. Your actions will speak volumes to people around you and mean more, even though you are just one individual, than the meaningless words of most politicians.

It comes down to a simple idea. You are free, and always were. All you must do is realize this within yourself.

## FREEDOM ALWAYS WINS

However, freedom goes beyond individuality. It is a principle of reality. Reality is free and unbounded.

The universe is in fact ruled by the free interplay of forces. Here, freedom means that possibilities are always open, not forever fixed within certain boundaries. Forces are always adjusting in order to keep all things in balanced movement. Reality always imposes itself because, in this interplay of forces, the most efficient always wins.

Individuals do not fully control these forces. For instance, different ideological groups will fight, just as peoples or countries go to war on a large scale.

The winner is the most powerful one—the one who best followed the rules of reason and logic in his specific field. Winning does not mean that the victorious force was necessarily right or wrong or good or evil.

For example, communism won for a time in Russia, Cuba, and China because its leaders were more able than their opposition. They won because they had reason on their side in how they used tactics and strategy to seize power.

Nevertheless, capturing power did not mean that their ideas were strong or true at the economic and political level. They were not. They denied human nature and its political and economic foundations. Though communism won power temporarily, it lost at the economic level and condemned the countries it enslaved to poverty, misery, and deprivation.

We say this to indicate a higher interplay of forces. Here too the invisible hand is at work, at a higher level. In this higher sense, too, laissez-faire is fully functional.

This means that freedom is the ground of reality itself. Ultimately, freedom wins. At the level of human action, freedom necessarily wins, because freedom means going with the flow of human nature.

So, we can confidently believe that freedom and the enhancement of human nature are in our future. This is not a blind belief, but one based on reason, logic, and the lessons of history.

When you strive for individual freedom, you are in harmony with the sense of history, its meaning and its destiny.

# Chapter 14

# Politicians! Do Not Read This Chapter!

*The basic tool for the manipulation of reality is the manipulation of words. If you can control the meaning of words, you can control the people who must use the words.*

—Philip K. Dick, "How to Build a Universe That Doesn't Fall Apart Two Days Later," 1978

Politicians depend on votes—your votes. This makes political action a contest to win votes. The more loyal voters he has, the greater the probability that the politician will win the election. He knows that and acts accordingly.

## GOVERNMENT IS YOUR ENEMY

This means that he will say or promise whatever will ensure that he will obtain the raw numbers he needs. Quantity rules, not truth. Quantity of voters is a mathematical need of the political game itself. When you go against it, you lose. It's a law of politics. All efforts against it are useless.

## *All politicians are liars*

Of course, this is because, once the politician has been elected, the people are defenseless and have no way to force him to fulfill his promises. What must be emphasized is that politicians cannot act differently. They must lie or perish, whatever their political programs may be. They lie because the system has no safeguards against their lies.

Politicians should be legally bound by their promises and pay indemnities when they lie. They are not so bound today because they have a captive and defenseless population, their willing victims, whose opinion they control.

However, things could—and perhaps soon will—be different. To understand this, let us contrast the entrepreneur with the politician.

## *All entrepreneurs tell the truth*

True entrepreneurs are the opposite of politicians. Politicians have a no-risk monopoly over a defenseless population on which they can prey at will. Not so entrepreneurs.

While a politician must lie and prey on his constituents to survive, an entrepreneur must take risks and must tell the truth if he is to survive. The population can freely accept or refuse the products and services that entrepreneurs propose. Nothing requires you to buy a car if you don't want to. And when you buy a car, nobody points a gun at you to ensure that you choose a particular brand.

The entrepreneur makes his living by real votes in a real, invisible democracy. When you buy from him, you choose what to buy and your choice is at the same time a vote. Voting and choosing are truly one. As Ludwig von Mises wrote, "The market is a democracy in which every penny gives a right to vote," and thus, "the consumers are supreme."[70]

When the entrepreneur stops delivering quality, you, the consumer, can stop buying from him and go to someone else who satisfies your needs. Recall the example from chapter 13 of a restaurant where quality declines: you can simply choose to eat elsewhere, and in so doing withdraw your support from the owner. Having choices is not only true capitalism, but true democracy.

The way that entrepreneurs are is the way that governments should be. However, governments do not like to be told this. Instead, many politicians would like to see businesses behave as governments do. This is why socialists, left-wingers, and collectivists of all kind are against competition. They would like to have uniform markets with uniform products and single prices that don't fluctuate. In other words, they would like to see markets behave like governments, and businessmen behave like politicians.

All their efforts are bound to fail. The invisible hand and laissez-faire will win in the end.

## *Lies self-destruct*

What is not real can survive as an illusion for a while, but sooner rather than later it will self-destruct and disappear. This happened to the Soviet Union and to all governments that have attempted to rule against human nature.

Truthful governments could arrive sooner than we think, as the new technologies make lying more and more difficult. Today, all is known and exposed. No one can hide behind a cloak of invisibility. People can see who the politicians are on television. Blogs and online videos expose their lives and actions and, most importantly, what people actually think about them.

---

[70] Ludwig von Mises, *Planned Chaos* (Auburn, AL: Mises Institute, 2009).

Society is changing at an increasing rate. A silent and invisible revolution, led by the microchip, is on its way.

The power of logic, mathematics, and the computer, made possible by electronics, is making this revolution unstoppable.

Children are more familiar with these media today than adults, who are still living with the memories of the precomputer age. Children are also symbols of the destruction of lies that this new technology is causing. Children have an innate ability to spot lies. In this sense, the new media have made children of all of us. They have given us a new awareness of the world.

The fear of this awareness is why bureaucrats and collectivists often hate new technologies and think of all kinds of arguments to try to control them. But attempts to control technology will be in vain. Technologies and the industrial society are the result of human intelligence surviving and thriving. They cannot be stopped.

## THE POLITICIANS HAVE ALREADY BEEN DESTROYED

### *Politicians self-destruct*

A further word about politicians. We have proved they must lie to survive in their jobs. Lying is the foundation of their self-destruction. Today, the politicians cannot hold their positions for much longer, because people realize who they truly are.

Politicians today are accepted only as necessary evils. A politician is a kind of puppet who must abase himself to please the population in order to remain in office. Politicians will go to events they hate, endorse people they despise, dress in ridiculous ways, and do whatever is needed to be popular.

The people know and feel this. They are not fooled, and a distance is now opening up between them and the politicians. People accept politicians as necessary evils that they hate and revere at the same time. This hatred and reverence generates a schizoid behavior in society.

## *Politicians don't even believe in themselves*

I have explained why politicians must lie. We have seen that this cannot be avoided while populations are defenseless against predation.

The primary victims of this state of affairs are the politicians themselves. They know that they lie and they know that they must do so. This awareness erodes their confidence and renders them mediocre and shallow.

So politicians are constantly and subconsciously reinforcing their own corruption and weakness. They progressively lose confidence, strength, and ultimately power.

Politicians would love to believe in themselves, but they know that they can't. The politicians feel like traitors to themselves. They too feel helpless.

The people rightly feel that politicians do not have self-respect, and the people have witnessed the politicians' failures to keep their promises. This means that the politician has already lost power and authority.

All of these politicians will become more and more powerless and less and less respected and feared. As a result, their political world will slowly vanish. Governments and states in their present form will disappear.

## *Why states are doomed*

Today's politicians are anti-entrepreneurial: their behaviors and attitudes are opposed to the entrepreneurial spirit. The same can be said of most governments.

Governments are collectivist incursions into a capitalist world. They would like to make the market a mirror of what they are. Because they have failed at this, they are forced today to compromise with entrepreneurial forces.

The socialist structure of most governments, even in capitalist countries, is what makes them fail. People, even in the first world, have no say in the decisions of government, just as the Soviet people could do nothing against the Politburo in Moscow. Once the voters put the government in office, they can do nothing about it.

However, the failure of these governments to serve their people will give rise to a political system where people will have a real choice and elective power. As today's politicians lie more, work less, and depredate more, many of them will disappear. A tendency toward the truth will arise, and a new kind of politician will appear. However, he will not be a politician in the sense that the word has today.

He will be a political entrepreneur in a true democracy, not in a simulated parody of a democracy, like the majority of countries have today.

Then the world will experience a new leap in prosperity.

## *A happy world without politicians*

The old politicians will be replaced by a new kind of politician. This new kind of politician will in fact be an entrepreneur. He will sell services to the population, who will buy them on the condition that the services deliver what the consumers actually want. Politicians will abandon all welfare programs. Instead, the politician will be hired to manage affairs for those who pay him to deliver results.

He will sign a contract that specifies exactly what he will deliver during his term of office. This contract will include severe penalties for any failure to fulfill its clauses. For the first time in history, the politician will be accountable to society. Any citizen will have the power to sue a politician who fails to deliver—and receive a payment in indemnity.

Anyone who does not want to live in a territory where free individuals make the law will go somewhere else. For example, there could be socialist countries where the fans of old-style politicians and socialists could go to live in poverty and misery.

Just as you choose a car, you could choose the country that has a system you like. One who did exactly this was Socrates, Plato's mentor. Socrates said that people were free to choose where to live and under which constitution or form of government. For Socrates, you could choose the country that endorsed your way of life.[71]

For Socrates, this link to one's life was that, once you had chosen the country in which you wanted to live, you had to abide by its rules, defend it, and live by its ideals. Abiding by your own choice is logical and sensible. The country becomes an extension of you as a free individual.

As a sidenote, Socrates warned us of politicians. He said that politics was a risky business in which life was at stake. And he became an example of the danger he had warned of. Although Socrates was not a politician his ideas were so troublesome because of their truth that the jury condemned him to death.[72]

## THE INTELLIGENT ALTERNATIVE

True revolutions follow reality. They never go against it. They never begin aggression. They break down limits and defend themselves from those who initiate aggression.

True revolutions are silent. They operate from the bottom up. They start in the deepest core of reality and thought. This core is human action itself.

---

[71] Socrates, in "Crito," explains why he complies with his death penalty instead of fleeing from Athens. The reason was that he had chosen Athens and its laws as fully compatible with his being a free man with an educational vocation. Socrates could have chosen to flee Athens and live in another city, but he did not. He chose to live and to die by the laws of his city, because accepting exile would have meant abdicating his freedom and life. The emphasis is on Socrates as a free man, His choice of Athens as the country he lived in was a consequence of his freedom.
No one has any obligation to live in a country that restricts his freedom and ends his life. Socrates knew this better than anyone and lived and died accordingly. See Plato, *The Trial and Death of Socrates: Four Dialogues*, trans. Benjamin Jowett (New York: Dover, 1992).

[72] Ibid.

True revolutionaries are people like Socrates, Aristotle, Gutenberg, Leibniz, Newton, the Wright brothers, Edison, Tesla, Einstein, and Gödel.

Once again, free individuals rule. The reason for human change is to make life better. All creators, philosophers, scientists, and successful entrepreneurs did what they did because they enjoyed it. They loved what they did. If they had had to stop, they would have died. In fact, Socrates preferred to receive the death penalty rather than abandon his teaching of free thought.

## *True revolutionaries change themselves for their own sakes*

Only our actions as free individuals create the tools that change society for the prosperity of all. As Leibniz understood, each individual is a monad, a kind of center that radiates outward to the whole and, at the same time, mirrors the whole.

This is why self-change to make ourselves freer and better develops our inner and outer possibilities, and in turn reflects and improves the world. We contribute best to the world by creating value and wealth for our own sake.

Selflessness is not only a contradiction, but an insult to humanity. The selfless person gives what he does not need or does not want for himself. The value generator is never selfless. He loves and enjoys what he creates, and he thinks it is so valuable that he rejoices in giving it to himself. He becomes so wealthy through his value creation that he wants to share it with others, rather than merely giving it away and losing it for himself.

We can only give what we have. The selfless man values nothing and finally gives nothing. He is a parody of generosity that hides an egocentrism dependent on other people's opinions.

This kind of person lives for others and not for himself, because he has nothing to give except his time and space. Imagine for a moment Edison and Einstein devoting their entire lives to helping the poor.

If they had done that, the world would have lost electricity and nuclear power plants. The world would be less prosperous and the poor would be much poorer than today. The same goes for all the other inventors and entrepreneurs—indeed, all the other creative people—in history.

So, the best thing that you can do for the world and society at large is to become valuable and wealthy yourself. When you do, you will contribute to changing the world for the better in the fastest possible way.

We must emphasize this point. Nothing changes the world like self-change. The best that can happen for other people is for you to realize the need for self-change.

By self-change, we mean concentrating on achieving maximum freedom and its benefits, including wealth. When the individual creates value and wealth, he benefits not only himself but also society.

A single individual—this is all that is needed to change a world or to create a new one.

## *The technological gap*

In a few generations, the technological gap relative to where we are today will be huge. We cannot anticipate what the new technology will be. We can only guess that it will further abolish the barriers of time and space, as all technology has done so far.

All of this will enlarge the individual. Today, governments are becoming powerless while individuals are gaining power and influence. World changes come mainly from individuals. Think of the important changes of the last forty years, and you will discover creative individuals behind many of them.

Think of the persons who invented the computer, or of the persons who developed the Web or the cell phone or computer operating systems. These people have done more to change the world than all politicians put together.

# Chapter 15

# Sailing to New Horizons

*God grants liberty only to those who love it and are always ready to guard and defend it.*

— Daniel Webster, speech before the US Senate, June 3, 1834

The printing-press revolution and the microchip revolution, along with advances in mathematics, logic, linguistics, and electronics, have given the mind new tools with which to expand its horizons and develop itself.

## THE LAST FRONTIER FOR THE TRUE ADVENTURERS

All of this helps us to discover our true nature, and the nature of the universe in which we live. New ways of looking at ourselves have enriched our self-knowledge and enhanced the adventures we experience in travelling through life. So, technology is a tool that the mind has given itself to enlarge its own scope.

## *The universe of mind is limitless*

The mind can continue to build on itself as long as it is free. The freer a mind is, the more developed it will be, the more value it will create, and the more wealthy it will become. The freer a mind is, the greater will be its contributions to society and to itself.

Now, these possibilities of the mind are the foundation of all prosperity, individual and social. However, they come with a condition: to be truly free, the individual must *choose* freedom. This means leading a responsible, conscious life that cares for itself and the lives of others. It also means choosing to respect other individuals in their time, work, and lives.

To be free, you must choose freedom. Nothing can replace your own choice.

## *Freedom is a choice*

There is freedom because the individual chooses to be free. A free society is a society in which the majority of its members have chosen freedom and developed its potential. They are conscious of the responsibility and advantages of freedom.

Where freedom is not valued, you don't have a free society, and where you don't have a free society, you don't have free individuals.

This is the case in third-world countries. Corruption, regulations, and bureaucratic hassles are common in third-world countries, because most of their people don't care to be free.

They don't value freedom because they don't understand it. This lack of understanding is why their bureaucrats act blindly, without respect or care for other people's time, work, or lives.

Here we encounter the paradox of freedom. Only when freedom is understood and valued can it be chosen as a way of life. But this choice for freedom is itself the foundation of an understanding of freedom and the beginning of the education of a free mind.

This makes us ask what comes first—education or freedom?

A possible answer is that freedom comes first as an attitude. In this sense, freedom would originate not in a theoretical kind of education, but in active principles of behavior learned in the family by tradition. If this is true, then tradition would be the root of freedom as an attitude towards life. A tradition of freedom would be ingrained in the life and mental habits of creators of all kinds and of independent-minded people and families .

However, we do not know the ultimate answer. All that we can be certain of is that some people and societies value their freedom more than others do. And we also know that there is a direct link between freedom and prosperity.

## *Happiness is a choice*

We can also say that happiness accompanies independence, and that unhappiness accompanies dependence. This means that unhappiness is the result of an individual not mastering his own life and of a society not mastering its life.

Happiness is the opposite. It means mastery over one's own life, either as an individual or as a society. Happy individuals and happy societies are in control of their lives. They are not mentally dependent on exterior events.

These two ways of being are attitudes. Unhappy societies blame an exterior cause for their misery. Happy societies accept responsibility for themselves and blame no one for their own failures.

Adopting the responsible attitude is a choice. This choice makes the difference between prosperity and wealth on the one hand or poverty and misery on the other—for countries and individuals alike. Either your life is in your own hands, or it is in the hands of a malevolent deity.

## *Life is a choice*

Once many of the people in a country have chosen freedom, the consequences manifest themselves.

These consequences are brought about by free-roaming minds that explore the possibilities of thought and action and make themselves effective in practical ways. When this happens, value creation and wealth conversion are the necessary and unavoidable outcomes.

Choosing freedom means having a will to live a life of value creation that generates many kinds of wealth.

Choosing not to be free is choosing against life and human nature. Additionally, whoever refuses freedom for himself refuses it also for his neighbors. He thus becomes, in a sense, an aggressor against human nature and free individuals.

Whenever a democracy chooses to let its people be enslaved, any insurrection of the few who want freedom against the many who do not is legitimate. An example was the struggle against Hitler, whose Nazi Party won elections democratically.

The free individual must put no boundaries on the defense of his freedom, so long as he does not restrict the freedom of others. He cannot allow anyone to transgress against his life and freedom.

## YOU ARE ABOVE ALL RULES

Rules are intended to serve you. You are not meant to serve them. The purpose of rules is to enhance human life. They are human creations that must be flexible and adapt to circumstances. When rules do not recognize you as a center, an autonomous individual, they are useless to you.

However, this is true not only of you, a center around which all that you call your world and society revolves. It is true also of all the other individuals around you, each of whom is a center around which the world and society revolve.

So, all individuals are in the same condition and circumstance. Government is a part of you, meant to serve you so that you will be able to exercise your freedom and develop all your possibilities of action and life.

Therefore, you must comply with government only so far as government complies with you. If you comply more than this, you will be the victim of predation and lose your true nature in favor of powers that will enslave you.

The way out is to realize that you are the reason for government's existence. The individual is above the collectivity. The reason for this is that you are free; you are your own center, and you are the center of the world as far as you are concerned.

Therefore, you do not belong to government, but government belongs to you.

## *You do not belong to the state*

You have no obligation or duty toward the government unless you so decide on the grounds that it is convenient for you.

A government only deserves your allegiance if it delivers what you are paying it for. Further, when it is acting for your benefit, you will benefit others too.

All other people, like you, are asking that you be yourself first. To love others, or to do something for others, you must love yourself and serve yourself first. No one can give what he does not have.

This is true in life, in logic, and in mathematics. Logic tells us that in order to give, you must have what you want to give. Mathematics tells us that from zero nothing can come but zero. What both logic and mathematics prove is that you can give only what you are.

All that comes from you originates in what you are yourself. The best gift that an individual can give to another is his own fully deployed being. Einstein's and Mozart's best gifts to humanity were themselves, which included their creations.

Protect your freedom and be yourself. Forget government. It is only the manager you have appointed to take care of a limited sector of your own reality.

## *Seed thoughts*

Once everyone realizes government's true function, everything will change.

No aggression or violent revolution is needed. A simple shift of focus is all we need to transform society. The revolution of the individual that we are witnessing today is the lazy man's revolution.

Once this shift of focus occurs in one individual, all the rest will follow naturally. Tiny causes can have exponential effects. Saint Augustine and other philosophers of ancient times had the right expression for this. They called these small causes *rationes seminales.* The meaning of the term is "seminal virtues" or "seed thoughts" All that is needed is a single "seed thought" to change the world. Tesla did so with his alternating-current generator. Here was a single inventor with his single invention and his single, nonviolent, silent revolution.

## *Have the courage to be yourself*

Once the individual recognizes that he is the center of power in his world, it is time for the next step: after recognition must come action. But not everyone can easily translate a concept or feeling into action. An individual needs courage to take this next step.

Many will abdicate their individuality for the sake of platitudes from the media and their entourage. They will stay under the spell of government employees who act as the arbiters of what the population should think and do.

To defend himself from predatory politicians, an individual must begin by realizing his own power. Once he recognizes his power and acts on that recognition, the politicians disappear and government fades into nothingness.

Recognize that you are already in control. Then take action to exercise that control.

## *Comply while acting*

Once the individual realizes his full control, his perspective will change. He will understand governments for what they are, management organizations that enable people to live together without being the victims of government whims.

Realizing his full power does not mean that the individual should refuse all politicians and all aspects of government. It means the refusal of politicians and governments *as depredators and victimizers of innocent and defenseless citizens.*

Some politicians have been exceptions to the rule and have tried to direct government along a path of noninterference with the individual's freedom. That was the case with Margaret Thatcher and Ronald Reagan. But politicians of this stature are rare. And of course, even they had to act within a predatory machine that could not be fully stopped.

The government under which you live has countless opportunities to prey on the individual. In such circumstances, it is important to comply with the rules when that is possible and convenient. However, compliance is not a duty. It means nothing more than trying to make the system work for you.

For example, in attempting to avoid taxes, you should work within the law—as long as the law does not enforce regulations that would spell the ruin of you, you family, or your business. The dividing line lies precisely where complying becomes more dangerous than refusing to comply.

However, even when complying, the individual should actively seek ways to avoid government predation. This might include such measures as relocating your business or your family or yourself. Similarly, you should not make it easy for government to part you from your money. Instead, put your money away safely.

This kind of compliance subtly exerts pressure on government in two ways. First, government cannot react violently against compliance. Second, the combination of complying and progressively minimizing what government can take away from you pulls the ground out from under predatory governments.

Government will discover that it is losing ground and has no opportunity for immediate attack, such as accusing you of tax evasion. It cannot recover its lost ground unless it changes its ways.

Finally, this nonviolent way of acting against the government by attempting to escape government aggression within the law has another benefit: it enables the individual to fight government in the most important arena of all, the arena of ideas and actions that support freedom. Government will be helpless to counter such actions when they come from lawfully complying individuals.

Supporting freedom within the law is the strongest weapon of all. In this mission, the individual will take full responsibility for freedom as the foundation of value, wealth, and prosperity, and will look for the best ways to defend it.

## *Find your true calling*

The best way to defend freedom is to use it in a fully conscious way in your life and business. Freedom starts by assuming that you are the source of what happens to you. You are responsible for your acts, so act for yourself.

You can defend freedom by outwardly supporting the causes, persons, or institutions that will help the cause of freedom. However, the best defense of freedom is the inner defense that efficiently uses the space of action and thought that freedom allows you.

This means having an entrepreneurial spirit. As an entrepreneur, you use your freedom to act as an independent, thinking being. The term entrepreneur, as stated earlier, is not restricted here to its normal use in the world of business. Broadly, being an entrepreneur means beginning new ventures and carrying them out to create new possibilities of value and wealth.

The entrepreneurial spirit assumes a dynamic concept of value and wealth. The entrepreneurial spirit thus sees the world as a field of opportunity where resources are unlimited.

Let us see how the entrepreneurial spirit can help change the world, especially today's third-world countries, and help them find the road to prosperity.

This change is governed by a simple formula. All that we must do is eliminate obstacles. Let us take a look at this formula.

# Chapter 16

# The Prosperous Economy Formula

The only way to achieve prosperity is by avoiding the misallocation of assets. Entrepreneurs naturally allocate assets optimally throughout society, because when they fail to do so, the market immediately punishes them and removes them from their positions. Thus, misallocation is almost always the result of an arbitrary, artificial government control that is not in harmony with the invisible hand of the market. A country can gain prosperity by simply avoiding this error.

## THE SIMPLE FORMULA FOR THE WEALTH OF COUNTRIES

To accomplish this, the entrepreneurs, who discover, invent, or produce value and then offer it, converting it to wealth, must be left free to decide for themselves how to use their earnings. This means the government must not take the products of their minds away from them.

Avoiding misallocation naturally makes the rich richer. That is what we want. In fact, the more efficiently the rich allocate their assets, the richer they will become. The gap between the rich and the poor creates a tension that builds energy and distributes wealth. Widening the wealth gap not only enables the rich become more rich, but also enables the poor become less poor.

## *Widening the gap through natural wealth distribution*

The wealth gap is the secret to wealth. It is a mistake to try to diminish this gap. Diminishing it abolishes the creative tension between rich and poor, and it also misallocates resources, letting them fall into the hands of unproductive people and thus preventing their most efficient use.

To understand this, we must take our point of view to its limit. Imagine that fifty years ago you had taken away all resources from computer entrepreneurs and given those resources to charities with the purpose of feeding the needy.

In that case, our world would be without computers, cell phones, or all the technologies that use them. We would be much poorer, and the number of people who live in misery would be overwhelming.

In contrast, by leaving entrepreneurs alone to widen the gap, we can efficiently build the productive energy and wealth tension that are conducive to prosperity. By simply not taking the product of entrepreneurs' work away from them, and by leaving them to decide what do with their own earnings, we can take a big step toward full world prosperity.

The first law of prosperity for countries is to widen the gap between the rich and the poor so that both can become richer.

Now let us examine the second law of prosperity.

## *Developing a creative critical mass: clustering talent*

We have explained that a critical mass is essential for a society to grow in a given direction. Society follows its critical mass. When a society has a critical mass of creators, inventors and entrepreneurs, it will become more and more prosperous.

Societies like those of Western Europe and the USA have a critical mass of creators and innovators that enables them to be technological and industrial societies.

Remember that a technological society is not merely one that uses technology but one that creates it. Most third-world countries call themselves technological, modern societies because they are on the receiving end of science and technology. A truly technological society is on the giving end of creation and research.

Most third-world thinkers and professors are at the receiving end only. They are followers and never leaders. They are directed by the influences and fashions of first-world academia. Unable to think for themselves, they borrow their thinking from the first world.

The physicist Richard Feynman became aware of this when he spent a year teaching at a Brazilian university.[73] He discovered a lack of creativity among professors and students alike. He realized that there is a difference between first-world minds and third-world minds.

Feynman observed that the first time the students were asked a question, they could answer it, but days later, when asked the same question, they could not answer it. This triggered Feynman's interest. He discovered many other student behaviors that had the same underlying cause as the first one he had observed.

For example, in an oral exam that Feynman observed, "one of the students was absolutely super: He answered everything nifty!" But by that time Feynman was suspicious. So after the exam, he asked the student to answer some questions that would have no effect on the results of his exam.

One of Feynman's questions was, "If this book was made of glass, and I was looking at something on the table through it, what would happen to the image if I tilted the glass?" The student gave a wrong answer. He

---

[73] *Surely You're Joking, Mr. Feynman!* (New York: W.W. Norton, 1985), pp. 211–219.

answered as if Feynman had asked about a mirror and not a transparent material.

What most struck Feynman was that the question was one of the questions that had just been asked in the student's exam. But in the exam, the question had been worded like this: "When light comes at an angle through a sheet of material with a certain thickness, and a certain index N, what happens to the light?" The student had answered, "It comes out parallel to itself, sir—displaced." Correct!

And, Feynman noted, "He had even figured out how *much* it would be displaced, but he didn't realize that a piece of glass is a material with an index, and that his calculation had applied to my question." The reason was that the student's knowledge was obtained by rote memorization that enabled him to answer theoretical questions (if they were worded pretty much the same way in the exam as they had been in his textbook or lecture notes) but without realizing their true significance and link to reality.

According to Feynman, all those students and their teachers understood nothing about physics.

Feynman says about his students, "One other thing that I could never get them to do was to ask questions." He tells us that, among students, "It was a kind of one-upmanship, where nobody knows what's going on, and they'd put the other one down as if they *did* know. They all fake that they know."

He also could not get them to work together and discuss the questions among themselves "because they would be losing face if they had to ask someone else. It was pitiful."

At the end of the academic year, Feynman was asked to give a talk for students and faculty about his experiences of teaching in Brazil. When he began his lecture, he told his Brazilian audience that the "main purpose" of his talk was to "demonstrate to you that no science is being taught in Brazil." Feynman noted that in Brazil many young people bought books on physics and started studying them earlier than in the USA. And he said, "It's amazing you don't find many physicists in Brazil—why is that? So many kids are working so hard, and nothing comes of it.

Then he gave an analogy of a scholar of Greek classics, who could not answer when asked for the relationship between Truth and Beauty according to Socrates, but who could answer readily when asked about what Socrates says to Plato in the Third Symposium. "But," said Feynman, "What Socrates was talking about in the Third Symposium was the relationship between Truth and Beauty." In other words, the scholar could recite, but had no understanding of the meaning.

Next, Feynman analyzed the Brazilian university's freshman physics textbook. He pointed out that there was only one experiment mentioned in the book, and then he showed that that experiment was a fake experiment. The experiment consisted of rolling a ball down an inclined plane and recording how far the ball had gone after one second, two seconds, three seconds, and so on. The author gave what he said were data from the experiment, and then he used those data to compute the acceleration constant.

Feynman pointed out that the data must be bogus because the author got the correct value for the acceleration constant, even though he used the wrong method to compute it. The method he used would have given him five-sevenths of the correct value if he had used real data from the experiment he had described. So, Feynman says, the author of the textbook did not even perform the only experiment mentioned in it.

Feynman told his audience, "I have discovered something else. By flipping the pages at random and putting my finger in, and reading the sentence on that page, I can show you what's the matter—how it's not science, but memorizing, in every circumstance." And he took the same Brazilian textbook and in front of his audience randomly selected a page in the book and read: "Triboluminescence. Triboluminescence is the light emitted when crystals are crushed." Then he told his audience that the definition he had just read was not science, but only the meaning of a word told in terms of other words.

Regarding the ending of his talk to students and faculty, Feynman says:

> Finally, I said that I couldn't see how anyone could be educated by this self-propagating system in which people pass exams, and teach others to pass exams, but nobody knows anything. "However," I said, "I must be wrong. There were two students in my class who did very well, and one of the physicists I know was educated entirely in Brazil."

But a little later, one after another, the two students and the professor whom Feynman had mentioned each got up and spoke to the audience. It turned out that one of the students had been educated in Germany and had just come to Brazil, and the other student had something similar to say. And the professor who had been educated in Brazil was self-taught during the war, when the university had no professors because they had all left!

Feynman heard later that a person in the State Department, having learned of Feynman's criticisms of physics education in Brazil, had said that Feynman was naive and could only cause trouble. Feynman said of that official, "I think this person…was naive to think that because he saw a university with a list of courses and descriptions, that's what it was."

Feynman' teaching in Brazil shows the difference between true science and fake science. What Feynman experienced is what happens in third-world countries where often not only is there no real understanding of science, but—what is worse—teachers and students think that they are really learning and doing science.

Mathematics and physics are not about formulas and definitions, but about the ideas and realities underlying them.

Feynman's experience shows in the area of science teaching what we have said about technology. Just as being technologically developed means not being surrounded by technology but the ability to create ex nihilo, having an understanding of science does not mean rote memorization or rote manipulation and application of formulas without understanding the ideas behind them and without the ability to create and discover.

Third-world countries are at the receiving end and not at the giving end of science and technology. This is not to deny that in the third-world there may be some first-rate minds. What we are saying is that these people do not form a critical mass sufficiently large to change the character of their societies.

Remember, no third-world country has invented anything of significance in technology. Fundamental inventions like the electric motor, the light bulb, the airplane, radio, television, and the computer were all invented in first-world countries. Only these countries have the critical mass that allows them to invent or create the foundation of their prosperity. Such prosperity and value creation can be checked by looking at the number of useful patents a country has.

So, the second law of prosperity is the law of critical mass: a critical mass of inventors, creators, and entrepreneurs must be accumulated.

Let us now examine the third law of prosperity, which tells us how to accumulate such a critical mass of creative and productive agents.

## *Creating the joy of living*

Many politicians ask themselves why capital and minds flee their countries. The answer is that the creators and entrepreneurs, and their money, receive better treatment elsewhere.

These politicians, instead of asking why capital and minds flee, should be asking a different question. They must seek to understand the secret of those countries that attract capital and minds to themselves.

We have seen that society can be like an emulsion. People who are alike go and join their peers. It is as if they were oil bubbles mixed with water by agitation. When the water has become calm, the oil particles gather together and coalesce.

The same happens with talent. Talent seeks talent. When talent is momentarily scattered, its tendency is to come together. The momentary emulsion of scattered talent tends to separate itself from the surrounding population and join the critical mass of talent in the main clusters. This is why talented people are clustered in specific geographical zones in our world.

Most mental talent is clustered in the northern hemisphere, and talent from around the world attempts to join the zones where the clusters are, whether in the USA, Canada, Western Europe, or, to a lesser degree, Australia and New Zealand.

Now, a question to ask is why this happens.

Talent clusters in a critical mass where it finds better conditions and opportunities for life. In other words, talent goes where it can find greater pleasure and joy in life.

The joy of living and creating, and the pleasure of inventing things or creating enterprises that require first-rate minds, comes from deregulation. Superior minds will flee the hassles and obstacles that regulation puts in the way of their work of creation.

Most poor countries are full of regulations that are not conducive to the development of first-rate minds. To begin with, these minds cannot find the tools or books that they need, nor can they import them easily. Bureaucratic hassles make this difficult, if not impossible.

Only in first-world countries do first-rate minds find the comfort and ease of work that enable their ideas and actions to reach their full potential. The number of first-rate minds in a country is in direct relation to the absence of government regulations, which place obstacles in the way of creative individuals.

These obstacles are the reason why third-world countries have easy, low-cost, living, in the form of low wages and cheap food and accommodations. In these countries, time and work have less market value, making the cost of living and space cheaper than in first-world countries. As always, you get what you pay for.

Regulations, and the obstacles they produce, kill the possibility of having first-rate individuals with first-rate minds gather together and increase in number. Those numbers, when they eventually reach a critical mass, are the only thing capable of transforming a society into a creative, inventive, truly technological society, which gives science and technology to the world.

Thus, the third law of prosperity is the law of deregulation as the path to a happy and joyful life that will attract first-rate minds and encourage them to stay and develop their talents and aptitudes.

To apply the third law, governments must deregulate everything. The more deregulation there is, the more stimulating will be the conditions for first-rate minds. And first-rate minds are both a measure and a cause of a society's prosperity.

## HOW TO PUT THE FORMULA INTO ACTION

As long as people perceive value and wealth as static, invention and creativity cannot uncover new value, and prosperity will lag. Third-world countries, as explained in chapter 2, see value and wealth as static and earthly, and their politicians use such words as "innovation" or "technology" without any understanding of their real meaning.

This static mentality conceives of value and wealth as limited (in the model of land possession within definite boundaries); thus, it assumes that wealth can be obtained only by taking it away, from someone else, legally or illegally. The world, in this view, is a gladiators' arena. This is a malevolent idea, conducive to exploitation and abuse. Its answer to poverty lies in class struggle, including violence, preying on other people's property and eventually even taking their lives.

The truth is that value is dynamic and is created by the mind, because the material world is a plastic reality full of possibilities, with no ultimate boundaries. The mind can exercise itself in new ways to shape this plastic material in what comes to be almost an alchemist's action of discovery, transformation, and invention.

## *Create a vision of dynamic wealth*

When people in a society consider value and wealth to be dynamic, fundamentally mind-based, and not tied to material resources or land, an important barrier to wealth comes down. This dynamic mentality is necessary to achieve a prosperity unconnected to material conditions.

In short, third-world countries need to learn to give. They are used to only receiving. As long as they stay at the static, receiving-only end of world development, they will reinforce the conditions conducive to misery, poverty, corruption, and violence.

Until they become able to give what they now receive from the inventive and creative countries, prosperity will elude them. The secret of having is giving, as perennial wisdom teaches us.

Third-world countries must change their static mentality and replace it with a dynamic concept of value and wealth. This change will necessarily bring prosperity. The remaining question is how to effect this change of mind-set, shifting it from static to dynamic, from receiving to giving.

The answer is so simple that it is often disregarded or minimized and undervalued. Here it is:

## *Enable the free circulation of minds and capital*

To generate a critical mass of people with a dynamic concept of value and wealth that will transform society, all that is needed is to enable the full and free circulation of minds, goods, and capital.

The elimination of obstacles to this movement will open the road to mental development and creativity. Individuals and entrepreneurs will find no obstacles to their creative nature, and, most importantly, they will feel happy.

Their happiness will benefit all. When entrepreneurial individuals and businesses find that all the prerequisites needed to create and develop their ambitious projects are easy to obtain, they will create and develop as much as they can.

All that is needed is to let the creative natures of individuals and enterprises follow their own inclination. Some will do better than others, but all will achieve what is possible for them.

So, the path to prosperity is not a matter of doing things but of not doing things. It is not a matter of regulating and adding obstacles but of removing them. When this path is followed, the result will be the development of a critical mass of people who have a dynamic mind-set—one that is able to achieve unbounded value and wealth creation.

When entrepreneurs and creators find themselves in environments full of limiting regulations, they are disheartened and diverted from their most efficient paths. No one can be happy, for example, when a customs official makes it unpleasant to import tools, books, or software.

When you ask why you cannot find the latest medicines, technologies, or informational materials in third-world countries, the answer is that regulations make it difficult to import them.

Abundant supply is why working in first-world countries is more efficient than working in third-world countries. In first-world countries, you find an infrastructure that simplifies action, instead of hindering it.

All that is needed to build a critical mass of creative and inventive individuals is to permit the unregulated, free circulation of minds, goods, and capital. When this is done, the best possible conditions for creativity, value, and wealth creation will have been established.

## *Let freedom define its own natural form*

We must not think that once we have implemented our formula, value and wealth creation will be the same everywhere. The formula elicits the best development from each environment, but the environment will play a role.

We are far from believing that value and wealth creation must be imitated along fixed parameters. On the contrary, once people adopt the dynamic concept of value and wealth, progress will seek its own path according to those people's specific circumstances.

So, we must not impose a particular way of being for a country and its population. All that we must ask from them is to adopt a dynamic concept of value and wealth.

The creation of wealth need not be exclusively the development of new technologies in mechanics or electronics. Creativity can be applied in many ways. Some countries will develop in electronics or chemicals, whereas others might employ their creativity in real estate, mining, tourism, or finance. As long as there are no boundaries to invention and creativity, they will explode with possibilities, creating value and wealth.

All that need be done is to not impose anything, to deregulate and remove all obstacles to the creation of value and wealth, and then to wait and see. Society acts alone; no government is needed.

In an environment free of obstacles, each individual will create value and wealth in his own way. All that we must do is to leave the free individuals to create value unhindered.

Let us see now how this program should be put into action.

## HOW YOU CAN BENEFIT TODAY FROM THE FORMULA

For this formula to work, nothing is needed except willing individuals who understand what is to be done and why it works.

The most important thing to remember is that the individual is the center of everything. Governments exist for individuals and because of individuals. People should ask nothing from government beyond noninterference and general administration.

So in putting our formula into action, we are not asking government to change its ways as a precondition. Instead, individuals will combine their actions in a way that will necessarily force change.

### *Show that you are a free individual, and governments will change for the better*

The dynamic mind necessarily creates value. Such a mind does not ask for government help. The actions of free minds will change the environment, as they always have.

All fundamental and valuable changes in human history have been made by individuals. Once the dynamic power of the individual is known and understood, the doors of social change are open.

We have our formula. It is:

**Gap Enlargement * Creative Critical Mass * Non-Regulation = Social Prosperity**

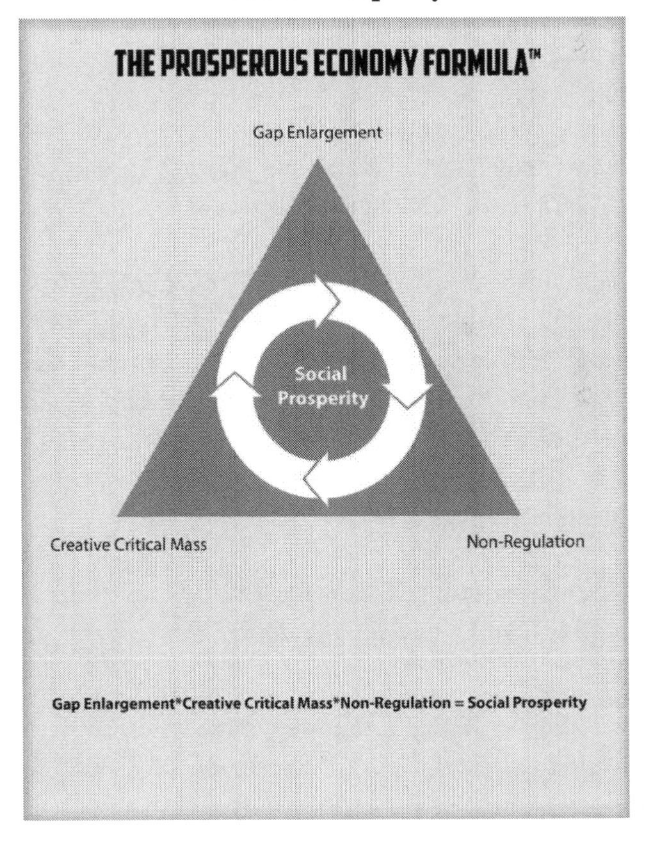


Figure 5. The prosperous economy formula.

To apply the formula, the individual needs to seek those three factors in his own life and business. This is all that is needed. When more people do this, the governments and social conditions will adapt to them.

Now we will apply the formula. Let us see how.

## *The formula and how to apply it*

The individual must look for the best conditions to help him with the three factors of the formula.

1. Gap Enlargement. The individual must seek a social environment that allows the rich to become more rich and the poor to become less poor. Gap enlargement is a consequence of value creation and entrepreneurship.

2. Creative Critical Mass. The individual must seek territories that have inventive, creative people in technology, science, and other fields conducive to the creation of value.

3. Non-Regulation. The individual must look for the least regulated environments that best satisfy his interests as an entrepreneur or value creator. This is not merely a theoretical consideration. It is a practical absolute. Although theoreticians waste their time and other people's time discussing whether all or some regulations should be abolished, the free individual goes where regulations hurt the least.

All that the free individual must do is look for the optimal conditions for himself and his family or fellow workers. The rest falls into place by itself.

Technology is there to help. Computers have changed the world, and they are still changing it. Never have communication and data transfers with the farthest regions of the world been easier.

In addition, transport technology is changing. Never has it been easier or cheaper to travel anywhere in the world. The same can be said of capital transfers.

Technology can help people seek the best locations in the world for what they do, with the fewest regulatory hassles.

## *Help others by freeing yourself*

To free others, first free yourself. To make others rich, first make yourself rich. To gain control over the outer world, first gain self-control. These are not empty words. They work. When you want to help others become free, you must act to gain your freedom first and teach by your example. Your example is the best lesson that any society can receive.

Remember that all great social changes have occurred because a single individual or a few people decided to behave in a certain way. If you apply the algorithm to yourself, society will follow sooner or later. Then, even governments will be motivated to help the algorithm work.

However, change—yours, that of people around you, and even of government—must begin with your own individual actions. Self-change has always been, still is, and always will be the law of social change.

Above all, the individual must make a conscious effort to acquire a mentality of dynamic value and wealth. The only thing that prevents entire countries and regions of the world from being prosperous is their static, earthly, violent concept of value and wealth.

The dynamic concept of value and wealth is all that is needed to free the forces of value creation and prosperity. This is why it is so important for individuals to learn and understand this concept.

## SUMMING UP

We have seen that the mind is the ultimate resource for generating value and wealth. The origin of all discoveries, all inventions, and all material resources is in the mind that discovers their usefulness.

Indeed, the mind goes beyond finding value in the world around us. The mind continues to use its transformative power to liberate matter from its boundaries. It is thanks to the mind that wood as a fuel was replaced by coal and coal by oil and, today, perhaps all of them by nuclear power. The transformative power of mind abolishes the limits of quantitative matter.

All discoveries and inventions have as their ultimate function the furtherance of mind and the enhancement of its own powers. The nature of mind is the key to understanding freedom and the dynamic origin of value and wealth.

Freedom is what human action seeks first. Freedom is what liberates matter and mind and spirit from their boundaries. Freedom is the core of our adaptation and survival.

The mind seeks freedom, not only to adapt and survive, but to live, enjoy, and achieve happiness. We adapt in order to live happy lives, in which the mind accomplishes its function of creating value and wealth in the largest sense of those words.

Every creation of mind is a tool that the mind uses to become freer. By freeing itself from its surrounding conditions, the mind ensures its happiness and survival.

In this sense, technology and science cannot go against man. They can oppose man temporarily, but eventually the feedback from technology and science will enhance freedom and give man additional tools with which to oppose any system that limits the exercise of a free mind.

Leibniz rightly thought that we live in the best of all possible worlds. Nothing unreal can survive for long. The evil of communism and the Soviet Union ended in collapse. Their dismissal by history was due to their inner irrationality.

The idea that technology is neutral and can be used for either good or evil is only true to a certain extent. In a deeper, more fundamental way, the direction of technology is toward good, not evil. For an example, consider guns. They can kill, but their truest use is for legitimate self-defense.

The greatest value of technology lies in its use to increase freedom and enhance human life, rather than the opposite. The benefits of science and technology largely outweigh their drawbacks.

Technology is a tool of freedom. Freedom comes from knowledge, and knowledge is the root of all science and technology. Technology and science give back to knowledge the existence that they received from it.

The gift to knowledge from science and technology is growing exponentially. The Gutenberg revolution, which was begun by the invention of the printing press, was the first step. The second step was the Leibniz revolution, which originated in the 18th century with Leibniz's development of the binary system, and then later enabled the invention of the computer and the microchip in the 20th century.

The first revolution transformed the world from the bottom up in all ways—technologically, scientifically, economically, politically, spiritually, and socially. A new world emerged from the ashes of the old one.

The second revolution has even greater power. Not only has it enabled us to process data and make calculations at tremendous speeds, but it has also linked the entire planet in an electronic web.

This information revolution will destroy the world and its institutions as we know them and create a new world from the wreckage. Again, the goal of this revolution, this explosion of information and knowledge, is freedom.

The Gutenberg revolution created our techno-scientific civilization. The Leibniz revolution is transforming it into an electronic and cybernetic civilization. The ultimate goal of both revolutions is to free the mind.

I am not a prophet, and it is not my task here to precisely forecast the details of the new world that will emerge from the present one. However, one thing we can reasonably foresee is that freedom will increase—and with it the power and consciousness of the individual.

Governments and all other powers will have to adapt to this new individual freedom or collapse and die. Government's transformation or destruction will happen naturally, without a need for special action by anyone.

## *Poverty, wealth, and the prosperous economy formula*

Poor countries are those that have the fewest conditions for freedom, whereas rich countries are those that have sufficient freedom to enable free, creative minds to gather and to work successfully.

We have defined a formula or algorithm that contains the elements necessary for value and wealth creation in any country. When the formula is applied, the result is value creation, wealth conversion, and prosperity.

Let us review the formula once more. It is Gap Enlargement * Creative Critical Mass * Non-Regulation = Social Prosperity.

The formula means that the first condition for prosperity is to have an environment in which the rich may become richer and the poor may become less poor. This natural enlargement of the wealth gap leads to the best possible allocation of resources.

The second condition is to have a critical mass of creative people that is sufficient in number to change the productive direction of a society, from being at the receiving end to being at the giving end—making the society a creative source of science, technology, business, and other human thought and action.

The third condition is lack of regulation. Here, non-regulation is not just a theoretical concept; it means that entrepreneurs and enterprising individuals in all fields must avoid, flee, or seek to abolish regulations that hurt their productive actions.

When an entrepreneur relocates his industry to avoid regulations that impinge on his creative productivity, or when a manual worker flees his third-world country to work in a better and more stimulating environment, both are acting rationally and increasing their freedom.

Both the entrepreneur and the worker in the above examples are creating more opportunities and a better and happier future for themselves by increasing their freedom. It is through individual actions of his kind, made possible by our new technologies, that conditions will change and prosperity will be achieved worldwide—and sooner than we realize.

Governments will not transform societies to make people freer and more productive. No, individuals will do it, by seeking free environments in which to create value and wealth in better and better ways.

These individuals, acting with free minds, will force governments to act in accordance with, and for the benefit of, their free minds. This is the key to all value, prosperity, and wealth.

# Bibliography

Abbattista, Guido. "European Encounters in the Age of Expansion." Published Jan. 24, 2011. EGO | European History Online. http://ieg-ego.eu/en/threads/backgrounds/european-encounters/.

Adams, Ray, and Margaret Wu, eds. *PISA 2000 Technical Report.* Paris: OECD (Organisation for Economic Co-ordination and Development), 2002. http://www.oecd.org/edu/school/programmeforinternationalstudentassessmentpisa/pisa2000technicalreport-publications2000.htm.

Aquinas, Thomas. *Summa Theologica.* Translated by the Fathers of the English Dominican Province. New York: Benziger Brothers, 1947.

Aristotle. "Metaphysics." In *The Basic Works of Aristotle.* New York: Random House, 1941.

Asimov, Isaac. *Caves of Steel.* New York: Bantam, 1991.

Bastiat, Claude Frédéric. *The Bastiat Collection.* 2nd ed. Auburn, AL: Mises Institute, 2007. http://mises.org/library/bastiat-collection.Bastiat, Claude Frédéric. *Harmonies Economiques.* Paris: Guillaumin, 1850.

Bastiat, Claude Frédéric. *Mélanges d'Economie Politique*, Brussels: Meline, Cans,1851.

https://books.google.com/books?id=JIABAAAAQAAJ&dq=Bastiat%2C%20Claude%20Fr%C3%A9d%C3%A9ric.%20M%C3%A9langes%20d%E2%80%99Economie%20Politique%2C%20Meline%2C%20Cans%20Et%20Comp.%20Libraires%20Editeurs%2C%201851&pg=PP9#v=onepage&q&f=false.

Bastiat, Claude Frédéric. *Sophismes Economiques*. Paris: Guillaumin, 1847.

Bastiat, Claude Frédéric *Propriété et Loi*. Paris: Guillaumin: 1848.

Batra, Ravi. *The Great Depression* of 1990. New York: Dell, 1988.

Belfiore, Michael. *Rocketeers: How a Visionary Band of Business Leaders, Engineers, and Pilots is Boldly Privatizing Space*. New York: HarperCollins, 2007.

Berra, Yogi. *The Yogi Book*. New York: L.T.D. Enterprises, 1998. Antoine de Saint-Exupéry. *The Little Prince*. Translated by Irene Testot Ferry. Ware, Hertfordshire, UK: Wordsworth, 1995.

Declaration of Independence of the United States.

Dick, Philip K. "How to Build a Universe That Doesn't Fall Apart Two Days Later." In *I Hope I Shall Arrive Soon*. Garden City, NY: Doubleday, 1985.

Doxiadis, Apostolos, and Christos H. Papadimitriou. *Logicomix: An Epic Search For Truth*. New York: Bloomsbury, 2009.

Easterly, William. *The Elusive Quest for Growth: Economists' Adventures and Misadventures in the Tropics*. Cambridge, MA: MIT Press, 2002.

Feyman, Richard. *Surely You're Joking, Mr. Feynman!* New York: W.W. Norton, 1997. Friedman, Thomas L. *The World is Flat: The Globalized World in the Twenty-First Century*. New York: Penguin, 2005.

Gore, Al. *Earth in the Balance: Forging a New Common Purpose*. New York: Rodale Books, 2006.

Graham, Loren, and Jean Michel Kantor. *Naming Infinity: A True Story of Religious Mysticism and Mathematical Creativity*. Cambridge, MA: Belknap Press of Harvard University Press, 2009.

Greenspan, Alan. *Gold and Economic Freedom.* In Ayn Rand, *Capitalism: The Unknown Ideal.* New York: Signet, 1966.

"Gutenberg Bible." *Wikipedia.* Last modified November 29, 2014. http://en.wikipedia.org/wiki/Gutenberg_Bible.

Hallak, Jacqes, and Muriel Poisson. *Corrupt Schools, Corrupt Universities: What Can Be Done?* Paris: UNESCO International Institute for Educational Planning, 2007. http://unesdoc.unesco.org/images/0015/001502/150259e.pdf.

Hayek, Friedrich August. *The Road to Serfdom.* Abingdon, U.K. England: Routledge, 2007.

Hogan, James P. *Kicking the Sacred Cow.* Riverdale, NY: Baen, 2004.

Hogan, James P. *Mind Matters.* New York: Ballantine, 1997.

Hopkins, Jasper. *On Learned Ignorance: A Translation and an Appraisal of "De Docta Ignorantia."* 2nd ed. Minneapolis, MN: Arthur J. Banning, 1985.

Koch, Charles G. *The Science of Success: How Market-Based Management Built the World's Largest Private Company.* Hoboken, NJ: John Wiley & Sons, 2007.

Konrad, Mike. "How to Destroy a Rich Country." *American Thinker,* September 20, 2013. http://www.americanthinker.com/articles/2012/10/how_to_destroy_a_rich_country.html.

Lamb, Annette. "Early Libraries: 1300s CE." On the History of Libraries website. 2012–2013. Eduscapes, IUPUI Online Courses. http://eduscapes.com/history/early/1300.htm.

Leibniz, Gottfried Wilhelm. *Essais de Théodicée, Sur la Bonté de Dieu, la Liberté de l'Homme et l'Origine du Mal.* Paris Flammarion, 1969.

Leibniz, Gottfried Wilhelm. *Principes de la Nature et de la Grâce, Monadologie et autres textes 1703–1716.* Paris: Flammarion, 1996.

Leibniz, Gottfried Wilhelm. *The Monadology.* Translated by Robert Latta. London: Forgotten Books. 2008.

Linehan, Dan. *SpaceShipOne: An Illustrated History*. Minneapolis, MN: Zenith, 2008.

Lord, Albert B. *The Singer of Tales*. Cambridge, MA: Harvard University Press, 1960.

Lowe, Janet. *Warren Buffett Speaks: Wit and Wisdom from the World's Greatest Investor*. Hoboken, NJ: John Wiley & Sons, 2007.

Maxfield, Clive. *Bebop to the Boolean Boogie: An Unconventional Guide to Electronics Fundamentals, Components, and Processes*. Burlington, MA: Newnes, 2003.

McLuhan, Marshall. *The Gutenberg Galaxy: The Making of Typographic Man*. Toronto: University of Toronto Press, 1962.

Mises, Ludwig von. *A Critique of Interventionism*. Auburn, AL: Mises Institute, 2011.

Mises, Ludwig von. *Human Action*. 3rd rev. ed. Chicago: Henry Regnery, 1966(1949).

Mises, Ludwig von. *Planned Chaos*. Auburn, AL: Mises Institute, 2009.

Mises, Ludwig von. *Socialism: An Economic and Sociological Analysis*. New Haven, CT: Yale University Press, 1951.

Mugasha, Agasha. *The Law of Letters of Credit and Bank Guarantees*. Sydney: Federation Press, 2003.

Nagel, Ernest, and, James R. Newman. *Gödel's Proof*. New York: New York University Press, 2001.

Osterfeld, David. *Prosperity versus Planning: How Government Stifles Economic Growth*. Oxford, Oxford University Press, 1992.

Paulet de Vásquez, Sara Madueño. "Pedro Paulet: Peruvian Space and Rocket Pioneer," *21st Century Science and Technology Magazine*, Winter 2001–2002. http://www.21stcenturysciencetech.com/articles/winter01/paulet.html.

Peters, Edgar E. *Patterns in the Dark: Understanding Risk and Financial Crisis with Complexity Theory*. New York: John Wiley & Sons, 1999.Plato. *The Trial and Death of Socrates: Four Dialogues*. Translated by Benjamin Jowett. New York: Dover, 1992. Plotinus. *The Essential Plotinus*. Translated by Elmer O'brien. New York: New American Library, 1964.

Popper, Karl. *The Open Society and Its Enemies*. London: Routledge, 2002.

Rand, Ayn. *Answers: The Best of her Q&A*. New York: Penguin, 2005.

Rand, Ayn. *Atlas Shrugged*. New York: Penguin, 1966.

Rand, Ayn. *Capitalism: The Unknown Ideal*. New York: Signet, 1966.

Rifkin, Jeremy. *The End of Work: The Decline of the Global Labor Force and the Dawn of the Post-Market Era*. New York: G.P. Putnam's Sons, 1996.

Roth, Gabriel. "Federal Highway Funding." Cato Institute, June 2010. www.downsizinggovernment.org/transportation/highway-funding.

Rothbard, Murray N. *For a New Liberty: The Libertarian Manifesto*. 2nd ed. Auburn, AL: Mises Institute, 2006.

Say, Jean-Baptiste. *Traité d'Economie Politique*. Guillaumin, Paris, 1876.

Schiff, Peter D. *Crash Proof 2.0: How to Profit from the Economic Collapse*. Hoboken, NJ: John Wiley & Sons, 2009.

Skousen, Mark. *EconoPower: How a New Generation of Economists Is Transforming the World*. Hoboken, NJ: John Wiley & Sons, 2008.

Skousen, Mark. *The Making of Modern Economics*. Armonk, NY: M.E. Sharpe, 2001.

Smith, Adam. *The Wealth of Nations*. New York: Modern Library, 1965 (1776).

Smith, L. Neil. *Lever Action: Essays on Liberty*. Las Vegas, NV: Mountain Media, 2001.

Smithies, Michael. "Reading Habits at a Third World Technological University," *Reading in a Foreign Language* 1, no. 2 (Oct 1983): pp. 111–118.

Solzhenitsyn, Aleksandr I. *The Gulag Archipelago, 1918–1956: An Experiment in Literary Investigation, Books I-II.* Translated by Thomas P. Whitney. New York: Harper & Row, 1973.

Sorman Guy. *La Nouvelle Richesse des Nations.* Paris: Fayard, 1987.

Spooner, Lysander. *Natural Law.* 2nd ed. Boston, MA: Williams, 1882.

Spooner, Lysander. *No Treason, No. 1.* Boston, MA: Lysander Spooner, 1867.

Steinrich, Dale. "75 Years of Housing Fascism." *Mises Daily*, July 9, 2009. http://mises.org/daily/3544.

Stirner, Max. *The Ego and His Own.* New York: Dover, 2005.

Tooley, James. *The Beautiful Tree: A Personal Journey into How the World's Poorest People Are Educating Themselves.* New Delhi: Penguin, 2009.

Vansina, Jan. *Oral Tradition as History.* Madison, WI: University of Wisconsin Press, 1985.

Victor L. Ochoa Papers, 1894 -1945. Archives Center. National Museum of American History, Smithsonian Institution, Washington, D.C.

Webster, Daniel. *The Works of Daniel Webster.* 15th ed. Vol. 4. Edited by Edward Everett. Boston: Little, Brown, 1861, Google Books.

Weinberger, Sharon. "The Navy's Electric Cannon Fires Its First Shots." *Popular Mechanics,* Feb 28, 2012.

Wirthlin, Richard, David R. Gergen, Arthur B. Laffer, and United States White House office staff. *President Ronald Reagan's Initial Actions Project.* New York: Threshold, 2009.

Woods, Thomas E. Jr. *Meltdown.* Washington, D.C.: Regnery, 2009.

*The World Factbook.* Washington, DC: Central Intelligence Agency, Continually updated. https://www.cia.gov/library/publications/the-world-factbook/.

# Index

## A



## B

# C



# D



# E

## F



## G



## H



## I



## J

## P



## R



## S

# T



# U



# V



# W



# Y

# About the Author

Felipe Tudela is an international investor and economic theorist. He is passionate about showing individuals, families, and countries how to escape poverty and take control of their destinies. Travelling for business through many countries, he was struck by a nagging question that just wouldn't go away: Why are some countries so rich while those next door are so poor?

This is the conundrum of our age. Despite all their promises, governments and world leaders have not succeeded in bringing better economies and livable wages for all. So far, none of the available social and economic theories have been successful in explaining inequality. That has spurred Tudela to create a new model of economic growth, the "the prosperous economy formula," which not only explains why income inequality exists, but also explains why that inequality is actually necessary for prosperity.

This new book offers a pathway for a better life for billions of people around the world. It gives insight and hope for those who would strive for a brighter future.

Felipe Tudela's expertise has been sought by major financial institutions, including the Bank of France, the Société Générale Asset

Management (SGAM), the French Association of Technical Analysis (AFATE), the London Society of Technical Analysis, the FOW group, and many others.

He is the author of *The Secret Code of Japanese Candlesticks* (John Wiley & Sons, Ltd, 2008), and of *Trading Triads, Unlocking the Secrets of Market Structure and Trading in Any Market* (John Wiley & Sons, Ltd, 2010).

This new book draws deeply from the best of philosophy, history, mathematics, economics, and finance to gain a truer understanding of wealth creation in the many countries Tudela has visited.

When he is not working, Felipe enjoys being with his family, reading, playing, studying chess, and walking in nature.

You can contact the author at www.felipetudelasite.com.

Made in the USA
Middletown, DE
09 July 2018